JESUS IS AWESOME

Christian Life and Evangelism

DANNY LOVETT

"If any man be in Christ...all things become new."
— II Corinthians 5:17

Jesus Is Awesome: Christian Life and Evangelism

Published by 21st Century Press, P.O. Box 8087, Springfield, MO 65801.

Cover and Book Design: Lee Fredrickson

Scripture quotations are from the *New King James Version.*

Requests for permissions should be addressed to:
Liberty University
Office of the President
1971 University Blvd.
Lynchburg VA 24502

ISBN 0-9700639-1-1

Printed in the United States of America

Contents

Chapter One

A NEW STORY

—Your Testimony —

Therefore, if anyone is in Christ, he is a new creation; old things have passed away; behold, all things have become new.

—2 Corinthians 5:17

But sanctify the Lord God in your hearts, and always be ready to give a defense to everyone who asks you reason for the hope that is in you, with meekness and fear;

—1 Peter 3:15

Having a Testimony

It's amazing how simple little things can change the course of a person's life forever. The choice of where you live — whether in a city or in a farming community, the choice of where you go to college and what you study, the choice of who you marry, all of those things set your life in a specific direction. However, sometimes our lives are changed by things beyond our control. One young man was hang-gliding just weeks before his high school graduation. He flicked his wrist to adjust his grip at the wrong moment and a gust of wind carried him into the side of a cliff. From that day on, he lost control over his lower body, but he uses his active imagination to invent devices to help disabled people. That flick of a wrist became part of his story — the story of his life.

When you accepted Christ as your Savior, your story changed. The course of your life changed. To some extent, you chose those changes because you rejected the life of sin and self-direction in order to live a Christ-directed life; but in other ways, your salvation was beyond your control. You had no control over who shared the gospel with you or the circumstances that led you to make a decision for Christ. What God has given you in this package called salvation goes far beyond what you understood when you received it. You put your life in God's control. Your story changed. You now have a new story to tell the world about what Christ has done in you.

Every person who has been born again of the Spirit of God has a new story to tell, a story of God's saving and changing power. This story is called a testimony. Your testimony is the story of how God's grace has changed your life. 1 Corinthians 15:10, *"But by the grace of God I am what I am, and His grace toward me was not in vain; but I labored more abundantly than they all, yet not I, but the grace of God which was with me."*

There are lots of stories in the Bible of how God changed people. There is the story of how God blessed Abram, changed his name to Abraham, and made him become the father of many nations. There is the story of how God saved Moses from death as an infant and later called him to be the one who led Israel out of bondage. David's story begins when he is a simple shepherd boy and tells how God made him king of Israel.

In the New Testament, there is a story about a blind man whom Jesus healed. His testimony was very simple: *"One thing I know: that though I was blind, now I see,"* (John 9:25). A woman named Mary told a story of how Jesus led her away from prostitution, forgave her, and, as a result, she devoted her life to serving him (Luke 7:37-50). Peter's testimony would have to include the story of how fearful he was in denying Jesus three times on the night Jesus was arrested, yet God changed him into a bold preacher of the Gospel.

These are all marvelous stories of changed lives. Not everyone has seen a burning bush or been healed of blindness, but that doesn't make his testimony less powerful. It doesn't mean that the change in his life is less significant. Sometimes the most powerful testimonies come from ordinary people who found God in ordinary ways, but share their story with passion because they know where they would be without Jesus. John 15:5, *"I am the vine, you are the branches. He who abides in Me, and I in him, bears much fruit; for without Me you can do nothing."*

Using Your Testimony

The story of your salvation — your personal testimony — can be a tool for evangelism. If a Christian is to be an effective witness for his Savior, he needs a clear, forceful testimony. Your experience of salvation is the substance of your testimony.

Sharing your testimony is the first aspect of witnessing — simply telling what eternal life has meant to you. By doing that, you show that your faith has substance — there is a reality behind it. It is not just your opinion or an attitude that has helped you. There is really a God who stands behind His promises and has changed your life. This testimony helps people feel that if God did that for you, maybe He can change the course of their lives too. Sharing your personal testimony personalizes your message and makes it attractive to the listener.

If you cannot tell the story of how you became a Christian, if you are not sure how knowing Christ has changed your life, then perhaps you need to back up and make certain that you have indeed been born again. If you are truly a Christian, then you should be able to point to a time when you invited Christ into your life, and He started making a difference. In order to witness for Christ, you must have the assurance that you have been forgiven and that Christ Jesus is your Savior.

There are three essential elements to a personal testimony. The first is your "Before" picture. It is the part of the story that tells what you were like before you met Christ. The second part of the story is your conversion. It is the tale of how you came to faith in Christ — how you heard about salvation, what you realized that made you change your mind, and how you made a decision to receive the gift of salvation. The last element is the "After" picture — the picture of what knowing Jesus has meant to you. It is the account of how you have changed because you know Jesus.

You don't have to pretend that everything in your life is perfect now. You just need to tell what ways your life is better than it was and show how Jesus has provided for the needs in your life. Phil 4:19, *"And my God shall supply all your need according to His riches in glory by Christ Jesus."*

Paul gives his testimony three times in the book of Acts. Each time, he includes those three essential elements — a "Before" picture, how he came to believe, and an "After" picture. But it sounds different each time. Why is that? First, your testimony is not a speech that you have memorized. It is your story which you should be able to tell spontaneously and creatively. Paul simply shared from his heart.

But he also tailored his testimony to his audience. Look closely at these three passages. When he was speaking to the Jewish people (Acts 22), he emphasized his own Pharisaical education and zeal for Judaism. When he was speaking to Roman authorities (Acts 26), he portrayed himself as an obedient citizen of Rome. To the philosophers in Athens (Acts 17), Paul's approach was to show that his teaching agreed with the thoughts of philosophers with whom they were familiar , and went beyond that to teach the power of the resurrection. In each case Paul adapted the message to the listeners. In 1 Corinthians 9:22, he says, "*I have become all things to all men, that I might by all means save some.*" We need to use the same kind of approach and make sure that we adjust what we include in our testimony so that the people we are talking to can relate to it best.

Preparing a Personal Testimony

Has anyone every asked you, "What is it about you that makes you different?" Or, "How do you stay so stable? Why don't you panic like everyone else?" Or, "Don't you ever just feel like going out and getting drunk to relieve the pressure?" The Apostle Peter challenged us to be ready for those types of questions. "*Always be ready to give a defense to everyone who asks you a reason for the hope that is in you,*" (1 Peter 3:15). Part of that answer should be your story of what God has done in your life.

One of the most effective tools you have for sharing your faith is the story of how Jesus Christ gave you eternal life and how He has enriched your life. John wrote, "*that which we have seen and heard we declare to you, that you also may have fellowship with us; and truly our fellowship is with the Father and with His Son Jesus Christ*" (1 John. 1:3) concerning eternal life and his relationship with God.

When Paul stood before King Agrippa in Acts 26, he told him simply, logically, and clearly about his life before salvation, how he met Christ, and what his life was like after conversion. Paul's testimony takes three or four minutes to read aloud in a conversational manner. You should be able to tell your testimony simply and clearly in just a few minutes also. It is easy if you just do a little preparation to know the basics of what you are going to say.

Although you will be writing your testimony in this exercise, the purpose is not to memorize it and repeat it verbatim. The purpose is to help you express your experience in words that convey your sincerity and your genuine appreciation for the change that God has made in your life. The choice of the right words, the flow of your story, and the knowledge of how to begin and end are all important; however, the most important thing is to prepare so that the words can come when you need them.

As you begin this project, ask the Lord for wisdom and insight into just how to share your story. John 1:5, "*And the light shines in the darkness, and the darkness did not comprehend it.*" Also, be open to suggestions from friends, your teachers, your pastor, and others who have experience in witnessing. The testimony you will prepare here is designed to share with a non-Christian in a one-on-one context or in a small group. It will be a "door-opener," a conversation starter, not a "convincing tool." Many people are not ready to be convinced that they need Christ, but they can often be led to talk about the Gospel after an inoffensive presentation of a personal testimony.

Trust God and work diligently. Give time, thought, and prayer to preparing your personal testimony.

Guidelines for Preparing Your Personal Testimony

The outline you will follow is the simple plan of the three essential elements about which we have already talked:

1. *Before* — a short sketch of what your life was like before you became a Christian
2. *How* — how, specifically, you took the step of becoming a Christian
3. *After* — what changes have taken place in your life because you accepted Christ.

To help you get started, first identify when you actually became a Christian. What influenced that decision? Were there any specific realizations that led to that decision? Who was involved in leading you to Christ? What did they say that made a difference?

The next thing to identify is what you want to say about your Before picture. What was in your life that made you aware of your need for Christ? What was the best evidence of your sinfulness? Most people have a way to rationalize why they don't need Christ. What did you use to justify yourself before God?

Finally, look at your life now. What has changed? Why has it changed? What is the single biggest difference you see between the old you and the new you?

As you write your testimony, here are some general suggestions that will help:

Make it sound conversational — the way you normally talk. Don't make it all flowery and poetic. No literary stuff like, "I viewed the crimson sunset and pondered." Nobody talks like that. Don't use your "stain-glassed voice" to read it. This is a testimony, not a sermon.

Make "I" and "me" statements, not "you" statements. This is sharing, not preaching. It helps to keep the testimony warm and personal. It breaks down barriers when you are open and honest about your self, people like hearing about other people's experiences told in the first person.

Avoid religious words, phrases and jargon. Sometimes we get so wrapped up in speaking "Christianese" that we forget that most people don't understand it. Use terms that everybody will understand.

Religious Words	Possible Substitutions
Believe	Invited Christ to come into my life through prayer
Sin	Disobedience, breaking God's law, turned my back on God
Went forward	Decided to turn my life over to God
Under the blood	God forgave me of my failures
Accepted Christ	(Same as believe)
Saved	Became a Christian, delivered from the penalty of disobedience
Prayed through	Sincerely prayed
Christian	Committed Christian, real Christian
Born Again	Received a new life with Jesus as my Lord

Use general terms so that more people can relate to your story. Don't name specific churches, denominations, or groups. Avoid using dates and ages. Those kinds of things exclude people who didn't have exactly the same experience.

Include some humor and human interest. When a person smiles or laughs, it reduces tension. Humor is disarming and increases attention. It also makes your serious point carry a little more weight.

Word pictures increase interest. Don't just say, "I grew up on a farm." Describe the farm in a couple of sentences so that a person listening can visualize it.

Avoid dogmatic statements that skeptics can question. If you say, "I prayed and I know Christ came in," you are opening yourself up to the question, "How do you know that?" What kind of answer can you give? "Well, I just know." Stick with verifiable statements of your experience: "I prayed and asked Christ into my life. Since then I have experienced peace..." He can't argue with that.

Speak from an adult perspective, even if you were converted at an early age. "My dad helped me understand about Jesus," sounds like you were simply indoctrinated as a child. Your conversion was a major decision in your life and it was *your* decision. It is better to describe the discussions you had with your father that led you to understand who Jesus was.

Simplify. Keep the story free of unimportant facts, names, places, jobs, moves, houses, etc. Just reduce the clutter around your story. Use first names only whenever possible, but don't mention a name without explaining the person's relationship to you. You don't want to say, "Bill Smith, Thomas Van Buren, and his cousin, Ed Matthews, came by my office at Acme Plumbing and Appliance Company." All you have to say is, "Bill and two other men talked to me at work one day." You can also combine information saying, "After living in five states and attending six universities, I found my first engineering job." You don't have to give us the addresses and phone numbers of each place.

In the Before section:

- Have a cushion of interesting non-spiritual material at the beginning. Your goal is to draw the listeners in to hear what you have to say.

- Include both good and bad aspects of your life. Don't make yourself out to be Charles Manson. No one can relate to you if you were purely evil. For example, include things like "hard working," "desire for education," "wanted to excel," "had concern for others." Those are good qualities that people can see in themselves. When you speak of the bad things, try to use general descriptions: selfish, inferiority complex, get ahead at any cost, temper, greed.

- You may want to include the specifics of one event that capsulizes your sinful state. Do this only if you feel comfortable revealing it, and remember that your audience may not be able to handle details that are too graphic. Use discretion to protect both yourself and your listeners.

In the How section:

Communicate the Gospel clearly and briefly. You need to include how you came to understand:

The fact of sin - Rom. 3:10-12, 23; *As it is written: "There is none right-*

eous, no, not one; There is none who understands; there is none who seeks after God. They have all turned aside; they have together become unprofitable; there is none who does good, no, not one for all have sinned and fall short of the glory of God"; 1John 1:8, *"If we say that we have no sin, we deceive ourselves, and the truth is not in us.")*

The penalty of sin - Rom. 6:23, *"For the wages of sin is death, but the gift of God is eternal life in Christ Jesus our Lord."* Ephesians. 2:1, *"And you He made alive, who were dead in trespasses and sins."*

Christ's payment of the penalty - Rom. 5:8, *"But God demonstrates His own love toward us, in that while we were still sinners, Christ died for us."* John 3:16, *"For God so loved the world that He gave His only begotten Son, that whoever believes in Him should not perish but have everlasting life";* 1 Pet. 3:18, *"For Christ also suffered once for sins, the just for the unjust, that He might bring us to God, being put to death in the flesh but made alive by the Spirit."*

The requirement to receive Christ - Rom. 10:9-10, *"That if you confess with your mouth the Lord Jesus and believe in your heart that God has raised Him from the dead, you will be saved. For with the heart one believes unto righteousness, and with the mouth confession is made unto salvation";* vs.13, *"For whoever calls on the name of the Lord shall be saved";* John 1:12, *"But as many as received Him, to them He gave the right to become children of God, to those who believe in His name."*

Make the Bible the authority. If I call someone a sinner, that is being judgmental. If the Bible calls someone a sinner, then he has to take it up with God. If we make the Bible our authority, it takes the burden off of our opinions and makes us deal with the truth of what God says. His word is living and active. We must trust it to do its work in our hearts. Nothing we have to say could be as powerful.

Bad example: "Bill told me that I was a failure and needed forgiveness."

Better example: "Bill shared with me that the Bible said ..."

When referring to receiving Christ, use the word ***pray***. That is what you want them to do, so tell them what you have done. You prayed to receive Christ and so should they. For instance, "I prayed and asked Christ to come into my life and give me the gift of eternal life."

In the After section:

- Share briefly two or three personal benefits of becoming a Christian. It is best if those benefits correspond to problem situations that you spoke of in the Before section, but that is not necessary. They just need to hear that there is a real difference between the Before and After pictures.

- Your closing statement should be something like this: "But the greatest benefit of all is that I know I have eternal life." Listeners often comment on the last thing that you say, so if you end in this way, then you have directed the conversation to the subject of eternal life. The door is then open for presenting the Gospel to them.

You should be well on your way to writing a testimony that simply, effectively and clearly presents the Gospel. Your testimony will be a tool you use constantly. David said, *"I will praise You, O Lord my God, with all my heart, and I will glorify Your name forevermore. For great is Your mercy toward me, and You have delivered my soul from the depths of Sheol,"* (Psalm 86:12-13). In your testimony, you can declare God's love for you and how he has rescued you from the death of sin to live in His marvelous life.

Chapter Two

A NEW NOURISHMENT

— Memorizing Scripture —

"As newborn babes, desire the pure milk of the word."
—1 Peter 2:2

Some time ago, I heard an interesting story about a missionary in Africa. One day while the missionary was walking through the jungle, a lion began to chase him. He ran and ran as fast as he could go, but the lion was gaining on him. He saw that the end was near, so in utter desperation he fell upon his face and began to pray. "Dear Lord, please make the lion a Christian." Suddenly, all was quiet. The missionary slowly looked around to see what had happened and to his amazement, the lion was praying: "Thank you, Lord, for answering my prayer. Bless this food to the nourishment of my body."

Now, we all laugh at that and know that it couldn't really happen, but it does bring to mind something that is very real and very serious. The Bible warns us that Satan is like a roaring lion and he is out to devour every one of us. 1 Peter 5:8 reads, *"Be sober, be vigilant..."* In other words, exercise self-control and be watchful. Awake! Be on the alert! Why? *"Because your adversary the devil, as a roaring lion, walketh about seeking whom he may devour."* He is just waiting to eat your lunch if you give him a chance. Satan would like to destroy every Christian if God would permit him to do so. If he can get Christians entangled in sin, frozen in guilt, and devastated by shame, they cannot be effective in building the kingdom of God.

Ephesians 6:10-12 gives additional instruction about the battle between the believer and Satan. *"Finally, my brethren, be strong in the Lord and in the power of His might. Put on the whole armor of God, that you may be able to stand against the wiles of the devil."* ***Wiles*** means the methods, the tricks, and the traps that Satan has laid for the believer. *"For we do not wrestle against flesh and blood, but against principalities, against powers, against the rulers of the darkness of this age, against spiritual hosts of wickedness in the heavenly places."* Principalities, powers, and rulers are all terms that mean angelic beings who are under the authority of Satan — his demons. It is a spiritual battle, and it must be fought with spiritual weapons.

Satan does everything in his power to destroy, discourage, deceive, and decommission as many of God's children as possible. In seeking to defeat us, he uses the world, the flesh, and demons.

As a result of his opposition, there is lack of growth in the lives of many Christians. They have been saved for years, yet they are still spiritual babies. There is lack of victory in the lives of God's children. Defeat is the rule rather than the exception. There is a lack of spirituality and holiness in the lives of multitudes of professing Christians. I am horrified and deeply disturbed at the percentage of carnal, complacent, backslidden, worldly Christians in our churches today. There is a lack of witnessing for Christ. Less than five percent of the Christians witness regularly. There is a lack of ministering among believers. Very little follow-up is ever done on new converts. Seldom, if ever, do we see believers building one another up and ministering to one another as the Scriptures teach.

We cannot allow these conditions to continue. We must face our fierce opponent and through spiritual warfare defeat him. The Word of God tells us how.

First, you have to know where the battleground is. This is a spiritual battle.

It is a contest between real forces that have no material being. It is a war of ideas — thoughts. The spiritual battleground is the mind of each individual believer. When Paul describes this battle he says, *"For though we walk in the flesh, we do not war according to the flesh. For the weapons of our warfare are not carnal but mighty in God for pulling down strongholds, casting down arguments and every high thing that exalts itself against the knowledge of God, bringing every thought into captivity to the obedience of Christ,"* (2 Corinthians 10:3-5). Our battle is against arguments — rational defenses of some idea — and pretensions — the ways we lie to ourselves and justify our own desires. When these things set themselves in the way of our knowledge of God (that is, knowledge of the Truth), it is clear that they come from Satan, who Jesus called the Father of Lies. John 8:44, *"You are of your father the devil, and the desires of your father you want to do. He was a murderer from the beginning, and does not stand in the truth, because there is no truth in him. When he speaks a lie, he speaks from his own resources, for he is a liar and the father of it."*

How do we win this battle? What is our battle strategy? Paul tells us about that in Roman 12:1-2. He says that we must first dedicate ourselves to God, as if we were putting ourselves on the altar as a living sacrifice. Then he says we are not be conformed to this world, but to be transformed by the renewing of your mind, that you may prove what is that good and acceptable and perfect will of God. The battle will be fought, and we will be transformed into warriors, as we get rid of the thought patterns of the world and renew our mind with God's truth. The battle plan is to change God's people by changing the way they think — renewing their minds. Then we can be the warriors who attack Satan's lies and tear down his strongholds with the Truth.

But what are the weapons that Paul talked about? He said they were "divinely powerful." If they have God's power behind them, then they must be stronger than any weapon Satan or his demons have. What are they? In Ephesians 6:13-17, *"Therefore take up the whole armor of God, that you may be able to withstand in the evil day, and having done all, to stand. Stand therefore, having girded your waist with truth, having put on the breastplate of righteousness, and having shod your feet with the preparation of the gospel of peace; above all, taking the shield of faith with which you will be able to quench all the fiery darts of the wicked one. And take the helmet of salvation, and the sword of the Spirit, which is the word of God."* Paul describes our arsenal as the "full armor of God". He says we have a big wide belt that does more than hold up our pants. It supports our whole torso that we stand upright and don't bend. This belt is truth. He says we have a breastplate of righteousness that fends off any arrows or blows that might seriously damage our vital organs. This righteousness is not ours, but Christ's righteousness credited to us, which can withstand any attack; for we cannot be separated from His love. Our feet are shod with shoes called "readiness" — the readiness to share the gospel. We also have a shield. In ancient times, shields were covered with layers of leather which were not only hard to penetrate, but if hit by a fiery arrow, the leather would smother the flame. Our faith is our shield. No matter what accusations Satan may cast our way or doubts he may try to instill, our confidence that God is true to His word will extinguish the flame. There is a helmet that protects our head, which is our assurance that we are saved and are adopted as sons of God.

Wait a minute! Belts, helmet, shield, shoes — all of those things are protection. With what do we attack? The only offensive weapon on the list is "the sword of the Spirit, which is the Word of God." The one weapon we have, given by the Spirit and empowered by the Spirit, with which we can fight the spiritual battle is the Bible — the Word of God. It is the only weapon that can cut through the web of falsehoods and lies that Satan uses to deceive us. It is the only thing in the world that can cut to the heart of a man's soul and convince him of his need for a Savior.

But how well do you know how to use this sword?

Let's suppose that you were living in ancient times when men fought with swords and you went out to the battlefield with your armor on and sword in hand. However, the enemy noticed that you were holding your sword with only two fingers. If this were the case, he could easily knock the sword out of your hand and you would be at his mercy. If, on the other hand, you gripped the sword firmly with your whole hand, you could put up a good fight and even win the battle.

There is a parallel here between physical battle and spiritual warfare.

Most Christians go into the battle with only a very flimsy grasp of what the Scriptures actually teach. It is like holding the Bible, their sword, with only two fingers and hoping the enemy doesn't knock it out of their hands. But the warrior who has a firm grip on his weapon knows how to counter every blow, how to attack, and how to disarm the enemy. It never occurs to him that his weapon might be ineffective because he has firm confidence in its power and he understands how to use it effectively. This is the man who clearly understands the Word of God and who, through diligent study, has prepared himself for battle.

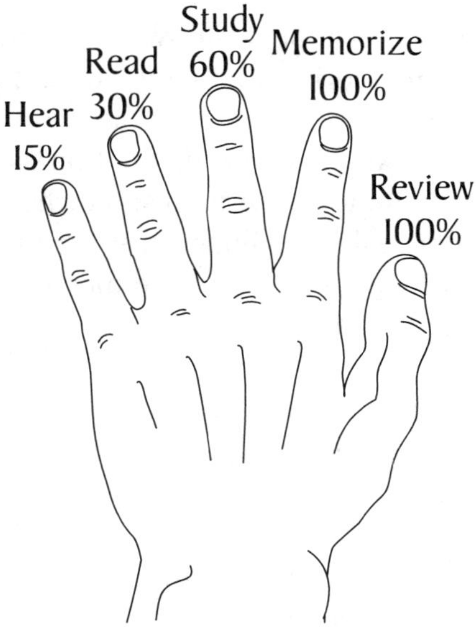

What kind of preparation does that take? Isn't going to Sunday School and listening to sermons enough? The drawing of the hand points out that we remember about 15% of what we hear twenty-four hours after we have heard it. We remember about 30% of what we read and about 60% of what we study. But we remember 100% of what we memorize and review. All five of these methods of retaining Scripture are both commanded and recommended in the Word of God. They are not optional, but are an obligation. They are binding upon every believer.

So, continuing the illustration, let's suppose you went to church yesterday and heard a good sermon; however, today you can only remember 15% of what you heard yesterday. Therefore, when Satan comes to tempt you, he can easily knock the sword of the Spirit out of your hand and cause you to fall into sin, because you are only holding it with two fingers - hearing and meditation. After confessing your sin, you purpose in your heart to get a better grip on your weapon. Now you are hearing, reading, and meditating upon the Word. You are still no match for the enemy because you are still only holding the sword by three fingers and only have about 30% control. You want victory, so you begin studying the Word. This gives you greater victories because it is harder for Satan to disarm you, but you are still losing some battles. You still have only a 60% grip on your sword. In order to have 100% victory over the enemy, you have to have a 100% grip on your sword — the Word of God. You must hear, read, study, memorize, and meditate on the Word of God.

Now in that illustration, we gave you meditation as a freebie, assuming that you gave some thought to the sermon somewhere along the way. The truth is that you cannot really meditate on something that you have not committed to memory. Only after you have memorized it can real meditation begin to have its full effect.

Let's look at two examples: Eve and Jesus. When Satan tempted Eve, he was able to raise doubts in her mind as to just what the command was and whether it was good to obey it. She had only heard God's Word secondhand. Jesus, on the other hand, was able to fend off Satan's temptations from Scriptures he had committed to memory from the book of Deuteronomy. Not only did he have these Scriptures memorized, but he was also able to contradict Satan's attempts to twist the meanings of Scripture because Jesus had also meditated on the meaning of these verses. Jesus' memorization was not rote memorization of a series of words; He had taken the Scriptures to heart and made them his own thoughts — His own words.

Our minds don't like to be lifted out of their old ruts. We enjoy pampering our flesh and taking the path of least resistance. But we have decided to put to death the deeds of the flesh, to crucify the old man, and to start memorizing the Word of God. Now you can fend off the attacks of Satan in the same way Jesus did. Remember that phrase Jesus used, "Get thee behind me Satan, for it is written..." Memorization gives you the best possible grip on the sword of the Spirit.

It is very important that we grip the sword fully and firmly because

1. The Word of God is the only offensive weapon we can use against the world, flesh, and devil.
2. The Word is the Christian's only guidebook. The will of God is revealed in the Word of God.
3. The Word is the Christian's only source of spiritual food.
4. The Word is the Christian's primary tool for ministering to the saints and winning the sinners. 2 Timothy 3:15-17, *"That from childhood you have known the Holy Scriptures, which are able to make you wise for salvation through faith which is in Christ Jesus. All Scripture is given by inspiration of God, and is profitable for doctrine, for reproof, for correction, for instruction in righteousness, that the man of God may be complete, thoroughly equipped for every good work."*

What the Bible Teaches about Scripture Memory

Memorizing Scripture is not just for pastors, evangelists, and those considered fanatics. EVERYBODY SHOULD BE MEMORIZING SCRIPTURE! That is not just my personal opinion; that is what God has commanded. Just look at the things God has said.

Deuteronomy 6:6-9, *"And these words which I command you today shall be in your heart. You shall* teach *them diligently to your children, and shall talk of them when you sit in your house, when you walk by the way, when you lie down, and when you rise up. You shall bind them as a sign on your hand, and they shall be as frontlets between your eyes. You shall write them on the doorposts of your house and on your gates."*

The commandments of God are to be in our consciousness always, especially if you are a parent. Some Jews today take the latter part of this passage literally and tie a small box containing tiny scrolls on their forehead. Of course, what God really wants is the Scripture to be so much a rule of our life that it is as evident as writing Scripture on our foreheads and on our doorframes. But that only happens when we have memorized it and internalized it so that it is truly on our hearts. This is the key to being effective and a real influence on our children and others as well.

Job 22:22, *"Receive, please, instruction from His mouth, and lay up His words in your heart."*

The only way to deal with adversity in your life, as Job had to, is to humble yourself and listen carefully to God's wisdom. If you do not have His words laid up in your heart (remember that to the Hebrews, the heart was the seat of rational thought), you will not stand in the day of trouble. We must have a rich reserve of God's Word stored permanently in our minds.

Proverbs 3:1-2, *"My son, do not forget my law, but let your heart keep my commands; For length* of *days and long life and peace they will add to you."*

Are you a son or daughter? This command applies to you: keep God's commands in your heart. Do not forget — memorize! And the promise applies to you also, that you will have a long and prosperous life. The benefits of Scripture memory are amazing.

Proverbs 4:20-21, *"My son, give attention to my words; incline your ear to my sayings. Do not let them depart from your eyes; keep them in the midst of your heart."*

Not only do we need to memorize the Scripture, but we need to make sure we don't let it out of our sight. We need to go back and review so that we don't forget what we have memorized.

Proverbs 6:2, *"You are snared by the words of your mouth; you are taken by the words of your mouth."*

How else can you bind Scripture to your heart but to memorize and meditate on it?

Proverbs 7:1-3, *"My son, keep my words, and treasure my commands within you. Keep my commands and live, and my law as the apple of your eye. Bind them on your fingers; write them on the tablet of your heart."*

Storing the Word within you means you are not dependent on having a Bible handy or listening to a preacher to know what the Word of God says. You know it, you keep it, and you guard it. How well do you protect the iris (the colored part) of your eye? Do you ever let anything just smash into it? No, you treat it as a precious possession and never let even a speck of dust in. That is the way you have to treat your knowledge of the Word.

In spite of these clear commands, there are still many Christians who, like King Saul, chose the convenient way rather than God's way. 1 Samuel 15:22-23, (*Then Samuel said, "Has the LORD as great delight in burnt offerings and sacrifices, as in obeying the voice of the LORD? Behold, to obey is better than sacrifice, and to heed than the fat of rams. For rebellion is as the sin of witchcraft, and stubbornness is as iniquity and idolatry. Because you have rejected the word of the LORD, he also has rejected you from being king.")* reveals God's displeasure toward those who refuse to obey His commands. Saul had been told to wait for Samuel to arrive before offering the sacrifice, but he grew impatient and offered up the sacrifice himself, though he was not a priest. Samuel showed up while the animal was still burning and confronted Saul's disobedience. Saul rejected the Word of God and was cut off from the blessings of God. We have a choice: to be like Saul, or to be like Job, who said, "*I have not departed from the commandment of His lips; I have treasured the words of His mouth more than my necessary food,*" (Job 23:12). "*David, who was made king in Saul's place, said, 'I delight to do Your will, O my God, and Your law is within my heart,'*" (Psalm 40:8).

Scripture memorization is not only commanded in the Bible, but it is also taught by implication. *"All Scripture,"* whether in the Old Testament or the New Testament, *"is given by the inspiration of God and is profitable for ..."*

> "doctrine" - that's what is right and good teaching
> "reproof" - that's confronting what is not right
> "correction" - that's how to get right
> "for instruction in righteousness" - that's how to stay right
> "*...that the man of God may be complete, thoroughly equipped for every good work,*" 2 Timothy 3:17

In other words, the Word of God is all that we need. Romans 15:4 says, *"For whatever things were written before were written for our learning, that we through the patience and comfort of the Scriptures might have hope";* therefore, let us consider what the Scriptures imply concerning Scripture memorization. Reflect on the following verses. Each one contains both a command and a benefit.

Joshua 1:8, *"This Book of the Law shall not depart from your mouth, but you shall meditate in it day and night, that you may observe to do according to all that is written in it. For then you will make your way prosperous, and then you will have good success."*

Psalm 1:2, *"But his delight is in the law of the LORD, and in His law he meditates day and night."*

Jeremiah 15:16, *"Your words were found, and I ate them, and Your word was to me the joy and rejoicing of my heart; for I am called by Your name, O LORD God of hosts."*

Ezekiel 2:3, *"And He said to me: "Son of man, I am sending you to the children of Israel, to a rebellious nation that has rebelled against Me; they and their fathers have transgressed against Me to this very day."*

Ezekiel 3:4, *"And He said to me: 'Son of man, go to the house of Israel and speak with My words to them.'"*

Matthew 22:29, *"Jesus answered and said to them, 'You are mistaken, not knowing the Scriptures nor the power of God.'"*

Colossians 3:16a, *"Let the word of Christ dwell in you richly in all wisdom..."*

1 Timothy 4:5, *"For it is sanctified by the word of God and prayer."*

How to Memorize Scripture

Many Christians believe that they cannot memorize Scripture. They think it is too hard or that it takes too much time. Some even believe that they are not smart enough to remember it. However, I am of the opinion that anyone who wants to memorize Scripture can. If this were not true, then God would be unjust in commanding His children to memorize the Word. I am convinced that no matter how young or old you are, you can memorize Scripture and that whatever effort it takes will be rewarded many times over.

The main reason most people never memorize Scripture is because they have never had a practical method to aid in memorizing and reviewing Scripture. In this section, we are going to learn a practical method and aid to help you begin a Scripture memory program.

1. Make up your mind to do it!

   The most important step in doing something is to make up your mind that you will do it. No method will help you unless you first purpose in your heart that you will do it. At the age of twenty-four, Augustus Van Reign learned that he was going blind. It was at that time that he decided to use all of his free time to memorize God's Word. By the time he reached thirty-five years of age, he had memorized the entire New Testament.

   Someone has said, "By the street of by-and-by one arrives at the house of never." Someone else has said, "The greatest waste of time is the time wasted getting started." Purpose in your heart to spend time daily memorizing and reviewing God's Word. Psalm 46:10 says, *"Be still, and know that I am God."* In order to do that, we have to make up our minds now to spend time every day memorizing God's Word.

2. Select the verses to memorize.

   It is best for you to select your own verses. The more meaningful the verse is to you, the more significance you attach to it and the easier it is to memorize. You will retain it more easily, enjoy it more, and be highly motivated.

   However, not everyone has the background to begin a memory

program in that way. So we are going to give you a list of verses to help get you started. The verses we have chosen are ones every Christian should know for his own benefit and for sharing with others. While you are memorizing these, start a list of other verses that you would like to memorize. That way, when you are finished with this program, you can keep going without having to think about what verse you are going to memorize next. When a verse comes alive to you, then add it to your list.

You may want to memorize a number of verses on a particular topic or doctrine. That's great, but it is better to memorize three verses on ten different topics than to memorize thirty verses on one topic. Likewise, it is best to learn three or more verses on all of the doctrines before attempting to memorize all of the verses on a particular doctrine. A concordance, a topical Bible, or a basic Bible doctrine book will assist you in selecting your verses.

Another method you may want to try later on is memorizing whole chapters or whole books of the Bible. This method can be very profitable because it allows you to meditate on the meaning of larger portions of Scripture and add more significance to each verse as you understand its context. Some good passages with which to start are Philippians 2:5-10, Psalm 1, Romans 8, Matthew 5 (Sermon on the Mount), or a shorter book like 1 John or 2 Peter. You will be surprised to find that some verses that don't mean anything to you at first become filled with significance when you understand them in context. But develop the habit with single verses first.

3. Use a card system.

It is believed that in 1898, Dr. Oscar Lowry, author of *Scripture Memorizing and Successful Personal Work*, started what has become a very popular practice of putting Scripture on cards. Dr. Lowry memorized twenty thousand (20,000) verses, almost two thirds of the Bible using the card method. The Navigators and many other groups have used cards to aid in Scripture memory since that time. There are a number of advantages in putting the verses you plan to memorize on cards. Some of these advantages are as follows:

a. Cards can be carried in a pocket or a purse and reviewed any time and any place.
b. Cards make it easier to file or rearrange your verses.
c. Cards can be fastened to the wall, mirror, or curtain and memorized while using your hands for other things.
d. They enable you to use spare moments that would otherwise be wasted.

4. Understand the principles of memorization.

A basic understanding of the principles of memorization helps one to memorize more effectively. The human mind has an unlimited capacity for storing facts. Most psychologists would agree that the majority of people never use more than five or ten percent of their mental capacity. What a shame for Christians to let such a vast storehouse go unused. The brain reacts very similarly to the muscles when one embarks on a physical program. When you first start to exercise, it is very difficult and the muscles become sore; but the more you exercise and use those muscles, the easier it becomes. The soreness leaves and the muscles develop a greater capacity to exercise. In like manner, when you first begin to memorize, it may seem difficult. But as you persist, memorizing becomes easier and your capacity to memorize grows.

There are three basic principles that should be applied to every verse that is memorized. I use the acrostic AIR:

A — Association
I — Impression
R — Repetition

The principle of association would involve studying the context and background of the verse and associating it with the context. This helps you to understand what the verse is talking about and avoid misinterpretation.

Impression means to impress it in your mind every way possible. People learn in different ways. Some learn by reading, some by hearing, some only learn through physical activity, and some people need pictures. So just cover all the bases:

a. read the verse in other translations
b. quote the verse out loud
c. write the verse
d. visualize the verse - try to picture what is being said

Another way to impress a verse on your mind is to set it to music. Sometimes songs can get stuck in your head easier than words alone, and many verses already have melodies written for them. There are thousands of people around the world who never intended to memorize the Lord's Prayer, but could recite most of it from memory simply because they have heard the music so often. In the same manner, listening to a tape where your memory verses are repeated can stamp the words not only into your memory, but also into your subconscious mind where you begin to believe them more deeply.

Walking or jogging also aid the memory. The more senses you involve in the memory process, the greater the impression that is made.

Repetition is the process of over-learning. Consistent, spaced repetition is a key to successful memorization. Memories are created by literally burning electrical pathways on the brain. Lasting memories are either very intense incidents, or things that were repeated over and over. The more repetition, the more deeply entrenched the pathway is that brings that verse up from your memory. To maintain access to that pathway, we have to use it on a semi-regular basis. So reviewing your memorized verses is just as important as memorizing it in the first place.

There are no short cuts to spiritual success. There is a certain amount of work involved and the flesh usually rebels against that type of discipline, but it can be done.

5. Utilize a method of spaced repetition.

Let us assume that you have decided to memorize a verse a day for the next year. You have already selected fifty verses and have written them on small cards. The verse you select to memorize is Psalm 119:11. The front of the card has the words of the verse, the reference, and the topic. The back of the card has today's date on it — the day you begin memorizing it. Using the three principles of memorization, you work on the verse until you can say it word perfect with reference. If it is a long verse, break it into phrases after applying the principles of association and impression. Repeat the first phrase with the reference a number of times and then add the second phrase, then continue until you can quote the entire verse with the reference.

Now, you begin the process of spaced repetition. The first day quote the verse out loud with the reference twenty-five (25) times. Check the card from time to time to be sure you are saying it correctly. Each time you quote the verse, make a mark with your pen on a piece of scrap paper. When you complete your work for that day, you will have made twenty-five (25) marks. These marks may seem unnecessary, but they will aid you in several ways. They give you a specific goal to work towards, they help you to concentrate, and they give you a feeling of accomplishment and success when you finish. They prevent you from omitting any portion of this important process. Remember, if you take short cuts, you will come up short. After quoting the verse twenty-five times, write "25" on the back of the card on which the verse is written.

On the second day, you use the above procedure to memorize a new verse. However, when you look at the reference from the day before, Psalm 119:11, you may be unable to recall the words, but with a little work it will all come back and you can quote it word perfect once again. Quote it aloud with the reference twenty times, making marks as you go, and write "20" on the back of the card.

The third day you memorize a new verse saying it twenty-five times. You quote yesterday's verse twenty times, after refreshing your memory. Then you return to Psalm 119:11. You might not remember every word perfectly, but that's ok. Don't be discouraged, because this is the learning process.

In order to memorize something, you must learn it, forget it, learn it, forget it, learn it and you've got it. Sometimes it may even take four or five sessions of working on a verse before you can recall it word perfect and well. So on the third day, you quote Psalm 119:11 fifteen times and write "15" on the back of the card.

On the fourth day, you quote it ten times, and on the fifth day, say it five times. For the next forty-five days, you quote it once a day, just to lock it in. Psalm 119:11 is then placed in a weekly review and is reviewed once a week for seven weeks. It is placed in a monthly review and is reviewed once a month thereafter.

If at any time you cannot quote a verse that is in the weekly or monthly review, it should be placed in a special daily review until you are satisfied that you know it. Somehow that verse missed part of the vital process. It took a short cut and came out short.

At the end of five days, the back of the card will look like this:

Psalm 119:11
September 19, 2000
25, 20, 15, 10, 5

The date will assist you in keeping the verses in the order they are memorized so each will be reviewed for fifty days before being moved to the weekly review.

6. Consider the time cost.

At the end of 365 days, if you have faithfully followed this method, you will know 365 verses. Your daily verse pack will contain fifty verses. Each day, you will be adding a new verse to the top and take one from the bottom to place it on the top of your weekly review pack. At this point, the monthly review contains three hundred and sixteen verses.

The time required will vary depending upon the person, the length of the new verses, the amount of time spent meditating, and the amount of interruptions. On the average, however, it will take thirty to forty minutes to review the daily memory, and ten to fifteen minutes each week for the weekly review. This is reviewing four or five verses per minute and sixty minutes each month for the monthly review. These estimated times do not allow for meditation or interruptions.

7. Schedule the time.

Most people find it best to do their memory work early in the morning, shortly after rising for the day. At this time, the mind is fresh, there are fewer distractions, and you can meditate upon the Word all day. If you wait until the evening to memorize, your mind is usually tired and filled with the activities of the day. Many evenings you will be involved in activities that may interfere with your memory work. Your schedule may dictate a later time in the day, but the earlier the better. In fact, the Scriptures repeatedly encourage us to meet with God in the morning. Genesis 19:27, *"And Abraham went early in the morning to the place where he had stood before the LORD";* Genesis 22:3, *"So Abraham rose early in the morning and saddled his donkey, and took two of his young men with him, and Isaac his son; and he split the wood for the burnt offering, and arose and went to the place of which God had told him"* Gen 28:18, *"Then Jacob rose early in the morning, and took the stone that he had put at his head, set it up as a pillar, and poured oil on top of it";* Exodus 9:13, *Then the LORD said to Moses, "Rise early in the morning and stand before Pharaoh, and say to him, 'Thus says the LORD God of the Hebrews: Let My people go, that they may serve Me'";* Joshua 6:12, *"And Joshua rose early in the morning, and the priests took up the ark of the LORD"*; Psalm 5:3; *"My voice You shall hear in the morning, O LORD; in the morning I will direct it to You, and I will look up"*; Mark 1:35, *"Now in the morning, having risen a long while before daylight, He went out and departed to a solitary place; and there He prayed."*

8. Review, review, review!

The weekly and monthly review serves two very important functions. It enables you to meditate upon God's Word and it keeps the verses fresh in your mind, available for the Holy Spirit to use as the need arises. So let me stress that the value of review cannot be over-emphasized. Jack Van Impe has memorized all of the New Testament. He knows over eight thousand (8,000) verses and for the past twenty years, he has sought to spend two hours per day memorizing and reviewing the Word of God.

9. Use the verses you have memorized.

You, no doubt, have heard the true saying, "If you don't use it, you will lose it." This statement applies to memorizing Scripture. The more you use your verses, the less likely you are to lose them. Scripture memorization is not an end in itself, it is a means to an end. We want to know the Word so we can meditate upon the Word; we want to meditate so we can understand the Word; and we want to understand so that we might grow, help others, and obey God's Word. Therefore, the goal of Scripture memorization is obedience to God's Word. The following are some of the ways that you may use the memorized Word:

a. in witnessing
b. in letters to friends and relatives
c. in teaching and preaching

d. in counseling and comforting
e. in defending the faith
f. in answering questions
g. in prayer
h. in Bible study
i. in discussing doctrines
j. in combating temptation, worry, and evil thought
k. in meditation
l. in refuting false doctrine

The more you use the verses, the more you will want to memorize and review.

Why Some Do Not Memorize Scripture

There are many Christians who do not memorize Scripture. Some simply do not want to and therefore make excuses for their disobedience. Let us look at some of the excuses.

1. Some say they don't see the value of Scripture memorization. They give the impression that Scripture memory is for Sunday School children. This excuse shows ignorance of the Bible and may be one of the reasons that so many have been saved for years but are still babes in Christ.

2. Some excuse themselves by saying they cannot memorize. These fail to recognize how many names, numbers, and other things they have memorized almost effortlessly. I imagine those who offer this excuse would gain great memory skill overnight if they were offered ten dollars for each verse they memorized.

3. The most popular excuse is, "I don't have time" or "I'm too busy." The practice of putting the physical before the spiritual is not new by any means. You will no doubt remember how Martha who was cumbered about much serving asked the Master to rebuke Mary for sitting at His feet instead of working. Instead of rebuking Mary, *"Jesus answered and said to her, 'Martha,*

Martha, you are worried and troubled about many things. But one thing is needed, and Mary has chosen that good part, which will not be taken away from her,'" (Luke 10:41-42). Certainly the Lord wants us to serve Him, but He first wants us to take in the Word before we seek to give it out or concern ourselves with physical tasks. Yes, doubtless, many will make the excuse that they cannot afford to take the time for this extra work. But I would put it the other way — you cannot afford NOT to do it. You can find time for everything else you wish to do. Why not find the time for this also? Though it will mean for many that they must cut short their early morning nap, yet they cannot afford to miss this great blessing. I really believe that this poem puts it as well as it could be said:

"I have only just a minute just sixty seconds in it,
Forced upon me
Can't refuse it
Didn't seek it
Didn't choose it
I must suffer if I lose it
Give account if I abuse it
Just a tiny little minute
But eternity is in it."

I have known several college students that have carried heavy academic loads as well as many hours devoted to a job, yet they find time to memorize Scripture. Many of them do it early before class; many of them recite the verses while walking to class or waiting in the lunch line. There is always enough time to learn what you need to know. Memorization has greatly aided my personal life and my witnessing. I promise you that it will aid your life also.

I am convinced that there are basically two kinds of people in the world: There are the way-finders and the excuse-finders. When we really want to do something, we join the way-finder's club because we always find a way to do what we want to do. If we do not want to do something, we join the excuse-finder's club, for we can always find an excuse not to do what we don't want to do. You must leave the excuse-finders behind and find the way-finders club and find a way to memorize the Word of God.

While some make excuses for their lack of Scripture memorization, others are truly hindered for various reasons. However, solutions can be found to each of the following obstacles.

1. Not saved

   Naturally, an unsaved man would not be interested in memorizing Scripture. The Bible is foolishness to the lost man (1 Corinthians 2:14, *"But the natural man does not receive the things of the Spirit of God, for they are foolishness to him; nor can he know them, because they are spiritually discerned.)* Only God knows how many church members and Sunday School members are not Christians. Those who have never been born again would have no appetite for the Word. 1 Peter 2:2 says, *"As newborn babes, desire the pure milk of the word, that you may grow thereby."*

2. Backslidden

   Proverbs 14:15 says, *"The simple believes every word, but the prudent considers well his steps."* A backslider, a Christian who has fallen into sinful patterns, will have no interest in Scripture memorization because he is out of fellowship with God. If a man has sin in his life, he avoids the Word until he is ready to get right with God again. The Word of God reveals what he really is (Hebrews 4:12, *"For the word of God is living and powerful, and sharper than any two-edged sword, piercing even to the division of soul and spirit, and of joints and marrow, and is a discerner of the thoughts and intents of the heart"* and that is the last thing he wants to be reminded of.

3. Laziness

   Some do not memorize because they are not willing to put forth the necessary effort. Paul gives a solution to this weakness in

Romans 13:14, *"But put on the Lord Jesus Christ, and make no provision for the flesh, to fulfill its lusts."* In other words, rely on God's strength to overcome your laziness and do it anyway.

4. Rebellion

Rebellion is as the sin of witchcraft, just as stubbornness is. They are both very much like iniquity and idolatry. In each of these, you are asserting your own authority over God. Yet I have known people to refuse Scripture because they were rebelling against God, or some person, or some method.

5. Lack of follow-through

Some have become discouraged and quit because they were unable to retain either the verses or the references. Forgetting is a result of insufficient review. One must give the same attention to the reference as he does the text. The method recommended in this text solves the problem. The only people this method has not worked for are those who failed to follow the instructions.

6. Procrastination

The thief of procrastination has robbed some of the blessings of Scripture memorization. You no doubt have heard the procrastinator saying, "I am going to start next semester," or, "I'll start when I finish school," or, "I'll start when I get into the ministry." The procrastinators are like the man in this verse of poetry:

"The man who slept beneath the moon
and basked beneath the sun,
he lived a life of going to do
and left with nothing done."

Another poem gives a vivid description of the results of procrastination.

"Mr. Meant To" has a comrade and his name is "Didn't Do It"
Have you ever chanced to meet them?
Did they ever call on you?
These two fellows live together in the house of Never Win.
And I'm told that it is haunted
by the ghost of Might Have Been.

Yes, the person who waits for the convenient time or the perfect time to serve God usually never does anything but wait. If you have been waiting, why not start today, right now, memorizing Scriptures.

7. Lack of purpose or goal

Others find it difficult to memorize the Word because they have no purpose for memorizing. To be motivated to faithfully memorize Scripture, you must link it with a definite purpose or goal. Therefore, you should select and memorize verses you know will help you in your personal life — verses that you can use to help others.

"Onward and upward your course plan today
Seeking new heights as you walk Jesus' way;
Heed not past failures, but strive for the prize
Aiming for goals fit for His holy eyes."

I trust that you will realize, as I have, that the rewards of Scripture memorization are so great that no one can let any excuse or hindrance stand in his way of memorizing God's precious Word.

The Rewards of Memorizing Scripture

Proverbs 3:3-4 says, *"Let not mercy and truth forsake you; bind them around your neck, write them on the tablet of your heart, And so find favor and high esteem in the sight of God and man."* Down deep in the heart of every normal person born into this human race there is a threefold desire: (1) a desire to be happy, (2) a desire to be wise, and (3) a desire to be successful. Anyone who will obey God's command in memorizing Scripture will have all three of these desires realized in his life. Let us look at the results and rewards for memorizing Scripture.

1. Memorizing Scripture leads to loving obedience to God.

In Deuteronomy 6:5, Moses tells the people of God that *"You shall love the LORD your God with all your heart, with all your soul, and with all your strength."* Then in the next few verses, he tells them to memorize the Word and keep it before themselves and their families constantly. He went on to say that this would result in obedience to God.

Likewise, God told Joshua (1:8): *"This Book of the Law shall not depart from your mouth, but you shall meditate in it day and night, that you may observe to do according to all that is written in it. For then you will make your way prosperous, and then you will have good success."* God wanted Joshua and all of His people to memorize and meditate upon His Word so that they might obey His commands. Then the blessings He promised would flow through their lives. When people desire to love and obey God, they should memorize the Word of God because it never returns void (Isaiah 55:11, *"So shall My word be that goes forth from My mouth; it shall not return to Me void, but it shall accomplish what I please, and it shall prosper in the thing for which I sent it."*)

2. Memorizing Scripture helps us teach our children.

Right after God called Israel to love Him, He told them to teach His Word to their children. In Deuteronomy 6:6-7, *"And these words which I command you today shall be in your heart. You shall teach them diligently to your children, and shall talk of them when you sit in your 1house, when you walk by the way, when you lie down, and when you rise up."* Moses told the people to memorize God's Words and to "teach them diligently unto thy children, and shalt talk of them when thou sittest in thy house, and when thou walkest by the way, and when thou liest down, and when thou risest up." These words they memorize would enable them to teach their children at all times and in all places. Most Christian parents do not teach the Word to their children because they do not know the Word or do not know the Word well themselves. The New Testament describes new converts as spiritual children. Anyone who has ever been a spiritual parent knows how helpful the memorized Word is in answering questions and guiding new converts.

3. Memorizing Scripture causes us to prosper and be successful for God.

There is much being said about success in the world today. Sinners and saints alike are seeking shortcuts to success. However, there are no shortcuts to true spiritual success. The word ***success*** appears only one time in the King James Version of the Bible. It is found in Joshua 1:8, *"This Book of the Law shall not depart from your mouth, but you shall meditate in it day and night, that you may observe to do according to all that is written in it. For then you will make your way prosperous, and then you will have good success."* This verse hints at the definition of success and gives a clear, concise formula to follow for finding success.

First, let us consider the definition. The word "prosperous" in this verse conveys the idea of making progress. Success for the Christian is progressing in the will of God. It is daily finding and doing the will of God. It is the progressive realization of a worthwhile goal. The only worthwhile goal in this world for the Christian is the will of God. God wants His children to prosper and succeed in His will. But what is the will of God? *For this is the will of God, your sanctification: that you should abstain from sexual immorality";* (1 Thessalonians 4:3), or as Paul put it is Romans, *"For whom He foreknew, He also predestined to be conformed to the image of His Son, that He might be the firstborn among many brethren,"* (8:29). True prosperity and success is progressively becoming more and more obedient to God, as Jesus was.

Joshua 1:8 also gives a three-fold formula for finding success. We must (1) memorize the Word by repeating it constantly, (2) meditate on it day and night, and (3) obey all that is written in it. It is not easy, but God promises success and prosperity to all who will follow this simple, three-step formula. For those who think the task is too great, God offers the power of His abiding presence in the next verse.

4. Scripture memorization brings great happiness and joy.

Probably the two things most sought after by the world are happiness and success. Most believe that success brings happiness. It is interesting to me that God makes it very clear in His Word how His children may obtain both of these. God has placed them in easy reach of every believer and yet I wonder how many really enjoy these much sought after intangibles. Joshua 1:8 gave us the formula for success, and Psalm 1 gives us the formula for happiness. It says, *"Blessed* (happy) *is the man that walketh not in the counsel of the ungodly, nor standeth in the way of sinners, nor sitteth in the seat of the scornful. But his delight is in the law of the Lord and in His law doth he meditate day and night. And he shall be like a tree planted by the rivers of water that bring forth his fruit in his season; his leaf also shall not wither; and whatsoever he doeth shall prosper."* Most Bible teachers agree that the word ***blessed*** in verse one could be translated "happy," "jubilant," or "content." The formula for happiness, according to these verses is to. . .

a. **REJECT** the way of the wicked
   1) Reject his advice
   2) Reject his sinful ways
   3) Reject his scornful attitude

b. **RECEIVE** the way of the Word
   1) Delight in it — love spending time in it
   2) Meditate on it — which means you have to memorize it first so that you can think about it and mull it over in your mind.

c. **REJOICE** in the results of the above
   1) It produces a *stable* life
   2) It produces a *fruitful* life
   3) It produces a *vibrant* life
   4) It produces a *prosperous* life

Psalm 19:8 says, *"The statutes of the LORD are right, rejoicing the heart";* Jeremiah 15:16 says, *"Your words were found, and I ate them, and Your word was to me the joy and rejoicing of my heart; for I am called by Your name, O LORD God of hosts."* The memorized Word brings great joy and happiness to the believer's life.

I think of joy as being created within the believer by the Word and the Holy Spirit, and happiness is the outward manifestation of the inner life. This being the case, the believer is not dependent upon the stimulus outside himself for his joy. He can be happy at all times regardless of his circumstances. Have you been missing out on this aspect of the Christian life? Jesus says, *"These things I have spoken to you, that My joy may remain in you, and that your joy may be full."* (John 15:11).

5. Memorizing Scripture enables us to meditate upon the Word day and night.

Meditating on Scripture is a great advantage because we become what we think. It is not what you think you are, but what you think, you are. A paraphrase of Titus 1:5 reads, "*For this reason I left you in Crete, that you should set in order the things that are lacking, and appoint elders in every city as I commanded you"*— for his dirty mind and rebellious heart color all he sees and hears. This is why Proverbs 4:20-23 admonishes us to exercise great control over what enters out hearts and minds. "*My son, give attention to my words; incline your ear to my sayings. Do not let them depart from your eyes; keep them in the midst of your heart; For they are life to those who find them, and health to all their flesh. Keep your heart with all diligence, for out of it spring the issues of life."* Our attitudes, speech, and actions all come from our minds. We can control our attitudes, speech, and actions by controlling what enters our minds and the thoughts upon which we focus our attention.

The goal of every Christian should be to be more Christ-like every day. Paul said, "*Let this mind be in you which was also in Christ Jesus,*" (Philippians 2:5). "*Meditate on these things; give yourself entirely to them, that your progress may be evident to all,*" (1 Timothy 4:15). If you were to focus your attention upon committing a crime each day, if you would daily think it through, you would soon find yourself committing that crime. On the other hand, if you would daily visualize yourself thinking and acting like Christ, you would soon find yourself manifesting these attitudes and actions. Scripture memory enables you to select, plan, and shape your character. Proverbs 20:7 says, "*The righteous man walks in his integrity; his children are blessed after him.*"

A cow chewing her cud illustrates meditation. A cow's stomach has four sections. When a cow eats food, it is stored in the first two compartments for a time. The food is formed into balls so it can be returned to the cow's mouth for additional chewing. While chewing her cud, the cow can extract from her food the energy and nutrients her body will need to carry on the activities of the day. In like manner, the Christian can store God's Word in his mind by memorizing and then calling it to mind whenever possible or necessary, and extract from it additional spiritual energy and nourishment.

6. Memorizing Scripture produces a vibrant, stable, and consistent life.

The Psalmist describes the individual who memorizes and meditates upon the word as "*...planted by the rivers of water, that brings forth its fruit in its season, whose leaf also shall not wither,*" (Psalm 1:3). This idea conveys a stable, consistent person overflowing with life. This person has built his life upon the unchanging principles of God's Word and he is not tossed to and fro, and carried about by every wind of doctrine. He knows what he believes and why he believes it. He cannot be shaken because his roots are deep in the rich soil of God's Word. Usually you leave his presence blessed or inspired because he overflows with the Word of Life.

7. Memorizing Scripture produces a fruitful life.

The Psalmist also said that the one who memorizes the Word *"brings forth its fruit in its season,"* (Psalm 1:3). In other words, he produces when he is supposed to produce. It is easy for one who is daily memorizing and meditating upon the Word to confess his sins and yield to the control of the Holy Spirit. When this is done, he blossoms as a tree with the fruit of the Spirit (Galatians 5:22-23, *"But the fruit of the Spirit is love, joy, peace, longsuffering, kindness, goodness, faithfulness, gentleness, self-control. Against such there is no law.*). The Spirit also prompts him to go and bring forth fruit and guides him in teaching his new converts so that his fruit might remain. Thus, the memorized Word equips this happy one to be fruitful and multiply and reproduce after his kind.

8. Memorizing Scripture converts the soul.

"The law of the LORD is perfect, converting the soul; the testimony of the LORD is sure, making wise the simple," (Psalm 19:7). The Word of God plays a part in the salvation of every soul that is saved. Paul said of Timothy *"That from childhood you have known the Holy Scriptures, which are able to make you wise for salvation through faith which is in Christ Jesus,"* (2 Timothy 3:15). The name ***Timothy*** means "honoring God." It may be that his mother, Eunice, taught him the Scriptures as a child so that he might be saved at a young age and honor God all of his life. My wife and I made it our goal and purpose to teach our children Scripture from the moment they were able to talk. I am convinced that one of the ways we are to train up our children is by teaching them to memorize Scripture. A child's mind is most impressionable between the ages of two and twelve, and many Christian parents pass up this golden opportunity while the world takes advantage of it. As a result of spaced repetition, most Sunday School

children, at the age of six, can quote word perfect scores of television commercials and know names of movie stars, but few, if any, Bible verses. Is it any wonder America is in its present condition?

9. Memorizing Scripture gives great wisdom.

Most people crave wisdom. Wisdom is the ability to apply knowledge to everyday situations. *"For the LORD gives wisdom; from His mouth come knowledge and understanding";* (Proverbs 2:6). The following verses clearly teach that the one who memorizes the Word is growing in wisdom daily.

"The law of the LORD is perfect, converting the *soul; the testimony of the LORD is sure, making wise the simple,"* (Psalm 19:7).

"I have more understanding than all my teachers, for Your testimonies are my meditation," (Psalm 119:99).

*"I have chosen the way of truth; your judgments I have laid before me," (*Psalm 119:30).

"My son, do not forget my law, but let your heart keep my commands; For length of days and long life and peace they will add to you. Let not mercy and truth forsake you; bind them around your neck, write them on the tablet of your heart, And so find favor and high esteem in the sight of God and man," (Proverbs 3:4).

This last verse reminds me of a story told to me by a man who held a psychology degree. He started using a memory system the day he was saved and, after memorizing sixty verses of Scripture, he told me he had learned more about getting along with people in those sixty days than in the entire forty years of studying psychology. My friends, if any man lacks wisdom, let him memorize Scripture.

10. Memorizing Scripture gives guidance.

Every surrendered Christian wants to know and do the will of

God. God has given us a road map to guide us: the will of God revealed in the Word of God. Therefore, the will of God will never lead a man to violate the Word of God. The man who disobeys the Word and says God led him is a liar and a blasphemer. The better I know the Word, the better I will know His will for my life. If a man took a long trip, got lost many times, but never consulted the map God had with him all the time, we would consider him to be very foolish. Yet how many times we have gotten out of the will of God and ended up in the hard place because we failed to consult the map He has given us. From now on, let us memorize the Word and be able to say with the Psalmist, *"The law of his God is in his heart; none of his steps shall slide,"* (Psalm 37:31). Psalm 40:8, *"I delight to do Your will, O my God, and Your law is within my heart." "Your word is a lamp to my feet and a light to my path."* (Psalm 119:105). Keep in mind that He only leads us one step at a time.

11. Memorizing Scripture gives victory over sin, Satan, temptation, strange doctrines, and strange women (Ephesians 4:14, *"That we should no longer be children, tossed to and fro and carried about with every wind of doctrine, by the trickery of men, in the cunning craftiness of deceitful plotting";* 2 John 9-11, *"Whoever transgresses and does not abide in the doctrine of Christ does not have God. He who abides in the doctrine of Christ has both the Father and the Son. If anyone comes to you and does not bring this doctrine, do not receive him into your house nor greet him; for he who greets him shares in his evil deeds";* Proverbs 6:21-33).

David asked the question in Psalm 119:9, "*How* can *a young man cleanse his way?"* In verse 11, he answers the question: "*Your word I have hidden in my heart, that I might not sin against You!"* Indeed, the memorized Word enables one to have the victory over sin, Satan, temptation, strange doctrines, and strange women. Adam and Eve, while in the garden of Eden, were having wonderful fellowship with God. But one day, Satan came in the form of a serpent and began to talk to Eve. Perhaps their conversation went something like this.

Satan:	"Hello, Eve."
Eve:	"Oh, hello. Who are you?"
Satan:	"I am the serpent, Eve."
Eve:	"A serpent? But snakes don't talk."
Satan:	"That's a beautiful tree in the midst of the garden, Eve."
Eve:	"Yes, it is pleasant to the eyes."
Satan:	"It looks like it would be good for food. Why don't you eat some of it?"
Eve:	"Oh, no! God told us we mustn't eat it, neither should we touch it, lest we die."
Satan:	"Ha, Ha, Ha, Eve! You won't die! You don't really believe that, do you? God just told you that; he is controlling you; he's holding you back; he doesn't want you to have any liberty or fun; he doesn't want you to live your own life. If you throw off this restraint and eat, you will be wise. You'll be like God. Why don't you try just a little bit?"
Eve:	"I guess a little bit won't hurt."

"So when the woman saw that the tree was good for food, that it was pleasant to the eyes, and a tree desirable to make one wise, she took of its fruit and ate. She also *gave to her husband with her, and he ate,"* (Genesis 3:6). So after Eve had dialogued with the Devil, she and Adam dove into sin and dragged the human race down into the depths of depravity. Ever since that time, every human being that has been born possesses a sinful nature. Mankind has a built-in sin factory. Sin is standard equipment on all models, and it is working when it comes off the assembly line, producing sinful thoughts, words, and deeds. This sin nature is subject to three areas of temptation: the lust of the flesh, the lust of the eyes, and the pride of life (1 John 2:15-16, "*Do not love the world or the things in the world. If anyone loves the world, the love of the Father is not in him. For all that is in the world— the lust of the flesh, the lust of the eyes, and the pride of life— is not of the Father but is of the world."*) You and I daily face the same

temptations that Eve faced in the garden.

Likewise, these are the same temptations Jesus faced in the wilderness. However, he dealt differently with the Devil than Eve did. Let's listen to the *conversation* after Jesus had fasted forty days and forty nights. Satan came to tempt him.

Satan:	"Jesus, if you are really the Son of God, prove it by turning these stones into bread."
Jesus:	"Get out of here, Satan, for it is written: '*Man shall not live by bread alone; but man lives by every word that proceeds from the mouth of the LORD.'"* (Deuteronomy 8:3)

Then Satan took him up on a high mountain, and showed him all the kingdoms of the world.

Satan:	"Jesus, all these things will I give thee if thou will fall down and worship me."
Jesus:	*"You shall not go after other gods, the gods of the peoples who are all around you."* (Deuteronomy 6:13)

Then Satan took Him up to the highest part of the temple, and I imagine he said:

Satan:	"Jesus, there's a large crowd in town. If you really want to become popular and famous; if you really want to make a name for yourself and be praised by men, jump off of the temple. Remember, God has promised to give his angels charge over you and they will come and swoop you up before you hit the ground. (Psalm 91:11-12, *For He shall give His angels charge over you, to keep you in all your ways. In*

	their hands they shall bear you up, lest you dash your foot against a stone.) This spectacular event will make you famous and you'll be the praise all men."
Jesus:	"Get out of here, Satan, for it is written: *'You shall not tempt the LORD your God.'"* (Deuteronomy 6:16)

Satan went away and left Jesus, and the angels of God ministered to Him. Whose example will you follow — Jesus or Eve? Will you do as Eve did: dialogue with the Devil, believe the way he twists God's Word, and dive into sin? Or will you memorize the Word, confront Satan, and send him on his way with the sword of the Spirit as our Savior did?

Tom Maharis, pastor of Manhattan Bible Church in the Bronx, New York, drew three columns in the back of his Bible. In each column he listed ten references. Ten verses dealt with the lust of the flesh, ten with the lust of the eyes, and ten with the pride of life. Tom memorized all thirty verses, and, now, when he faces temptation, he quotes an appropriate verse and prays for victory. If the temptation does not go away, he quotes another verse and prays for victory. He continues to quote Scripture and pray until God gives the victory — and He does!

Yes, the Bible teaches that you do not have to sin. 1 John 2:1 reads, "*My little children, these things I write to you, so that you may not sin. And if anyone sins, we have an Advocate with the Father, Jesus Christ the righteous.*" God does not want His children to sin. You may ask, "How can I prevent it?" I will paraphrase 1 Corinthians 10:13, which gives the answer, "*No temptation has overtaken you except such as is common to man; but God is faithful, who will not allow you to be tempted beyond what you are able, but with the temptation will also make the way of escape, that you may be able to bear it.*" In other words, every time you are tempted, if you will look around, you will see a door, and over the door you will see written, "Emergency Exit: Use in Case of Temptation." If you will always take that way of escape, you can have victory over sin. If you have already sinned, confess your sins and God will forgive you. What does God do with our sins when we confess them? He washes us whiter than snow; He removes them as far as the east from the west; He casts them behind His back; He dumps them into the depths of the sea and remembers them against us no more. If you have sinned, confess your sins, thank God for His forgiveness, and do as Tom Maharis did. When Tom was tempted, he quoted the Word of God.

12. Memorizing Scripture gives comfort in times of affliction.

Nothing soothes the soul of the saint like Scripture. When the seas of life are raging, the Psalmist said, "*Unless Your law had been my delight, I would then have perished in my affliction,*" (Psalm 119:92). In times of great heartache, sorrow, and trouble, the Holy Spirit is faithful to bring to mind the memorized Word to comfort and console the soul of the saint.

13. Memorizing Scripture gives a better understanding of the Word and results in spiritual growth.

The Psalmist wrote, "*I have more understanding than all my teachers, for Your testimonies are my meditation,*" (Psalm 119:99). Peter wrote, "*As newborn babes, desire the pure milk of the word, that you may grow thereby,*" (1 Peter 2:2). Paul said, "*All Scripture is given by inspiration of God, and is profitable for doctrine, for reproof, for correction, for instruction in righteousness, that the man of God may be complete, thoroughly equipped for every good work,*" (2 Timothy 3:16-17). These men are telling us that, if we will get a good grip on the Word, we will understand it better, grow faster, mature in Christ, and be fully equipped to serve God and to defeat Satan.

I am of the opinion that the best way to help Christians to grow and mature in Christ is to teach them how and motivate them to memorize the Word. When a Christian has the memorized Word in his mind, the Holy Spirit is able to select the appropriate verse and preach the appropriate message to that believer anytime, anywhere. The Holy Spirit always knows what every believer needs and when he needs it. The wife of the president of a Bible school said, "Daily memorizing and reviewing verses has helped me more in my Christian life than anything I have ever done." A pastor said, "I have memorized almost 400 verses with this plan." I think it is the best plan because of the constant review that it includes. I promise you, if you will memorize this Book, God will bless you greatly.

14. Memorizing Scripture gives victory over evil thoughts.

"I hate the double-minded, but I love Your law," (Psalm 119:113). Probably the greatest battle faced by most Christians is the struggle we have with our thought life. The past comes up, worry presses in, discouragement passes by, evil thoughts about others drop in, and the Devil suggests things unheard of. To my knowledge, the only way to real victory is to fill your mind with the Word of God. It has an interesting effect. The Bible says in 2 Corinthians 10:5 that we are to be *"casting down arguments and every high thing that exalts itself against the knowledge of God, bringing every thought into captivity to the obedience of Christ."* Remember this familiar statement, "Garbage in, garbage out." I say, "Righteousness in, righteousness out." That is why we have to be so careful what we put into our minds through movies, television, literature, filthy jokes, and sitting under the teaching of lost and worldly-minded teachers. I am so thankful for solid Christian educational institutions, where students are taught by men and women of God who are filled with the Word of God and the Spirit of God, and the knowledge of God.

You must remember that it is not a sin when an evil thought enters your mind. It becomes a sin when you entertain that thought or desire that thing. James comments on this by saying, *"Let no one say when he is tempted, 'I am tempted by God'; for God cannot be tempted by evil, nor does He Himself tempt anyone. But each one is tempted when he is drawn away by his own desires and enticed. Then, when desire has conceived, it gives birth to sin; and sin, when it is full-grown, brings forth death,"* (James 1:13-15).

Therefore, if you have entertained an evil thought, confess it as sin. Reject it. Thank God for His forgiveness and think on Scripture. Meditate on Scripture and pray for victory. Someone has said, "It is not wrong to let a bird fly overhead, but you don't have to let him make a nest in your hair." Our objective should be to so fill the air of our minds with the bullets of God's Word that the birds of evil thoughts won't even want to fly over our heads, much less make a nest in our hair.

15. Memorizing Scripture gives great peace and victory over worry.

Great peace and perfect peace are the lot of the man who memorizes and meditates upon the Word. So says the Scripture, "*Great peace have those who love Your law, and nothing causes them to stumble,*" (Psalm 119:165). "*My son, do not forget my law, but let your heart keep my commands; For length of days and long life and peace they will add to you,*" (Isaiah 26:3).

16. Memorizing Scripture results in a longer life

According to Proverbs 3:1-2, a man who memorizes the Word of God will live longer than those who do not, and longer than he would if he did not memorize the Word. The verses read, "*My son, forget not my law, but let thy heart keep my commandments, for length of days and long life and peace shall they add to thee.*" The person who knows and obeys the Word will live longer because he will take better care of his body. He will eat the proper foods, get the proper rest, exercise, and stay at the proper weight. He will have less stress on his mind and body. He will avoid all things that tend to shorten life, such as drinking, smoking, drugs, or riotous living, and he will stay busy serving the Lord and others, making a worthy contribution for time and eternity. All of these things make for a long life.

17. Memorizing Scripture gives sweet sleep.

Proverbs 3:24 says, "*When you lie down, you will not be afraid; yes, you will lie down and your sleep will be sweet. When you roam, they will lead you; when you sleep, they will keep you; and when you awake, they will speak with you,*" (Proverbs 6:22). These two verses, in the context, indicate that, instead of taking sleeping pills, tranquilizers, and booze, the Christian should memorize and meditate upon the Word. This will bring sweet sleep.

18. Memorizing Scripture keeps us from evil men and women.

"My son, keep your father's command, and do not forsake the law of your mother. Bind them continually upon your heart; Tie them around your neck. When you roam, they will lead you; when you sleep, they will keep you; and when you awake, they will speak with you. For the commandment is a lamp, and the law a light; reproofs of instruction are the way of life, To keep you from the evil woman, from the flattering tongue of a seductress," (Proverbs 6:20-24).

"*My son, keep my words, and treasure my commands within you. Keep my commands and live, and my law as the apple of your eye. Bind them on your fingers; write them on the tablet of your heart. Say to wisdom, You are my sister, and call understanding your nearest kin, That they may keep you from the immoral woman, from the seductress who flatters with her words,"* (Proverbs 7:1-5).

Much of the first seven chapters of Proverbs is devoted to warning against being influenced by evil men and women. Knowledge of the Word of God is the only safeguard the wise man recommends to protect one from evil persons. He describes in great detail the awful results of getting involved with wicked women. Solomon, who knew women well, admonishes to memorize the Word. He implies that this is the only protection from those wicked women. The best thing this side of heaven is a good woman, and the worst thing this side of hell is a bad woman. Many Christians fall into Satan's trap with the wrong person.

19. Memorized Scripture can never be taken away from us

Amos 8:1-12 indicates that there is coming a time when the Word of God will be taken away from us. The prophet says, *"Behold, the days are coming," says the Lord GOD, "That I will send a famine on the land, not a famine of bread, nor a thirst for water, but of hearing the words of the LORD. They shall wander from sea to sea, and from north to east; they shall run to and fro, seeking the word of the LORD, but shall not find it."* If this does happen in our generation, those who have memorized Scripture will not suffer as much as those who have neglected the Word.

20. Memorizing Scripture protects us from error.

"You are mistaken, not knowing the Scriptures nor the power of God," (Matthew 22:29). The surest safeguard to protect one from being led astray by false cults, false religion, Catholicism, or liberalism is the memorized Word. Jack Van Impe, in preparing for his ordination council, memorized several verses on each of the major doctrines of the Bible. During the examination, he answered every question by quoting Scripture. How much stronger our churches would be if all Christians would do this!

21. Memorizing Scripture is an investment in that which is eternal.

Jesus said, *"Heaven and earth will pass away, but My words will by no means pass away,"* (Matthew 24:35). Peter said, "*But the word of the Lord endures forever. Now this is the word which by the gospel was preached to you,*" (1 Peter 1:25). If I understand the Bible correctly, the only two things in this life that will last through eternity are the souls of men and the Word of God. What a shame for Christians to spend so much time watching television or wasting their time in other ways, when they could be investing in that which is eternal. A man would be considered the fool of all fools if he deposited his savings in a bank he knew was going out of business shortly, when he could be depositing the same money in a bank he knew would pay him compounding interest forever. Many Christians are doing something just as foolish.

They are investing in the temporal rather than the eternal.

Memorizing Scripture makes the Word available for the Holy Spirit to call to our attention whenever it is needed *"But the Helper, the Holy Spirit, whom the Father will send in My name, He will teach you all things, and bring to your remembrance all things that I said to you,"* (John 14:26). One of the ministries of the Holy Spirit is to bring to the mind of the believer what the Lord has said. This verse has direct reference to the apostles and the inspiration of the New Testament. This truth also applies in the life of every believer. If you will memorize Scripture, you will discover that whether you are teaching, preaching, witnessing, counseling, needing guidance or comfort, the Holy Spirit will bring the right verse at the right time to your mind.

23. Memorizing Scripture greatly aids our prayer life.

Memorized Scripture aids our prayer life in several ways. First, it increases our chances of getting our prayers answered. John 15:7 says, *"If you abide in Me, and My words abide in you, you will ask what you desire, and it shall be done for you."* Jesus gives here two prerequisites to answered prayer: (1) abide in me (that means stay in fellowship), and (2) my words abide in you (keep the word in your mind). John gives us two more prerequisites to answered prayer in 1 John 3:22, "*And whatever we ask we receive from Him, because we keep His commandments and do those things that are pleasing in His sight*." The one who memorizes the Word is much more likely to keep His commandments and do those things that please Him than one who does not. Second, it aids our prayer life, because the one who knows what the Bible teaches about prayer can pray more intelligently. Third, it aids prayer because the will of God is revealed in the Word of God. The more one knows of the Word, the more one can pray in line with the will of God (1 John 5:14-15, "*Now this is the confidence that we have in Him, that if we ask anything according to His will, He hears us. And if we know that He hears us, whatever we ask, we know that we have the petitions that we have asked of Him.")*

24. Memorizing Scripture enhances one's teaching or preaching ministry.

Paul told Timothy to "preach the Word" (2 Timothy 4:2). It is believed that Apollos had memorized the entire Old Testament. Without question, he preached the Word. It is therefore no wonder that," *he greatly helped those who had believed through grace; for he vigorously refuted the Jews publicly, showing from the Scriptures that Jesus is the Christ,"* (Acts 18:24:28). In an interview, Jack Van Impe was asked why he thought God had blessed his ministry and used him mightily as a preacher. His humble reply was, "Because of the Word." He said that some evangelists built their ministries on stories or humor, while others built theirs on poetry. Though he uses some of each of these things, he tries to build every message on Scripture. He went on to say that the story-telling or humorous evangelists would be received well by some groups, but not by others. On the other hand, all types of people love the Word of God. It does not matter whether they are rich or poor, young or old, educated or uneducated, from the big city or the small town, from the mountains or the country, when they come to church, they want to hear the Word of God preached. In Nehemiah chapter 8, the people of Israel called out Ezra and said, "Ezra the preacher, go get the book (the Bible) and preach it." They may not like it or agree with it, but that what they want, and that's what they need.

25. Memorizing Scripture equips us for effective witnessing and counseling.

The story is told of a young convert who was witnessing to an atheist. The atheist was objecting to the new Christian showing him Bible verses.

Atheist:	"Don't be showing me verses in the Bible! The Bible's not true. It was written by men."
Christian:	"Oh, no! The Bible is God's Word. Every word of it is true!"

Atheist: "Oh, no it isn't. You can't even prove one verse to me."
Christian: "Oh, yes I can!"
Atheist: "No, you can't. If you can prove just one verse to me, I will believe all of it!"
Christian: "Just one verse?"
Atheist: "Yeah. Prove just one verse and I will believe all of it."

With that, the new convert grabbed the man by the nose and pulled and twisted until blood went everywhere.

Atheist (holding his nose): "You crazy religious fanatic! Why did you do that?"
Christian: "You said that if I could prove one verse, you would believe all of it. Well, Proverbs 30:33 says, "*and wringing the nose produces blood.*"

Stop right there: bloodying someone's nose is not a recommended witnessing technique. There are much better ways to handle the situation. The point of the story is that at least this guy had memorized the Word and was using it in his witnessing.

1 Peter 3:15 tells us, "*But sanctify the Lord God in your hearts, and always be ready to give a defense to everyone who asks you a reason for the hope that is in you, with meekness and fear.*" (Our friend in the story needs to work on the meekness and fear part.) We should memorize the Word so that we can answer any question put to us. It doesn't matter whether the person who is asking is saved or lost: we should have the answers.

Acts 1:8 says, *"But you shall receive power when the Holy Spirit has come upon you; and you shall be witnesses to Me in Jerusalem, and in all Judea and Samaria, and to the end of the earth."* This is not a command, but a statement of fact. When a person receives the Holy Spirit, he will witness. Jesus said, "*When the Helper comes, whom I shall send to you from the Father, the Spirit of truth who proceeds from the Father, He will testify of Me,"* (John 15:26). According to these verses, a person who does not witness for Christ is either lost or backslidden. I know these are strong words, but the Bible is clear: if you are not witnessing, either you do not have the Holy Spirit, or the Spirit does not have you. A person who is under the control of the Holy Spirit will witness. Read the book of Acts for yourself.

Moreover, if you are not winning people to Christ, probably one of three things is wrong. There is sin in your life, you are not witnessing to enough people, or you are not making the message clear. If your life is clean and surrendered, and if you make the gospel clear to enough people, you will see souls saved. The Word is a powerful tool for soulwinning. God describes it as a fire, a hammer, and a two-edged sword. He said, "*I am not ashamed of the gospel of Christ, for it is the power of God to salvation for everyone who believes, for the Jew first and also for the Greek,"* (Romans 1:16).

Preach the Word, because it never will return void. But in order to preach it, we must memorize it.

Chapter Three

A NEW SAVIOR

—Jesus Christ—

The Claims of Jesus Christ

What did Jesus claim concerning His identity? Who did He say that He was?

In John 10:30, Jesus said, *"I and my Father are one."* That may be obscure to you, but to the Jews of his day, who grew up saying every Sabbath, *"Hear O Israel, the Lord your God is One,"* (Deuteronomy 6:1). the meaning was crystal clear. He was claiming to be God. How do we know they understood that? Their response in the next verse was to immediately pick up stones to kill this blasphemer!

In John 14:6-7, He told his disciples, *"I am the way, the truth, and the life. No one comes to the Father except through Me. If you had known Me, you would have known My Father also; and from now on you know Him and have seen Him."* Again Jesus claimed to be God by claiming equality with the Father. When one of the disciples questioned this statement, Jesus clarified, *Jesus said to him, "Have I been with you so long, and yet you have not known Me, Philip? He who has seen Me has seen the Father; so how can you say, 'Show us the Father'?"* (John 14:9).

Jesus also claimed the authority of God saying, *"All authority has been given to Me in heaven and on earth,"* (Matthew 28:18). And he claimed to have existed before the world was created (John 17:5 *"And now, O Father, glorify thou Me with thine own self with the glory which I had with thee before the world was"*) and to have been alive before Abraham

(John 8:58, *"Jesus said to them, 'Most assuredly, I say to you, before Abraham was, I AM."*). In that last statement, He even used for Himself the sacred name of God which the Jews would not pronounce (Exodus 3:14. *And God said to Moses, "I AM WHO I AM'" And He said, "Thus you shall say to the children of Israel, 'I AM has sent me to you.'")*

His disciples clearly understood these claims. It was when Simon confessed, *"You are the Christ, the Son of the living God,"* (Matthew 16:16) that Jesus changed his name to Peter. Mary's sister Martha also said, *"Yes, Lord, I believe that You are the Christ, the Son of God, who is to come into the world."* (John 11:27). And Thomas, the doubter, became convinced and said to Jesus, *"My Lord and my God!"* (John 20:28).

This creates a dilemma for the unbeliever. Jesus cannot simply be respected as a wise man if He made these kinds of statements. He must either be rejected utterly or embraced and worshipped as God.

Jesus Claimed to be God

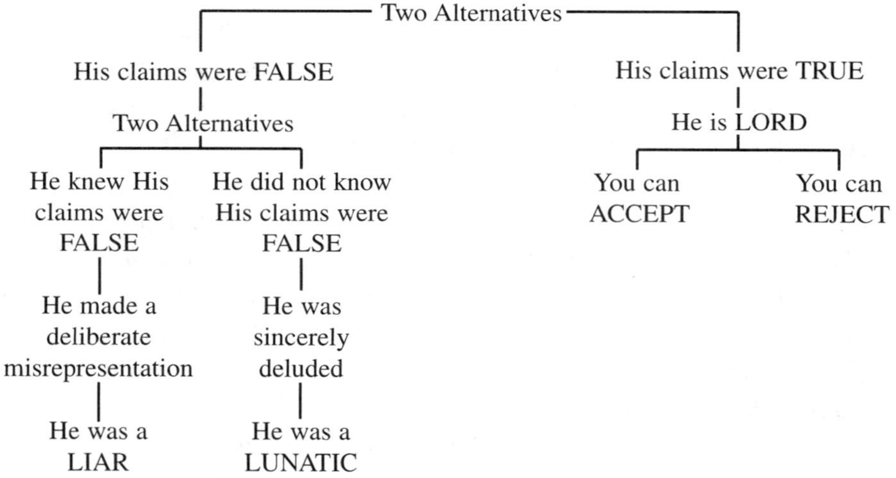

According to the above passages, Jesus claimed actually to be God. He made the kinds of claims that only a person who presumed he was God would make, and He was worshipped as God without ever attempting to deny it. (Matthew 8:2, *"And behold, a leper came and worshiped Him, saying, 'Lord, if You are willing, You can make me clean'"*; 14:33, *"Then those who were in the boat came and worshiped Him, saying, 'Truly You*

are the Son of God,'; 28:9, *"And as they went to tell His disciples, behold, Jesus met them, saying, 'Rejoice!' So they came and held Him by the feet and worshiped Him*"; John 9:38, *Then he said, 'Lord, I believe!' And he worshiped Him.")* He even commended His followers for thinking this.

Given the clear nature of Jesus' claims about himself, C.S. Lewis declared that there were only three possible conclusions: either Jesus was a liar, a lunatic, or Lord. If He claimed that He was God, knowing full well that it was not true, then He lied. This could not have been a simple lie, for it would have taken a great deal of planning and trickery to fake all of His miracles without the knowledge of His disciples, who clearly believed in Him enough that they all died for His cause. If He truly believed that He was God, but was wrong, then He was delusional. To persist in that kind of belief would require a schizophrenic break with reality that normally renders the person unable to function and deal with the basic responsibilities of life. But if He seriously claimed to be God, knowing it to be the truth and offering up proof to support that claim through His miracles and resurrection, then He must truly be Lord.

> *I am trying here to prevent anyone saying the really foolish things that people often say about Him: "I'm ready to accept Jesus as a great moral teacher, but I don't accept His claim to be God." That is the one thing we must not say. A man who was merely a man and said the sort of things Jesus said would not be a great moral teacher. He would either be a lunatic — on a level with the man who says he is a poached egg — or else he would be the Devil of Hell.*
>
> — C.S. Lewis,
> *Mere Christianity,* pp. 55-56

So who is this Jesus? Did he simply arrange to make it look as if over 300 prophecies were fulfilled? Did he fake all of his miracles? Did he deceive all of his disciples into believing it was all true? And most importantly, how did he manage to fake his resurrection? How did he come back to life in a transformed body after the Roman executioners pronounced him dead? Or maybe he was just so crazy that he talked to the wind and the sea. But why did they obey him? Maybe he was so delusional that he didn't know he couldn't walk on water. But why didn't he sink? And why would God set his seal of approval on such a man by raising him from the dead?

The only other option is that Jesus truly was the Christ, the Messiah, the God-man — a prophet, priest, and king who offered himself as a sacrifice for sin and will judge the world on the basis of whether or not they have trusted in that sacrifice to save them. If He is Lord, then that is why *"God also has highly exalted Him and given Him the name which is above every name, that at the name of Jesus every knee should bow, of those in heaven, and of those on earth, and of those under the earth, and that every tongue should confess that Jesus Christ is Lord, to the glory of God the Father,"* (Philippians 2:9-11).

Who is Jesus of Nazareth to you? A myth? A mere man? The Son of God? Your life upon this earth and for all eternity is affected by your answer to this question.

From the time sin first entered the world, God promised man a Savior. (Genesis 3:15, *"And I will put enmity between you and the woman, and between your seed and her Seed; he shall bruise your head, and you shall bruise His heel."*) As years passed, that prophecy expanded to say that this person would be a prophet, (Deuteronomy 18:18, *"I will raise up for them a Prophet like you from among their brethren, and will put My words in His mouth, and He shall speak to them all that I command Him"*), a priest (Psalm 110:4, *"The LORD has sworn and will not relent, 'You are a priest forever according to the order of Melchizedek'"*), and a king over the nation Israel. (2 Samuel 7:12-14, *"When your days are fulfilled and you rest with your fathers, I will set up your seed after you, who will come from your body, and I will establish his kingdom. He shall build a house for My name, and I will establish the throne of his kingdom forever. I will be his Father, and he shall be My son. If he commits iniquity, I will chasten him with the rod of men and with the blows of the sons of men."*) The person in whom all of these prophecies were united was called the Messiah - which is Hebrew for "the Anointed One." But this Messiah must also be God Himself (Isaiah 9:6-7, *"For us a Child is born, unto us a Son is given; and the government will be upon His shoulder. And His name will be called wonderful, Counselor, Mighty God, everlasting Father, Prince of Peace. Of the increase of His government and peace there will be no end, upon the throne of David and over His kingdom, to order it and establish it with judgment and justice from that time forward, even forever. The zeal of the LORD of hosts will perform this")*; (Daniel 7:13-14, "*I was watching in the night visions, and behold, One like the Son of Man, coming with the clouds of heaven! He came to the Ancient of Days, and they brought Him near before Him. Then to Him was given dominion and glory and a kingdom, that all peoples, nations, and languages should serve Him. His dominion is an everlasting dominion, which shall not pass away, and His kingdom the one which shall not be destroyed.*") It is clear that this Messiah was expected by the Jewish nation in the days when Jesus lived. When he arrived on the scene, Jesus clearly made the claim to be this Messiah.

Jesus Christ (the Greek word for "anointed") is the subject of more than 300 Old Testament prophecies made about the Messiah. His birth nearly 2000 years ago and the events of His life had been foretold by many prophets, from Moses to Malachi, over a period of 1500 years. History confirms that even the smallest detail happened just as predicted centuries before. It confirms beyond a doubt that Jesus is the true Messiah, the Son of God and Savior of the world.

Consider the following Scriptures and the amazing accuracy with which the Old Testament prophecies are fulfilled through the life of Jesus.

Old Testament Prophecy	New Testament Fulfillment
Isaiah 7:14 - Therefore the Lord Himself will give you a sign: Behold, the virgin shall conceive and bear a Son, and shall call His name Immanuel.	**Matthew 1:18** - Now the birth of Jesus Christ was as follows: After His mother Mary was betrothed to Joseph, before they came together, she was found with child of the Holy Spirit.
Micah 5:2 - But you, Bethlehem Ephrathah, though you are little among the thousands of Judah, yet out of you shall come forth to Me the One to be Ruler in Israel, whose goings forth are from of old, from everlasting.	**Luke 2:4** - Joseph also went up from Galilee, out of the city of Nazareth, into Judea, to the city of David, which is called Bethlehem, because he was of the house and lineage of David.
Hosea 11:1 - When Israel was a child, I loved him, and out of Egypt I called My son.	**Matthew 2:14-15** - When he arose, he took the young Child and His mother by night and departed for Egypt, and was there until the death of Herod, that it might be fulfilled which was spoken by the Lord through the prophet, saying, "Out of Egypt I called My Son."
Zechariah 11:12-13 - Then I said to them, "If it is agreeable to you, give me my wages; and if not, refrain." So they weighed out for my wages thirty pieces of silver. And the LORD said to me, "Throw it to the potter"— that princely price they set on me. So I took the thirty pieces of silver and threw them into the house of the LORD for the potter.	**Matthew 26:14-15** - Then one of the twelve, called Judas Iscariot, went to the chief priests and said, "What are you willing to give me if I deliver Him to you?" And they counted out to him thirty pieces of silver. (See also Matthew 27:3-10)

Old Testament Prophecy	New Testament Fulfillment
Psalm 16:9-10 - Therefore my heart is glad, and my glory rejoices; my flesh also will rest in hope. For You will not leave my soul in Sheol, nor will You allow Your Holy One to see corruption.	**Acts 2:31-32** - He, foreseeing this, spoke concerning the resurrection of the Christ, that His soul was not left in Hades, nor did His flesh see corruption. This Jesus God has raised up, of which we are all witnesses.

Among the things predicted of Jesus are his lineage (Isaiah 11:1, "*There shall come forth a Rod from the stem of Jesse, and a Branch shall grow out of his roots*"), his birthplace (Micah 5:2, "*But you, Bethlehem Ephrathah, though you are little among the thousands of Judah, yet out of you shall come forth to Me the One to be Ruler in Israel, whose goings forth are from of old, from everlasting*"), his miracles (Isaiah 35:5-6, "*Then the eyes of the blind shall be opened, and the ears of the deaf shall be unstopped. Then the lame shall leap like a deer, and the tongue of the dumb sing. For waters shall burst forth in the wilderness, and streams in the desert*"), his message, the manner of his death (Psalm 22:16, "*For dogs have surrounded Me; the congregation of the wicked has enclosed Me. They pierced My hands and My feet,*" the fate of his clothing. (Psalm 22:18, "*They divide My garments among them, and for My clothing they cast lots*," his companions in death (Isaiah 53:12, "*Therefore I will divide Him a portion with the great, and He shall divide the spoil with the strong, because He poured out His soul unto death, and He was numbered with the transgressors, and He bore the sin of many, and made intercession for the transgressors*"), and the type of grave used to bury him (Isaiah 53:9, "*And they made His grave with the wicked— but with the rich at His death, because He had done no violence, nor was any deceit in His mouth*"). But most importantly Jesus fulfilled both the Old Testament prophecies (Psalm 30:3, "*O LORD, You brought my soul up from the grave; you have kept me alive, that I should not go down to the pit*"; 118:17, "*I shall not die, but live, and declare the works of the LORD*"; Hosea 6:2, "*After two days He will revive us; on the third day He will raise us up, that we may live in His sight*") and his own prophecies (Matthew 12:38-40, "*Then some of the scribes and Pharisees answered, saying, 'Teacher, we want to see a sign from You.' But He answered and said to them, 'An evil and adulterous generation seeks after a sign, and no sign will be given to it except the sign of the prophet Jonah. For as Jonah was three days and three nights in the belly of the great fish, so will the Son of Man be three days and three nights in the heart of the earth'*" 16:21, *From that time forth, Jesus began to show unto His disciples that He must go unto Jerusalem and suffer many things of the elders and the chief priests and scribes, and be killed and be raised again the third day.*) that he would rise from the grave after his death. It is especially in the resurrection that God set his seal of proof that this Jesus was the Messiah. (Romans 1:4, "A*nd declared to be the Son of God with power according to the Spirit of holiness, by the resurrection from the dead.*")

There are many things that Jesus can do for us that no one else can do, but let us concentrate on four specific things. First of all, He is the only one who can pardon man from his sin. Second, He alone can give purpose for life. Third, only He can give peace to a troubled heart. Finally, Jesus alone can give us power to live an abundant life.

Pardons Sin

The Bible tells us that God is a holy God and that man is sinful. There is a great gulf between the two, and man cannot bridge this gulf. The Bible says that all have sinned and come short of the glory of God. The wages of sin is death — eternal separation from God; but the gift of God is eternal life through Jesus Christ our Lord. Because man is sinful, he cannot bridge this gulf between himself and God, no matter how good he is. God bridges the chasm to man through His Son, Jesus Christ. The Scripture says, "*For God so loved the world that He gave His only begotten Son, that whoever believes in Him should not perish but have everlasting life,*" (John 3:16).

Now, let us define our terms. What do we mean by sin? Sin is not necessarily a matter of lying, stealing, or immorality. Basically, sin is an attitude. Sin is going one's own independent way. It is a lack of relationship or fellowship with God. There is a throne in your life, and either God is on that throne or you are on it. If you are saying, "I am the master of my life; I will do as I please," you qualify as a sinner. If Christ is on that throne, He has brought you into relationship with Himself.

Picture, if you will, a floor lamp. Pull the plug out of the socket; contact with the current is broken, and the light goes out. Push the plug into the socket again; the light goes on. The current is constant, the variable is the plug. Man can be compared with that lamp. The current is God's love and it is constant. Our relationship to God is based on whether we are plugged into that current or not. But the only plug that fits the socket is Jesus Christ. When we reject Him, we have no relationship to God's love. Because we do not have fellowship with God, we walk in darkness. We have chosen to go our own way — we are guilty of sin.

Now what is God's provision? In the Old Testament, the Israelites brought their sacrifices to the priest — a lamb, a dove, and a bullock. These animals had to be perfect, without spot or blemish — the best in the flock. The sin of the one making the sacrifice was symbolically transferred to the innocent lamb. The animal was slain, the blood was sprinkled by the Priest on the altar as a temporary covering for his sins. This sacrificed pictured the coming of God's one special lamb, whose blood would not temporarily cover man's sins, but would wash them away forever. God sent His only Son, the Lamb of God, without spot or blemish, to give His life, to shed His blood upon the cross for the forgiveness of our sins. "*And according to the law almost all things are purified with blood, and without shedding of blood there is no remission.*" (Hebrews 9:22).

No provision is made for the forgiveness of sin apart from the cross of Jesus Christ. Basically most religions embrace the philosophy of good works as a means to salvation. Man subscribes to the concept that if his good works outweigh his bad works, he will go to heaven. But if his bad works outweigh his good works, he will go to hell, if there is a hell. Of course, he does not know until this life is over whether he will go to heaven or to hell. And most people assume that God either uses a standard to judge men that will justify themselves, no matter what sins they are engaged in. What a tragedy! How inadequate is such a religion or philosophy. God has promised that we can know Him and have fellowship with Him now and for all eternity through His Son, the Lord Jesus Christ. Only Jesus *can* pardon sin. Acts 4:12, *"Nor is there salvation in any other, for there is no other name under heaven given among men by which we must be saved."*

Gives Purpose

Not only is Jesus of Nazareth unique as the only one who can pardon our sins, but He is also unique as the only one who gives purpose, peace, and power to life.

Let us consider purpose. You will remember, according to the Bible, in Colossians 1:16, "*For by Him all things were created that are in heaven and that are on earth, visible and invisible, whether thrones or dominions or principalities or powers. All things were created through Him and for Him." It* was through the Son that God made the whole universe. God has said that all creation will ultimately belong to the Son. One can readily see that God has created everything for a purpose. There is order, system, and design to the whole creation; and the purpose of all of that order and of all things is to bring glory to God.

Man is the highest expression of God's creation. We are God's masterpiece. Man is the only thing in creation with creative intelligence. God created man with free will — with the power to choose. He can say "yes" or "no" to God, and for the most part man has chosen to say "no." Those who have said "no" have never discovered God's purpose for their lives.

No building contractor would think of constructing a beautiful building without consulting the blueprint of the architect, the designer. How can we be so foolish as to try to build our lives without first consulting the great architect of life, the One who created us for a wonderful purpose? The Bible says, "*The steps of a good man are ordered by the LORD, and He delights in his way,*" (Psalm 37:23). "*And we know that all things work together for good to those who love God, to those who are the called according to His purpose,*" (Romans 8:28).

There are great benefits to be derived from being where God wants you to be and doing what God wants you to do. God does not stand over us with a big stick to whack us before we get out of line. Rather, He has established His laws to govern the whole of creation, and, if we violate the laws, we must pay the consequences. Even as a man who violates the law of gravity must pay the consequences, so we must deal with the consequences of our sins. The man who violates the laws of traffic endangers not only his own life, but also the lives of others as well. In the same way, our decisions to break God's laws effect all of the people around us, and those who are injured by our choices may choose to retaliate. Or God may simply send someone else into your life to treat you in the way you have treated him. We do not break God's laws; they break us.

Take, for example, the matter of marriage. According to the 1998 Michigan Marriage Report, about 1 in 4 adults have divorced their partner at least once. Yet it is a well-established fact that a Christian husband and wife who daily read the Bible and pray together will experience a remarkably high degree of stability in their marriage. The same study found that about 71% of the people who pray together regularly felt that they were very effective at conflict resolution and 84% of them would marry the same person all over again. Less than half of those who didn't pray felt the same way.

Why the great contrast? Jesus Christ makes the difference. He brings real purpose to marriage. With these facts before us, who would dare take the gamble of marriage without Christ? You say, "I don't understand. How can Christ make such a great difference?" Simply in this way: if you are on the throne of your life, your ego and the ego of the one whom you marry will war against each other. Friction is inevitable. However, if Christ is on the throne of the lives of both husband and wife, He will not war against Himself and there will be peace. Discord will turn to harmony and hate will turn to love. Many times I have had the privilege of kneeling in prayer with men and women who have been on the verge of divorce. Their lives were in shambles, their homes were places of discord and strife. But as they have given their lives to Jesus Christ, harmony, peace, and love have come into their homes and hearts. Of course, the same truth applies to individuals as well, for no man is complete without Christ.

I have found through the years that people who know Jesus Christ have a purpose for life. Those who do not know Him are like a ship upon a rough sea without rudder and without sail, drifting with the tide. No matter how brilliant you might be or how successful as an athlete, as a student, as a business or professional person, unless you know Jesus Christ, you will never know real purpose in life. God has made us for Himself, and , as St. Augustine said centuries ago, "Thou has made us for Thyself, O God, and our hearts are restless until they find their rest in Thee."

Commenting on his own lack of fulfillment in life, H. G. Wells, famous historian and philosopher, said at the age of 61: "I have no Peace. All life is at the end of its tether." The poet Lord Byron said, "My days are in the yellow leaf, the flowers and fruits of life are gone, the worm and the canker, and the grief are mine alone." Thoreau, the great literary genius, said "Most men live lives of quiet desperation." Blaise Pascal, French physicist and philosopher, had a different perspective on a seemingly universal experience and noted, "There is a God-shaped vacuum in the heart of every man which only God can fill through His Son, Jesus Christ."

Dare I say that there is a vacuum in your life? I do not know you. But in all honesty, in the quiet of your own heart, if you do not know Jesus Christ, you are saying today, "Yes, there is a vacuum; I am not satisfied with my life." And you never will be until you invite Christ to show you the very purpose for which He created you. There is no one else who ever lived who can do this - no religion, no philosophy, no man. Jesus said, *"I am the way, the truth, and the life. No one comes to the Father except through Me,"* (John 14:6). As you come to know Him, He will show you that purpose for which He created you.

Gives Peace

Jesus alone can pardon sin. Jesus alone can give purpose to life. Third, Jesus of Nazareth is the only One who can give you peace. He is the Prince of Peace. There will never be peace in the individual heart or at the peace tables of the world until the Prince of Peace reigns supreme in the hearts of men. In John 14:27, Jesus says, *"Peace I leave with you, My peace I give to you; not as the world gives do I give to you. Let not your heart be troubled, neither let it be afraid."* In Matthew 11:28, He says, "*Come to Me, all you who labor and are heavy laden, and I will give you rest."*

Perhaps you are now experiencing fears and frustrations in your life. Perhaps you are worried about your grades, your social life, your finances, problems in your home. You say, "Of course I am; everyone has these problems." Yes, and the Christian is not exempt. Becoming a Christian does not mean that you will suddenly be ushered into a utopian situation where all problems disappear, but rather you will have One with you who said, "*Peace, be still; lo, I am with you always, even unto the end of the world, upon every occasion and at all times I am with you. I will never leave you, nor forsake you. My peace I give you."*

What is the peace of Jesus like? He showed us while He was here. He had finished a long day of preaching and told his disciples to take him across the Sea of Galilee for the next day's work. In the middle of the voyage, a storm came up, causing great turbulence and waves, tossing the boat so violently that even these professional fishermen, who had been sailing this lake all their lives, feared for their lives. Twelve guys were bailing like crazy and the boat was still filling up with water. This was a crisis! And where was Jesus? He was asleep in the back of the boat. That is His peace. While all others were panicking, he slept. Finally his disciples came to him and said, "Don't you even care that we are all going to DIE?!!!" The Bible says, *"Being aroused,"* — in other words, since he was awake, he decided to go ahead and do something. "*Then He arose and rebuked the wind, and said to the sea, 'Peace, be still!' And the wind ceased and there was a great calm,"* (Mark 4:39). Then He turned to His disciples and asked them, *"Why are you so timid? How is it that you have no faith?"* (Mark 4:40, *But He said to them, "Why are you so fearful? How is it that you have no faith?"*) You might imagine the following discourse wrapped up in that statement:

Jesus:	"Why were you out on the lake?"
Disciples:	"Because you told us to go out there."
Jesus:	"And who am I?"
Disciples:	"You're the Messiah."
Jesus:	"Am I finished with the work God gave me to do? Is this the way the Messiah is to die?"
Disciples:	"Well, no."
Jesus:	"So what were you afraid of? You were with me. Why didn't you have any faith that God would protect you? You knew He was going to protect me."

Jesus could sleep through the storm because He knew God would take care of him. He did not fear the storm and the wind and all the turmoil around him. His faith conquered fears about the circumstances of His life. That is the peace He can give to all who will trust in Him. It is the quiet confidence that God will accomplish His purposes in your life.

Gives Power

Heartache and sorrow will come into your life, too; but Christ, the Prince of Peace, waits to sit upon the throne of your life and to give you His pardon, His purpose, and His peace. Yet even pardon, purpose, and peace are not all that Christ can give, for Jesus of Nazareth is the only One who can give you power to live a new life.

Frequently men and women will say to me, "I would like to become a Christian, but if I do, I am sure that I will never be able to live the life of a Christian. You don't know the mistakes that I have made, the resentments that I have, the tendencies to sin, the immorality, the heavy drinking, the cruel tongue and many, many other problems. I do not believe I could live the Christian life."

But as these people have given their lives to Christ, they have discovered that the Christian life is a supernatural life. You and I cannot live it, no matter how good we are. Jesus Christ literally comes to live within us, and He lives His life in and through us. Therefore, it is no longer what we do, but what He does, because He is the One who provides the power and we are merely the instruments through which He releases that power.

This is what Jesus taught a man named Nicodemus who came to see Him one night. Nicodemus was a ruler of the Jews. He was a good, moral and ethical religious leader. He asked Christ, *"Rabbi, (meaning Teacher), we know that you have come from God as a teacher; for no one can do these signs that you do unless God is with him,"* (John 3:2).

Jesus said to Nicodemus, *"Truly, truly, I say to you, unless one is born again, he cannot see the kingdom of God"* (John 3:3). Nicodemus did not know what He meant. He asked if he must enter his mother's womb the second time to be born. Jesus replied, in essence, "No, you are born once in the flesh, but in order to enter the kingdom of God you must be born of the Spirit." You see, we are born with a physical body to live on a physical plane. But the kingdom of God is a spiritual kingdom and God is a spiritual being. If we are to have fellowship with Him, we must become spiritual creatures. Picture a caterpillar crawling in the dirt, It is just an ugly. hairy worm. If you could communicate with this caterpillar, you might say, "Why do you crawl in the dirt? Why don't you fly like the butterfly?" No doubt it would reply, "It is impossible for me to fly for I am earthbound; I can only crawl in the dust." Then you might suggest, "Let us perform an operation. We will attach some butterfly wings to your body." But that would do no good. Then you could say, "Why don't you take a course in aviation? Then you will be able to fly." But all of this would be to no avail.

So it is with people who try to become Christians by good works such as good conduct, church attendance, reading the Bible, praying, etc., rather than the way of the new birth, as Jesus commanded.

One day the caterpillar weaves about its body a cocoon, and later, out of that cocoon, emerges a beautiful butterfly. We do not understand fully what has taken place. We only know that where once a worm crawled in the dust, now a butterfly soars in the heavens. So it is in the life of a Christian; this new birth takes place when Jesus of Nazareth, the risen Lord and Savior, comes to live within you.

Intellect, Emotions and Will

There is a throne in every life. If you are on that throne deciding what to do with your life, it is quite likely that you are not a Christian. Christ knocks at the door. In Revelation 3:20 He says, *"Behold, I stand at the door and knock"* (the door of your heart, your will, your intellect, your emotions). He promises, *"If you will open the door, I will come in and have fellowship with you and you with Me."* The Bible says that as many as receive Jesus, to them God gives the power to become His sons. And if any man is in Christ, or if Christ is in any man, he is a new creature; old things are passed away and all things are new. Commitment to Christ involves the surrender of the intellect, the emotion: and the will — the total person.

Let us say for the sake of illustration that you had heard many fine compliments about a certain person of the opposite sex. You could hardly wait to meet that person. The actual meeting was even more exciting. Intellectually, you both liked what you saw. You liked each other's looks,

personalities and many other qualities. You liked everything about each other! Was this enough to launch a marriage? No. There is more to marriage than mutual respect and admiration.
As you spent more and more time together, you became better acquainted. Then it happened. Cupid found his mark, and you were in love. Is this marriage? No. There is more to marriage than the intellect and the emotions. One day you became engaged, and then the wedding day arrives. How exciting!

Intellectually, you believe that he or she is the most wonderful person in all of the world. Emotionally, your heart beats twice as fast when you are together; but now something even more important is about to take place. As the two of you exchange vows before the minister, you commit your wills, one to the other. The marriage is not a true marriage if there is no mutual commitment of one to the other. There you have it — a marriage relationship involves the intellect, the emotions, and the will.

So it is in becoming a Christian one must give himself wholly to Christ - intellect, emotions and will.

Someone may say, "I believe that Jesus Christ is the Son of God. I believe that He died for my sins. Why, I have believed this all of my life. Am I not a Christian?" Not if that person means only that he believes those statements are true, but has never personally trusted Christ for his salvation. It is one thing to believe *that* Jesus is the Son of God; it is another to place your faith *in* Him as your only hope for salvation. Peter reminds us, "*You believe that there is one God. You do well. Even the demons believe— and tremble!*" (James 2:19). Intellectual assent is not enough to save you.

Another may say, "I remember when I heard a wonderful sermon at a youth retreat or during a special series of meetings in our church. My heart was stirred and I had a great emotional experience! I even responded to the invitation to go forward for counsel. Am I not a Christian?" Not if that person has never relinquished the throne of his life, his will, to Christ. Having an emotional experience doesn't make you a Christian. Making a choice to trust Christ does.

Still another may say, "I go to church regularly, I read my Bible and pray daily. I try to live a good life. Am I not a Christian?" This person may be committed to the disciplines of a Christian life, but that does not mean he has committed his life to the Person of Christ as his only means of salvation. In fact, it is likely that he is trusting his own religious works rather than the finished work of Christ. Titus 3:5 says, *"Not by works of righteousness which we have done, but according to His mercy He saved us, through the washing of regeneration and renewing of the Holy Spirit."*

The surrender of the will is the key to becoming a Christian and the secret to living a victorious Christian life. We must give up our own ways to salvation and accept the one way that God has provided.

An outstanding young athlete and social leader wanted to become a Christian, but like so many, he was afraid to surrender his will to the will of God. He had worked out detailed plans for his life but was reluctant to become a Christian, for fear God would change those plans.

It was explained to him that God loved him dearly — so much that He sent His only begotten Son to die on the cross for his sins and that God had a wonderful plan for his life. He was challenged to trust the One who loved him enough to die for him and who was infinitely wiser than any man. After some thought, he made a decision to trust Christ, He invited Christ into his heart as Savior and Lord. Yes, his life was changed. But you may be sure that he has no regrets, for he is now devoting all of his time to challenging others to become Christians also.

Your Opportunity

At this moment, if you have not already received Christ as your Savior and Lord, Jesus may be knocking at the door of your heart (your intellect, your emotions. your will - your total personality). Will you, in the quiet of this moment, surrender your will to Him? Invite Him to come into your life to live His life in you, to pardon your sin, to give purpose to your life, to give you His peace and power.

Though the Lord is *"not slack concerning His promise, as some count slackness, but is longsuffering toward us, not willing that any should perish but that all should come to repentance,"* (2 Peter 3:9), He will not force His way into your life. He comes only by personal invitation. Just deciding to do something is not enough. All decisions are meaningless until accompanied by action.

Bow your head just now and in this moment of decision, pray: "Lord Jesus, come into my life. Pardon my sin. I surrender my will — the throne of my life — to You. Show me Your purpose for my life, Give me Your peace and power that I may please and honor You. Amen!"

According to Scripture, we are promised, *"But as many as received Him, to them He gave the right to become children of God, to those who believe in His name,"* (John 1:12). When you receive Christ, you become a child of God. We are also told in 1 John 5:11-12, *"And this is the testimony: that God has given us eternal life, and this life is in His Son. He who has the Son has life; he who does not have the Son of God does not have life."* When you receive Christ, you have eternal life here and now.

As you receive Christ into your life, you begin the great adventure for which He created you. And as you continue in obedience to His commandments, you will experience the fulfillment of His promise of an abundant life. If you have understood what it is to give your life to Christ and have just now invited Jesus to be your Savior and Lord, please share that decision with me and others so we can celebrate with you!

Chapter Four

A NEW LIFE

— Regeneration —

When you received Christ as Savior and Lord you were born again, The Bible speaks of two births: the physical, which takes place when you are born into your earthly family, and the spiritual, which takes place when you are born of the spirit into the family of God. The Bible also describes two deaths, the first death is temporal and the second eternal (Revelation 20:15, *"And anyone not found written in the Book of Life was cast into the lake of fire"*). If a person is born only once, he will die twice; but if he is born twice, he will have to die but once.

Our physical birth is the day we celebrate as the beginning of our life, but with that beginning comes an inevitable end. We are born with a sinful nature. (Psalm 51:5, *"Behold, I was brought forth in iniquity, and in sin my mother conceived me,"*; Romans 5:12, *"Therefore, just as through one man sin entered the world, and death through sin, and thus death spread to all men, because all sinned."* — a part of us that wants to rebel and does not understand the things of God. We inherited this sin nature from Adam along with a subconscious awareness that we, as a race, have opposed God. Eventually, every one of us acts from that part of our nature and becomes guilty of our own sins as well. Then we are also under the curse of Adam, and the penalty for sin is death. That is why we need a new birth to overcome that death sentence that we carry with us.

Your Condition before Experiencing the New Birth

So Paul makes it clear exactly what the condition of the unsaved is in Ephesians chapter 2. *"And you He made alive, who were dead in trespasses and sins,"* (v. 1). We were dead because of the deeds we had done

— trespasses and sins. We had violated God's laws and bore the decree of death in our souls. But, because of our rebelliousness, we would not admit it. *"In which you once walked according to the course of this world, according to the prince of the power of the air, the spirit who now works in the sons of disobedience,"* (v. 2). Being natural men, with only a natural birth, and being sinful by nature, it was only natural for us to follow the course of this world. But this world is under the influence of Satan — the prince whose realm is our atmosphere. Satan also opposes God and is in rebellion, so he loves to drive us to sin and disobedience. Hence, Paul says that we all *"... once conducted ourselves in the lusts of our flesh, fulfilling the desires of the flesh and of the mind, and were by nature children of wrath, just as the others,"* (v. 3). We were destined and appointed to being the object of God's judgment. That was the road that we were on.

> *But God, who is rich in mercy, because of His great love with which He loved us, even when we were dead in trespasses, made us alive together with Christ (by grace you have been saved), and raised us up together, and made us sit together in the heavenly places in Christ Jesus,* (2:4-6)

Your Condition after Experiencing the New Birth

Jesus first taught about the new birth very early in his ministry to a Jewish leader named Nicodemus. Even with his knowledge of the Torah, Nicodemus was totally baffled at the idea of a spiritual birth. Jesus explained, *"Most assuredly, I say to you, unless one is born of water and the Spirit, he cannot enter the kingdom of God. That which is born of the flesh is flesh, and that which is born of the Spirit is spirit,"* (John 3:5-6). John also wrote, *"But as many as received Him, to them He gave the right to become children of God, to those who believe in His name: who were born, not of blood, nor of the will of the flesh, nor of the will of man, but of God"* (John 1:12-13), equating belief in Christ with being born again.

What does the new birth do? Does it erase our sin nature? No, but it breaks the power of sin in three important ways. It does away with the penalty of sin. Once you are born again, you have eternal life; death is only a transition to your true home where you will live forever (John 5:24, *"Most assuredly, I say to you, he who hears My word and believes in Him who sent Me has everlasting life, and shall not come into judgment, but has passed from death into life."*) Second, it gives you the ability to suppress the inclinations of your flesh (your sin nature) and choose to obey God instead. We had been slaves to sin, but sin no longer is our master if we remember that we have died to sin with Christ and now live a new life in his power. And finally, it gives us the power of transformation in our lives. God has promised to complete the work that he began in us (Philippians 1:8, *"For God is my witness, how greatly I long for you all with the affection of Jesus Christ,"*) and that work is to conform us to the image of His Son (Romans 8:28-30, *"And we know that all things work together for good to those who love God, to those who are the called according to His purpose. For whom He foreknew, He also predestined to be conformed to the image of His Son, that He might be the firstborn among many brethren. Moreover whom He predestined, these He also called; whom He called, these He also justified; and whom He justified, these He also glorified."*)

But the most important thing the new birth does is to establish a new relationship between us and God, giving us a new identity. *"Beloved, now we are children of God; and it has not yet been revealed what we shall be, but we know that when He is revealed, we shall be like Him, for we shall see Him as He is,"* (1 John 3:2); *"having predestined us to adoption as sons by Jesus Christ to Himself, according to the good pleasure of His will,"* (Ephesians 1:5). The enmity we once had with God is replaced by the relationship He has with our mediator; therefore, we have become sons, just as Jesus is His Son. We have the rights and privileges of sons: we can ask for things, we can enjoy the Father's presence and blessing, and we can have full assurance of the Father's constant love. But we also have the responsibility of sons to honor our Heavenly Father through obedience and praise. And if we are disobedient, he treats us as sons and chastens us (Hebrews 12:5-7, *"And you have forgotten the exhortation which speaks to you as to sons: My son, do not despise the chastening of the Lord, nor be discouraged when you are rebuked by Him; For whom the Lord loves He chastens, and scourges every son whom He receives. If you endure chastening, God deals with you as with sons; for what son is there whom a father does not chasten?"*) While Jesus is a Son eternally by nature, our sonship is by adoption, making us fellow-heirs with Christ of all that the Father possesses (Galatians 4:5-7, *"To redeem those who were under the law, that we might receive the adoption as sons. And because you are sons, God has sent forth the Spirit of His Son into your hearts, crying out, 'Abba, Father' Therefore you are no longer a slave but a son, and if a son, then an heir of God through Christ."*)

A New Kinship

This new identity is paramount in the minds of the New Testament authors. *"Therefore, if anyone is in Christ, he is a new creation; old things have passed away; behold, all things have become new,"* (2 Corinthians 5:17). What a change! You are no longer the same old you! There is a new you, reborn of God by His Spirit. Paul says, "*Do not lie to one another, since you have put off the old man with his deeds, and have put on the new man who is renewed in knowledge according to the image of Him who created him,*" (Colossians 3:9-10).

Peter also calls us to behave as sons of God, because that is what we are (1 Peter 1:14-23) and to recognize that this new life is really new to us. We need to grow into it. So he refers to us as babies, *"as newborn babes, desire the pure milk of the word, that you may grow thereby,"* (1 Peter 2:2). Like all babes, we crave and cry for nourishment; however, our nourishment comes only from the Word of God.

Is our relationship with God the same as Jesus'? In many ways it is, but there are some important differences. Jesus was the Son of God, the second person of the Trinity, who existed as God from eternity past. That is not something we can be a part of because we are human. Jesus is called the "only begotten Son of God," indicating that He is the one son whom God has declared to be His own and has given a special place. The words ***only begotten*** were a legal term used at the time to indicate which son would be given the primary responsibility for the inheritance, having gained the father's trust and favor, and having the full authority of the father. Jesus is the only son that God named as his "only begotten," who has the authority to act on behalf the Father and who possesses all that the Father has. In these two ways, Jesus' relationship with the Father is totally unique.

We are adopted sons. As such, all that we have received from the Father comes through the "only begotten" son. We are heirs of God, but only through the Son. We have authority over angels, but only in the name of Jesus Christ. We can approach the Father with confidence, but only because of the Mediator of our faith.

Peter goes so far as to say, "A*s His divine power has given to us all things that pertain to life and godliness, through the knowledge of Him who called us by glory and virtue, by which have been given to us exceedingly great and precious promises, that through these you may be partakers of the divine nature, having escaped the corruption that is in the world through lust,"* (2 Peter 1:3-4). Yes, God has given us all that we could possibly need, but we can only have it through knowledge of Him. That is what Jesus said eternal life is: *"And this is eternal life, that they may know You, the only true God, and Jesus Christ whom You have sent"* (John 17:3). God has made amazing promises for those who know Him, so that by those promises we can be partakers of the divine nature. Does that mean we become Gods, or mingle our essence with God? It is impossible for finite humans to become infinite deity. To say that you begin to become what has no beginning is like saying you can draw a square circle - it is nonsense. But through our new birth, which is from God, we are promised a new relationship to the Holy Spirit who indwells us (Colossians 3:11, "W*here there is neither Greek nor Jew, circumcised nor uncircumcised, barbarian, Scythian, slave nor free, but Christ is all and in all"*), and transforms us (2 Corinthians 3:18, *"But we all, with unveiled face, beholding as in a mirror the glory of the Lord, are being transformed into the same image from glory to glory, just as by the Spirit of the Lord"*), so that our character and behavior will reflect the goodness of God and His love for the world. Goodness and Love are the divine nature (Matthew 19:17, *"So He said to him, 'Why do you call Me good? No one is good but One, that is, God. But if you want to enter into life, keep the commandments'"*; 1 John 4:8, *"He who does not love does not know God, for God is love"*), which we may share in as we are conformed to the image of Christ as promised to us.

A New Abundance

Jesus said, *"I have come that they may have life, and that they may have it more abundantly,"* (John 10:10b). What did he mean by that? *"As you have therefore received Christ Jesus the Lord, so walk in Him,"* (Colossians 2:6). We have received Christ by faith and we are admonished to live by faith. While we may not have experienced abundant life yet, it will come to us by faith — believing that Jesus wants us to have life abundantly.

You have been saved from the penalty of sin. *"He who believes in Him is not condemned; but he who does not believe is condemned already, because he has not believed in the name of the only begotten Son of God,"* John 3:18. *"For by grace you have been saved through faith, and that not of yourselves; it is the gift of God,"* (Ephesians 2:8).

You are being saved from the power of sin. *"Now to Him who is able to keep you from stumbling, and to present you faultless before the presence of His glory with exceeding joy,"* (Jude 24). *"But the Lord is faithful, who will establish you and guard you from the evil one,"* (2 Thessalonians 3:3).

You will be saved from the presence of sin. *"Beloved, now we are children of God; and it has not yet been revealed what we shall be, but we know that when He is revealed, we shall be like Him, for we shall see Him as He is,"* (1 John 3:2). *"Who will transform our lowly body that it may be conformed to His glorious body, according to the working by which He is able even to subdue all things to Himself,"* (Philippians 3:21). *"Behold, I tell you a mystery: We shall not all sleep, but we shall all be changed—in a moment, in the twinkling of an eye, at the last trumpet. For the trumpet will sound, and the dead will be raised incorruptible, and we shall be changed,"* (1 Corinthians 15:51,52).

You have trusted God for payment of your penalty for sin and for eternal life. Why not trust Him now for power over sin? Remember that you received Christ by faith, so you should now walk in faith. This is what having life abundantly means; it is having an existence full of life. Sin brings death into your life. Get rid of the sin, and all that is left is life.

The Basis of Abundant Living

Read Romans 6:1-16. This is the secret to living the Christian life - you have to die first. Not physical death, but you have to let your sin nature die. Paul makes it clear that when we became Christians and were baptized by the Spirit into Christ (water baptism is a symbol of that reality), we died with Christ. That is, our sin died on the cross where He paid the penalty for it. When He was buried, our sin was buried too. When He rose in a transformed body, we rose too with a transformed life. The problem is that we keep trying to dig up our sin and pull it out of that grave.

Paul gives us clear steps to correcting this problem. In verse 6, he says, *"Knowing this, that our old man was crucified with Him, that the body of sin might be done away with, that we should no longer be slaves of sin."* You have to understand completely that it is true - you died with Christ. Jesus said that the only way for a seed to grow is to be buried in the ground and die (John 12:24, *"Most assuredly, I say to you, unless a grain of wheat falls into the ground and dies, it remains alone; but if it dies, it produces much grain."*) Convince yourself one hundred percent that it is true. You were on that cross with Christ.

Then in verse 11, Paul says, *"Likewise you also, reckon yourselves to be dead indeed to sin, but alive to God in Christ Jesus our Lord."* How do you do that? You decide to make it so. That is what reckoning is. God saw Abraham's faith (*"For what does the Scripture say? Abraham believed God, and it was accounted to him for righteousness,"* Romans 4:3) —in other words, it was credited to his account by a simple decision. You have to do the same thing: reckon yourself dead to sin and alive to Christ. Why? Because you died with him. When? Every day and especially in times of temptation.

Verse 13, *"And do not present your members as instruments of unrighteousness to sin, but present yourselves to God as being alive from the dead, and your members as instruments of righteousness to God."* You also have to yield yourself unto God. When your are driving and you see a yield sign, you know to let the other guy go first. In this case, the other guy is God. You have to stop doing what you want to do and let Him do what He wants to do. That may mean giving up your plans, your desires, your ambitions — but that's okay. YOU'RE DEAD ANYWAY! So surrendering your good ideas to God's best is no problem. Once you have done all that, it is easy to obey God. It is hard to obey him as long as you are still alive and trying to run your life your way. But that was when you were a slave to sin. Now you have a choice: If you are dead and living God's life, you can be a slave to righteousness.

The steps are simple:

Know - *To be fully assured of a fact.*

Reckon - *To act upon a fact, to consider it, to depend upon it instead of upon feelings.*

Yield - *To give up, to surrender, to submit*

Obey - *To put instructions into effect, to comply with, to trust.*

The Practice of Abundant Living

As you are living a life of obedience to God, a new issue arises. What if things don't work out? How do I know that other people will treat me right when I obey God? If I give up control, how can I keep control of my life?

Psalm 37 teaches us that the practice of abundant living means that we have to quit worrying and start trusting God for all the things we can't control. *"Do not fret because of evildoers,"* (v. 1) is the attitude we are to adopt. God assures us that they will not ultimately prosper. Rather than worrying about others, the Psalmist tells us to *"trust in the LORD, and do good,"* (v. 3). Just do what you know is right and let God take care of the rest. There is a promise that goes along with this: *"Dwell in the land, and feed on His faithfulness,"* (v. 3). When you do what is right, God will take care of you. Jesus said, *"Seek first the kingdom of God and His righteousness, and all these things shall be added to you,"* (Matthew 6:33). He also reminded us, *"Look at the birds of the air, for they neither sow nor reap nor gather into barns; yet your heavenly Father feeds them. Are you not of more value than they? Which of you by worrying can add one cubit to his stature?"* (Matthew 6:26-27). Worry does not add anything to our life; it takes away from our ability to live abundantly.

With what are we to replace worry? Verse 4 says, *"Delight yourself also in the LORD, and He shall give you the desires of your heart."* Find your joy in knowing God, and the rest will work out. *"Commit your way to the LORD, trust also in Him, and He shall bring it to pass,"* (v. 5). Let God be the one in charge and trust him for the results. All that you can do is follow Him. *"Rest in the LORD, and wait patiently for Him; do not fret,"* (v. 7). Quit trying to work it all out yourself. Do what you can and stop trying to manipulate. You never really had any control in the first place. Finally, *"wait patiently for Him,"* (v. 7). God knows all that you are going through. If you have trusted Him and committed your way to Him, the only thing left is to wait until you see His hand move. It may not happen when you want it to or in the way you expect, but He will act on your behalf. However, you must wait *"casting all your care upon Him, for He cares for you,"* (1 Peter 5:7).

Now, review each of the above references and note the progression: Fret not thyself, trust in the Lord, delight thyself in the Lord, commit thy way unto the Lord, rest in the Lord, wait on the Lord.

Trust - *To rely on wholeheartedly.*
Delight - *To take great pleasure or joy.*
Commit - *To place in trust or charge, to entrust*
Wait - *To anticipate with confident expectancy*

The Secret of Abundant Living

The secret of the abundant life is contained in these words: know, reckon, yield, obey, fret not, trust, delight, commit, rest, and wait. Underline these key words in your Bible in Romans 6 and in Psalm 37. Whenever you are tempted to sin, go back and remind yourself of these things. When worry overcomes you, remind yourself of these things. These are the cornerstones of living a life of abundance and freedom.

Warnings a Christian Should Heed

1. Some people will make fun of you. They did the same to Jesus. *"Blessed are you when they revile and persecute you, and say all*

kinds of evil against you falsely for My sake. Rejoice and be exceedingly glad, for great is your reward in heaven, for so they persecuted the prophets who were before you," (Matthew 5:11-12). *"Remember the word that I said to you, A servant is not greater than his master. If they persecuted Me, they will also persecute you. If they kept My word, they will keep yours also,"* (John 15:20).

2. Some Christians will disappoint you. Keep your eyes on Jesus.

3. Satan is your enemy. You must put on your armor (Ephesians 6:11-18) and resist him. *"Therefore submit to God. Resist the devil and he will flee from you,"*(James 4:7). *"These things I have spoken to you, that in Me you may have peace. In the world you will have tribulation; but be of good cheer, I have overcome the world,"* (John 16:33). Be cheerful for God will use troubles for good. *"And we know that all things work together for good to those who love God, to those who are the called according to His purpose,"* (Romans 8:28).

Privileges of a Christian

Being a Christian gives you certain privileges which you did not have before. These privileges are yours whether you use them or not; therefore you may as well use them. These are keys which will enhance the abundance of your life.

1. To be called a friend by Jesus - *"No longer do I call you servants, for a servant does not know what his master is doing; but I have called you friends, for all things that I heard from My Father I have made known to you,"* (John 15:15).

2. To be recognized by God as a son - *"Behold what manner of love the Father has bestowed on us, that we should be called children of God! Therefore the world does not know us, because it did not know Him. Beloved, now we are children of God; and it has not yet been revealed what we shall be, but we know that when He is*

revealed, we shall be like Him, for we shall see Him as He is. And everyone who has this hope in Him purifies himself, just as He is pure," (1 John 3:1-3). We have a Father who knows our every need and causes all things to work together for good.

3. To be a part of the family of God, including all true Christians - *"Now, therefore, you are no longer strangers and foreigners, but fellow citizens with the saints and members of the household of God,"* (Ephesians 2:19).

4. To have the Holy Spirit as personal teacher - *"But the anointing which you have received from Him abides in you, and you do not need that anyone teach you; but as the same anointing teaches you concerning all things, and is true, and is not a lie, and just as it has taught you, you will abide in Him,"* (1 John 2:27).

5. To be able to pray directly to the Heavenly Father - *"Therefore, brethren, having boldness to enter the Holiest by the blood of Jesus,"* (Hebrews 10:19). *"But you, when you pray, go into your room, and when you have shut your door, pray to your Father who is in the secret place; and your Father who sees in secret will reward you openly."* (Matthew 6:6). *"For there is one God and one Mediator between God and men, the Man Christ Jesus,"* (1 Timothy 2:5).

Duties of a Christian

Along with the privileges of being a Christian, there are certain responsibilities or duties. God has commanded that those who belong to Him should live their life in a certain way. This is not a limitation of your freedom; it is, in fact, the only way in which you will be able to experience an abundant life. These things are commanded so that you can establish a solid relationship with the Source of Life and eliminate your inclination to include death in your life.

1. To be filled with the Spirit – *"Finding out what is acceptable to the Lord," (*Ephesians 5:10).

2 To pray - *"Then He spoke a parable to them, that men always ought to pray and not lose heart,"* (Luke 18:1). *"I desire therefore that the men pray everywhere, lifting up holy hands, without wrath and doubting,"* (1 Timothy 2:8).

3. To study - *"Be diligent to present yourself approved to God, a worker who does not need to be ashamed, rightly dividing the word of truth,"* (2 Timothy 2:15).

4. To be a witness and testimony of the grace of God - *"Those who are wise shall shine like the brightness of the firmament, and those who turn many to righteousness like the stars forever and ever,"* (Daniel 12:3). *"Go therefore and make disciples of all the nations, baptizing them in the name of the Father and of the Son and of the Holy Spirit,"* (Matthew 28:19). *"You did not choose Me, but I chose you and appointed you that you should go and bear fruit, and that your fruit should remain, that whatever you ask the Father in My name He may give you,"* (John 15:16).

5. To be faithful - *"Moreover it is required in stewards that one be found faithful,"* (1 Corinthians 4:2). *"And the things that you have heard from me among many witnesses, commit these to faithful men who will be able to teach others also,"* (2 Timothy 2:2).

6. To rejoice in the Lord always - *"Rejoice always,"* (1 Thessalonians 5:16)

Chapter Five

A NEW ASSURANCE

— Forgiven Forever —

The Forgiveness of the Believer

The Bible makes it crystal clear that we are all sinners. Many people console themselves that they have not committed murder or stolen anything (at least not anything valuable). But the first commandment is, *"Love the Lord your God with all your heart and all your soul and all your mind and all your strength."* Who can honestly say that everything they have done is motivated by love for God? If we can't get past the first commandment, why go on?

Paul puts all of the Old Testament statements together in Romans 3:10-18:

> *As it is written: There is none righteous, no, not one; There is none who understands; there is none who seeks after God. They have all turned aside; they have together become unprofitable; there is none who does good, no, not one. Their throat is an open tomb; with their tongues they have practiced deceit; The poison of asps is under their lips; Whose mouth is full of cursing and bitterness. Their feet are swift to shed blood; Destruction and misery are in their ways; And the way of peace they have not known. There is no fear of God before their eyes.*

And Paul forms his conclusions a few verses later, *"For all have sinned and fall short of the glory of God,"* (Romans 3:23). There may be some people who have done worse things than others, but if the standard is the glory of God, we have all fallen short. Guilt before God is the universal equalizer.

The Bible is equally clear about the punishment for sin. God told Adam in the Garden that if he ate from the tree, then he *"shall surely die,"* (Genesis 2:17). Paul says again, *"The wages of sin is death,"* (Romans 6:23). And Paul assures us that we can know that all men have sinned because all have died. *"Therefore, just as through one man sin entered the world, and death through sin, and thus death spread to all men, because all sinned,"* (Romans 5:12).

But God provided a way of salvation for us in His own Son. *"Who Himself bore our sins in His own body on the tree, that we, having died to sins, might live for righteousness— by whose stripes you were healed,"* 1 Peter 2:24). *"For Christ also suffered once for sins, the just for the unjust, that He might bring us to God, being put to death in the flesh but made alive by the Spirit,"* (1 Peter 3:18).

Why would God, a righteous judge who had all the evidence to convict us and punish us to the fullest, send Jesus instead to bear the punishment in our place? *"But God demonstrates His own love toward us, in that while we were still sinners, Christ died for us,"* (Romans 5:8). God didn't wait for us to deserve His love — we never could. He loved us anyway and proved that love by sending His Son.

The results of Christ's death are amazing. *"There is therefore now no condemnation to those who are in Christ Jesus, who do not walk according to the flesh, but according to the Spirit,"* (Romans 8:1). God does not hold any judgment against us. He sees us as having the righteousness of Christ (Romans 3:25-26; 4:3-9) which we have by faith, not the righteousness of our own works. Jesus' death paid for all the sins of mankind — past, present, and future (1 John 2:2, *"And He Himself is the propitiation for our sins, and not for ours only but also for the whole world."*). And we are forgiven, not in some small measure but *"in Him we have redemption through His blood, the forgiveness of sins, according to the riches of His grace,"* (Ephesians 1:7).

Believers are forgiven absolutely, not on the basis of works, but on the basis of their faith in Jesus' blood to cleanse them of their sin. The only way that forgiveness can be revoked is to cancel out the death of Christ, which is impossible.

The Security of the Believer

At the moment of salvation, you received a new kind of life, as we discussed in the last chapter. Jesus called it "eternal life" (John 3:16), and defined it as knowing God (John 17:3, *"And this is eternal life, that they may know You, the only true God, and Jesus Christ whom You have sent"*). This is a life that can never end, because it is from the eternal God whom we can never fully comprehend. Eternal life does not begin when we die; it begins when we believe and it lasts forever. Once we are born again, our life in heaven is assured.

Jesus said, *"My sheep hear My voice, and I know them, and they follow Me. And I give them eternal life, and they shall never perish; neither shall anyone snatch them out of My hand. My Father, who has given them to Me, is greater than all; and no one is able to snatch them out of My Father's hand,"* (John 10:27-29). Once Jesus has given us the gift of eternal life we are held securely in his hand, and the Father's hand is clasped over Jesus' hand. No one is greater than God, so it is impossible that anyone or anything could undo our salvation.

The requirement for knowing that you are saved is very simple: do you believe in Jesus? 1 John 5:12-13 says, *"He who has the Son has life; he who does not have the Son of God does not have life. These things I have written to you who believe in the name of the Son of God, that you may know that you have eternal life, and that you may continue to believe in the name of the Son of God."* Yes, you can know — absolutely and with full certainty — that you have eternal life and are going to heaven. The only requirement is faith in Jesus as your sin substitute. This verse does not say, "will someday have eternal life." It says "hath" which is present tense, meaning we have eternal life right now.

"Who shall separate us from the love of Christ? Shall tribulation, or distress, or persecution, or famine, or nakedness, or peril, or sword? As

it is written: For Your sake we are killed all day long; we are accounted as sheep for the slaughter. Yet in all these things we are more than conquerors through Him who loved us. For I am persuaded that neither death nor life, nor angels nor principalities nor powers, nor things present nor things to come, nor height nor depth, nor any other created thing, shall be able to separate us from the love of God which is in Christ Jesus our Lord," (Romans 8:35-39). What is left? That phrase "nor any other creature" seals it. If no created thing can take our salvation away, then only uncreated things can. But the only uncreated thing that can possibly exist is God Himself, who loves us and gave us salvation in the first place!

Peter tells us we *"are kept by the power of God through faith for salvation ready to be revealed in the last time,"* (1 Peter 1:5). It is God's power, not our own faithfulness, that keeps us saved. Ephesians 1:13-14 tells us that *"you were sealed with the Holy Spirit of promise,"* which means that the Holy Spirit, the third person of the Trinity, is given to us as a guarantee that we will live with God in heaven. We are a purchased possession, upon whom God has set His seal, so that no one else can take it until He is ready to bring us home to Himself.

Yet some believers still have trouble believing that they are saved. For most, it is a problem of perception. They don't always feel the way they think they should. They don't always have that same feeling they had in when they first received Christ. They don't always feel the exhilaration that they do after a church service. They don't always feel the joy that they think Christians are supposed to feel. So they wonder if maybe they aren't saved after all.

Your salvation does not depend upon feelings. It depends on Christ. If you have received salvation from Christ, it is yours forever, whether you feel like it or not. Feelings change, but God and His Word never change. Salvation is a fact, not a feeling. In 2 Timothy 1:12, the Word says that God is able to keep us *"For I know whom I have believed, and am persuaded that he is able to keep that which I have committed unto him against that day."* Leave the keeping of your salvation up to God, not your feelings.

Others become convinced that sins they commit after they become a

Christian are evidence that either they are not really saved or that they have lost their salvation. Jesus didn't just save us from past sins, but from all of our sin, including our sinfulness. The gift of life He gave us cannot be revoked, even if we sin. Go back to Romans 8. Paul said nothing can separate us from the love of God. Are you greater than God? Is your sin greater than the sins of all mankind? Isn't your sin a created thing - something you created? You did nothing to earn your salvation, and nothing you do can take it away; it is an act of God. Your salvation is one hundred percent dependent on the fact that Christ died for your sins and you, at some point, said "Yes, I believe."

It was your sin from which Christ saved you; it makes no sense to think that sin can separate you from Him after He saved you while you were still a sinner. There is nothing you can do that will separate you from your Savior. If you feel guilty about sins you have committed (now we are back to feelings), then you need to confess them as a believer. (1 John 1:9, *"If we confess our sins, He is faithful and just to forgive us our sins and to cleanse us from all unrighteousness."*) Your eternal life did not end; you don't have to be born-again again. Eternal life is yours forever if you have believed in the Son.

In order for a person to lose his salvation, the following things would have to fail:

The Word of God would have to fail. John 6:37, *"All that the Father gives Me will come to Me, and the one who comes to Me I will by no means cast out."*

The Power of God would have to fail. 1 Peter 1:3-5, *"Blessed be the God and Father of our Lord Jesus Christ, who according to His abundant mercy has begotten us again to a living hope through the resurrection of Jesus Christ from the dead, to an inheritance incorruptible and undefiled and that does not fade* away, *reserved in heaven for you, who are kept by the power of God through faith for salvation ready to be revealed in the last time."*

The Love of God would have to fail. Romans 8:35, *"Who shall separate us from the love of Christ? Shall tribulation, or distress, or persecution, or famine, or nakedness, or peril, or sword?"*

The Seal of God would have to fail. Ephesians 1:12-14, *"That we who first trusted in Christ should be to the praise of His glory. In Him you also trusted, after you heard the word of truth, the gospel of your salvation; in whom also, having believed, you were sealed with the Holy Spirit of promise, who is the guarantee of our inheritance until the redemption of the purchased possession, to the praise of His glory."* Ephesians 4:30, *"And do not grieve the Holy Spirit of God, by whom you were sealed for the day of redemption."*

The Seed of God would have to fail. 1 Peter 1:22-24, *"Since you have purified your souls in obeying the truth through the Spirit in sincere love of the brethren, love one another fervently with a pure heart, having been born again, not of corruptible seed but incorruptible, through the word of God which lives and abides forever, because all flesh is as grass, and all the glory of man as the flower of the grass. The grass withers, and its flower falls away."*

The Performance of God would have to fail. John 10:28-29, *"And I give them eternal life, and they shall never perish; neither shall anyone snatch them out of My hand. My Father, who has given them to Me, is greater than all; and no one is able to snatch them out of My Father's hand."*

The Prayer of God would have to fail. John 17:1-26, *"Jesus spoke these words, lifted up His eyes to heaven, and said: 'Father, the hour has come. Glorify Your Son, that Your Son also may glorify You, as You have given Him authority over all flesh, that He should give eternal life to as many as You have given Him. And this is eternal life, that they may know You, the only true God, and Jesus Christ whom You have sent. I have glorified You on the earth. I have finished the work which You have given Me to do. And now, O Father, glorify Me together with Yourself, with the glory which I had with You before the world was. I have manifested Your name to the men whom You have given Me out of the world. They were Yours, You gave them to Me, and they have kept Your word. Now they have known that all things which You have given Me are from You. For I have given to them the words which You have given Me; and they have received them, and have known surely that I came forth from You; and they have believed that You sent Me. I pray for them. I do not pray for the world but for those whom You have given Me, for they are Yours. And all Mine are Yours, and Yours are Mine, and I am glorified in them. Now I am no longer in the world, but these are in the world, and I come to You. Holy Father, keep through Your name those whom You have given Me, that they may be one as We are. While I was with them in the world, I kept them in Your name. Those whom You gave Me I have kept; and none of them is lost except the son of perdition, that the Scripture might be fulfilled. But now I come to You, and these things I speak in the world, that they may have My joy fulfilled in themselves. I have given them Your word; and the world has hated them because they are not of the world, just as I am not of the world. I do not pray that You should take them out of the world, but that You should keep them from the evil one. They are not of the world, just as I am not of the world. Sanctify them by Your truth. Your word is truth. As You sent Me into the world, I also have sent them into the world. And for their sakes I sanctify Myself, that they also may be sanctified by the truth. I do not pray for these alone, but also for those who will believe in Me through their word; that they all may be one, as You, Father, are in Me, and I in You; that they also may be one in Us, that the world may believe that You sent Me. And the glory which You gave Me I have given them, that they may be one just as We are one: I in them, and You in Me; that they may be made perfect in one, and that the world may know that You have sent Me, and have loved them as You have loved Me. Father, I desire that they also whom You gave Me may be with Me where I am, that they may behold My glory which You have given Me; for You loved Me before the foundation of the world. O righteous Father! The world has not known You, but I have known You; and these have known that You sent Me. And I have declared to them Your name, and will declare it, that the love with which You loved Me may be in them, and I in them.'"*

The Promise of God would have to fail. I John 2:25, *"And this is the promise that He has promised us— eternal life."*

The Evidence of a Believer

2 Corinthians 13:5 encourages believers to, *"Examine yourselves as to whether you are in the faith. Test yourselves. Do you not know yourselves, that Jesus Christ is in you?— unless indeed you are disqualified."* We can all ask the simple question, "Do I know that I have placed my faith in

Jesus Christ?" That is the only question that really matters. However, if we need more proof to convince ourselves, there are certain evidences that usually follow the new birth. I John 5:13, *"These things I have written to you who believe in the name of the Son of God, that you may know that you have eternal life, and that you may continue to believe in the name of the Son of God."*

One of the reasons the book of I John was written was to help believers establish in their own minds and hearts that Christ is really in them so that they might have fellowship with Him. Along the way, John gives six evidences that one is truly a believer. These evidences describe the life and thought patterns of people who are living in the light of the Son.

The first evidence is that true believers are honest about their sin. I John 1:8-10 says, *"If we say that we have no sin, we deceive ourselves, and the truth is not in us. If we confess our sins, He is faithful and just to forgive us our sins and to cleanse us from all unrighteousness. If we say that we have not sinned, we make Him a liar, and His word is not in us."* We can deny that we have a sin nature or that we have ever sinned, but we are only deceiving ourselves and calling God a liar. That is not the truth. But when we say the same thing about our sin that God does (which is the literal translation of the word ***confess***), then God is faithful to not only forgive us, but also to cleanse us so that we don't have to keep repeating that sin. Isn't it amazing how God is so willing to give us the healing help we need if only we will come to Him?

In I John 2:3-5, another evidence is seen. It says, *"Now by this we know that we know Him, if we keep His commandments. He who says, 'I know Him,' and does not keep His commandments, is a liar, and the truth is not in him. But whoever keeps His word, truly the love of God is perfected in him. By this we know that we are in Him."* Does that mean that all real Christians keep all of God's commandments all the time? Of course not. We are not under the Law anymore. That is not what Christianity is all about. But people who have been born again do try to do what God commands. The regular pattern of their life is that they obey what God has said is right. One of the most important criteria for their decision making is, "Will this be pleasing to God? Has God told me how I should handle this in His Word?" Unbelievers don't care what God thinks; only

Christians are concerned that their actions conform to God's commands. We can't keep His word perfectly until we are perfected, but Christians do make obedience a trademark of their lives. John 14:15, *"If you love Me, keep My commandments."*

"I write to you, fathers, because you have known Him who is from the beginning. I write to you, young men, because you have overcome the wicked one. I write to you, little children, because you have known the Father," (1 John 2:13). John addresses three different groups here: mature believers— those who are in the midst of the battle and those who are new to the faith. To both the fathers and the children, he says that they have known the Father. To the young men who are growing and actively pursuing righteousness in their lives, he says that they have overcome Satan. These are two sides of the same coin. If you have known the Father, then you can overcome Satan. If you overcome Satan, it is because you have known the Father. The evidence of which John is speaking of is that there is some amount of overcoming in your life as a result of your faith in God. If you really know God, then you can't let Satan keep winning the battles. God will win. Those who know God will obey Him and obedience breaks the power of Satan in their lives.

The fourth evidence, according to 1 John 3:9, is this: *"Whoever has been born of God does not sin, for His seed remains in him; and he cannot sin, because he has been born of God."* At first, reading that makes it sound as if it is impossible for a Christian to ever sin, but the tense of the verb indicates "to remain in sin" or "to keep on sinning." It is impossible for someone to be born of God — to have the seed of the new birth in him — and yet have his life marked by a pattern of continuing sin. A person who is born of God can't just keep on sinning. John repeats this point in I John 5:18 saying, *"We know that whoever is born of God does not sin; but he who has been born of God keeps himself, and the wicked one does not touch him."* Those who have eternal life don't live like the devil. Being born of God, having Christ's life, excludes the possibility of living in continual sin.

Another mark of a Christian is that he loves other people. *"We know that we have passed from death to life, because we love the brethren. He who does not love his brother abides in death,"* (I John 3:14). It was because of love that Christ saved us. The life that He has given us expresses itself through love for others, just as Christ has loved us. What we hate in other people is either the result of their sin or our own sin. But if we are born-again, our perspective on sin changes so that we see sinners as needing mercy just as much as we need it, and we have compassion on them, rather than hating them. John also puts this in practical terms, *"If someone says, 'I love God' and hates his brother, he is a liar; for he who does not love his brother whom he has seen, how can he love God whom he has not seen?"* (I John 4:20). Men are made in God's image. It is impossible to hate a man made in God's image and still love God. Rather than seeing sin in our fellow man, the new birth allows us to see the image of God in them, as defaced and corrupt as it may be. Each man has value and is precious because of the image of God in him. Christians see that, applaud it, defend it, celebrate it, and overcome their petty prejudices.

Finally, John gives us a very direct reference point: *"By this we know that we abide in Him, and He in us, because He has given us of His Spirit,"* (1 John 4:13). We know that we are Christians because of the presence of the Holy Spirit in our lives. We are given the Spirit at the moment of salvation both as a seal of our redemption and to indwell us, as our Comforter, teacher, and guide. It is this Spirit that cries out in our hearts, *"For you did not receive the spirit of bondage again to fear, but you received the Spirit of adoption by whom we cry out, 'Abba, Father.' The Spirit Himself bears witness with our spirit that we are children of God,"* (Romans 8:15-16). It is the Spirit that sheds the love of God abroad in our hearts, so that we know we are loved and can love others (Romans 5:5, *"Now hope does not disappoint, because the love of God has been poured out in our hearts by the Holy Spirit who was given to us."*) This is the one evidence that really separates believers from unbelievers. (Romans 8:9, *"But you are not in the flesh but in the Spirit, if indeed the Spirit of God dwells in you. Now if anyone does not have the Spirit of Christ, he is not His."*). The Spirit resides in all people who have the new birth, and those who do not have the Spirit do not have the Son either. Does that mean that everyone who has the Spirit knows they have Him? They ought to, but they may become confused by guilt or emotions. If you have any doubts about it, ask God to make it clear to you that His Spirit is living in you. But whether you have the Spirit or not is not based on your experience of His presence; it is a fact established in the Word of God as a result of your placing faith in Christ. It is your faith in the reality of His indwelling that will change your experience, not the experience that will change your faith.

Do these descriptions fit you? If not, then you need to examine yourself. Changing your life does not save you, but one effect of being saved is a changed life. A life change always occurs when you are born again, and the Holy Spirit indwells your life. Don't allow yourself to be deceived about the eternal destiny of your soul.

Dealing with Doubt

There are two kinds of people who doubt their salvation. The first is a lost man going through the motions of religious activities — blinded, thinking he is saved, but going to hell. As his conscience awakens by the conviction of the Holy Spirit, he becomes aware that his life does not match his confession. He must then choose to admit his need for a genuine relationship with Jesus Christ or continue his pretense. He has every reason to doubt his salvation because he is not saved.

Every Christian has days in which he does not *feel* saved. Christians should remember that their salvation is not based on feelings (which always change), but is based on the finished work of Christ on the Cross, which is eternal. Salvation is not based on the work of the Christian but on the work of the Christ.

The second kind of person who doubts his salvation is one who has trusted Christ for eternal life but is under attack from Satan. Doubts are actually good for us because they cause us to get into the Word of God and find assurance for our salvation. Your salvation is a fact guaranteed by God's Word. Answering the following questions will help you to understand the source of these doubts.

Peter warns us not to take Satan's attacks lightly. *"Be sober, be vigilant; because your adversary the devil walks about like a roaring lion, seeking whom he may devour,"* (1 Peter 5:8). He says we must be watchful and unflappable. We have an enemy who would love to eat us for lunch. Satan would love to stop your Christian growth and service. Jesus told us that

Satan only comes to "steal, kill, and destroy" (John 10:10). The image Peter gives us is a roaring lion — not the quiet lion who is hunting in stealth, but the one who is boldly strutting around trying to instill fear in everyone around and tell them that he is the king. Satan is trying to intimidate you so that you won't make any progress into his territory.

Peter's solution is amazingly simple: *"Resist him, steadfast in the faith, knowing that the same sufferings are experienced by your brotherhood in the world."* (I Peter 5:9). Just resist him. That may not sound like a great plan, but James says the same thing; *"Therefore submit to God. Resist the devil and he will flee from you",* (James 4:7). The devil is like a schoolyard bully who loves to make loud, bold, and frightening threats, but runs away if anybody ever stands up to him.

You can stand up to Satan's attacks by standing firmly on the foundation of your faith, the Word of God. Jesus would say, *"Get behind me, Satan,"* (Matthew 4:10) and confront him with the Word of God. It works every time. Don't be frightened by Satan's roaring. He knows that he can only win by intimidating you. But if you stand up to him with the truth from the Scriptures and in the power of the Spirit, he doesn't stand a chance. I John 4:4, *"You are of God, little children, and have overcome them, because He who is in you is greater than he who is in the world."*

To resist Satan we must put on the *"whole armor of God."* The armor that God gives us in Ephesians 6:10-18 will equip us to resist Satan's attacks. *"Having girded your loins with the truth"* means to protect ourselves and prepare ourselves with the truth that will expose Satan's lies. If your doubts concern the sins of your past, then gird yourself with the verses that say God remembers your sins no more and removes them as far as the east is from the west. If your own faithfulness is in doubt, cling to the truth that your salvation is based on Christ's faithfulness and not yours.

"To put on the breastplate of righteousness," means to fend off all personal attacks by relying on Christ's righteousness as your only basis for deserving to be saved. When Satan raises doubts about how a sinner like you can be saved, just point to the righteousness of Christ, not your own righteousness. You can always fall back on, "I don't deserve heaven, but Christ saved me while I was still a sinner and gave me his righteousness."

Satan can't argue with Christ's righteousness.

If you have shod your feet with the Gospel, then you are ready to share the good news. Satan would love to make you quit sharing your faith. If you share your faith anyway, even if you have doubts about God or about yourself, you are resisting Satan. If you will go against your natural instinct to freeze up and do nothing in the face of fear, Satan has lost. Even if you will just pray for someone who is lost, you are getting in Satan's face and he has to back off.

The fifth piece of armor is the shield of faith. *"Above all, taking the shield of faith with which you will be able to quench all the fiery darts of the wicked one,"* (Ephesians 6:16). Faith and fear cannot exist in the same mind at the same time. Nothing vanquishes doubt like a simple assertion of faith. To say, "I may have questions but not all the answers; however, I believe it because God said so," is one of the most powerful assaults you can use against Satan. If you have set your mind on belief, choosing to believe even without having all the answers, then you have closed the door on Satan's attacks. Ultimately, all doubt must be overcome by faith. 2 Corinthians 5:7, *"For we walk by faith, not by sight."*

The helmet of salvation is that solid steel brain-bucket by which you can say, "I am a son of God. I have Christ's righteousness. I am indwelt by the Spirit. Jesus Christ is my advocate. I am a new creature in Christ. I have full access to the Father to ask him anything in the name of Jesus. I will reign with Christ. I will be the judge of angels. ..." All of those things are bazooka rockets that hit at the heart of Satan's attacks, but they are simply all the things included in the package called salvation. You may need to just remind yourself of your own testimony — the date, the time, the circumstances, the people, — everything you can remember to assure yourself, and Satan, that you really did receive Christ and become one of God's sons. Your own testimony may be one of the most powerful tools you have to confront any doubts that arise about your salvation. If you will assert your salvation in specific terms, Satan cannot stand before you.

Finally, the basis for all of the other weapons, and the one offensive weapon you have, is the sword of the Word. With it, you can cut to the quick of Satan's lies and send him running. With it, you can be assured of the truth, Christ's righteousness, the Gospel, the value of your faith, and the benefits of your salvation. The sum total of the truth about your salvation is contained in His Word and it is the only truth you need to confirm your salvation. Luke 4:32, *"And they were astonished at His teaching, for His word was with authority."*

Since the battleground of Satan is your mind, in order to resist him, you must learn to put out of your mind all the doubts Satan puts there. Refuse to dwell on these doubts. Satan's greatest weapon against you is what your imagination can do with a little bit of misinformation. That is why Paul says, *"Casting down arguments and every high thing that exalts itself against the knowledge of God, bringing every thought into captivity to the obedience of Christ,"* (2 Corinthians 10:5). Don't let Satan cause fear in you by what you imagine might be — bring that thought into obedience. Don't let pride or self-importance convince you that you are different from the rest of mankind, that your sin is greater, or that you need Christ less than others — bring that thought into obedience. Don't keep thinking about some theory that only leads to greater doubt in your mind —bring that thought into obedience. Concentrate and meditate on what you know is truth, and there will be more than enough to occupy your mind and build your faith. John 8:32, *"And you shall know the truth, and the truth shall make you free."*

All Christians struggle at times with their faith, with their relationship with God and with the attacks of Satan; but the Word offers solutions. Even the apostle Paul struggled with obedience to God (Romans 7), with guilt over his former life (1 Timothy 1:15, *"This is a faithful saying and worthy of all acceptance, that Christ Jesus came into the world to save sinners, of whom I am chief."*, and with disappointments from people he trusted (2 Timothy 4:10, 14, *"For Demas has forsaken me, having loved this present world, and has departed for Thessalonica— Crescens for Galatia, Titus for Dalmatia. Alexander the coppersmith did me much harm. May the Lord repay him according to his works."*) *"Brethren, I do not count myself to have apprehended; but one thing I do, forgetting those things which are behind and reaching forward to those things which are ahead I press toward the goal for the prize of the upward call of God in Christ Jesus"* (Philippians 3:13-14).

Chapter Six

A NEW HOME

— Heaven —

The New Future of a Believer

As new creatures, our future and our destiny are changed forever. We can never really be at home in this world, because our citizenship, our hope, and all that we long for is in heaven. Just as we are assured of eternal life, we are also assured of what the future holds for us. The road that we travel to eternity will be the same for all of us — well, almost all of us.

Death

The next stop on the road that will lead us home is death. While many people fear death, Christians have a very different perspective on death. For us, death is not the end of our existence; it is the beginning of our life in heaven. It is not the end of life, but a transition from this earthly tabernacle (our bodies) to a heavenly tabernacle (2 Corinthians 5:1, *"For we know that if our earthly house, this tent, is destroyed, we have a building from God, a house not made with hands, eternal in the heavens."*) In fact, we can look forward to death knowing that this body, which houses our sinful nature and brings death to us, will be *"swallowed up by life"* (2 Corinthians 5:4) in our heavenly home.

Death came to mankind as a judgment on Adam's sin (Genesis 2:17, *"But of the tree of the knowledge of good and evil you shall not eat, for in the day that you eat of it you shall surely die.")*; Romans 5:12, *"Therefore, just as through one man sin entered the world, and death through sin, and thus death spread to all men, because all sinned."*) From the moment we are conceived, we carry in our bodies a death sentence. Hebrews 9:27 tells us that *"it is appointed for men to die once, but after this the judgment."* While most non-Christians simply see death as either an end to existence or a leap into the unknown, and those things are fearful enough, what they really fear without admitting it is judgment. Judgment is something to be feared by anyone who has not accepted God's love for them in Christ's work for their salvation.

But the Christian has passed out of judgment into life and no longer fears it. Death is a transition for us, not an end. Paul says that we approach death with confidence: *"So we are always confident, knowing that while we are at home in the body we are absent from the Lord. For we walk by faith, not by sight. We are confident, yes, well pleased rather to be absent from the body and to be present with the Lord,"* (2 Corinthians 5:6-8). When we leave this body, we get to be with God.

In fact, this posed a real dilemma for Paul, who also wrote, *"For to me to live is Christ, and to die is gain. But if I live in the flesh, this is the fruit of my labor: yet what I shall choose I wot not. For I am in a strait betwixt two, having a desire to depart, and to be with Christ; which is far better: Nevertheless to abide in the flesh is more needful for you"* (Philippians 2:21-24). Paul knew that his life after death would be better for him than his present life, but he also knew that God was not finished using him yet. The good that he was able to do for others outweighed his own desire to put an end to the struggles of life. Death is simply the completion of our earthly mission, but the beginning of our life in a new body in God's presence.

Jesus Is Coming Again

To many in the world, the idea of Jesus' coming again is associated with the end of the world and destruction of the planet. But to the Christian, it is homecoming. Jesus promised us, *"And if I go and prepare a place for you, I will come again and receive you to Myself; that where I am, there you may be also,"* (John 14:3). Christians understand Christ's return as His coming back to gather his people together and take them home.

Part of the confusion is that what we sometimes call "the second coming" or "the end times" is not one event, but several different events that happen over the course of more than a thousand years. On top of that, there is a considerable amount of disagreement as to the order of these events. What is presented here is my best understanding of the subject.

The Rapture

The first event, which is the next thing scheduled to happen, is the rapture of the Church. The rapture is Jesus' coming in the clouds and calls His Church to come be with Him in heaven. Paul tells us about this in 1 Thessalonians 4:15-17:

> *For this we say to you by the word of the Lord, that we who are alive and remain until the coming of the Lord will by no means precede those who are asleep. For the Lord Himself will descend from heaven with a shout, with the voice of an archangel, and with the trumpet of God. And the dead in Christ will rise first. Then we who are alive and remain shall be caught up together with them in the clouds to meet the Lord in the air. And thus we shall always be with the Lord.*

Paul's teaching is that Christ will come in the clouds and call to His Church. At that time, all Christians who have died will rise from their graves, and all believers living at that time will also be caught up with them to meet Christ in the air. From then on, we are with God. Christ does not descend all the way to the earth at this time, but only appears in the clouds. And clearly the apostles thought the rapture could happen at any moment even when they were writing the Scriptures in the first century.

The Tribulation

The next event is a seven-year period called the Tribulation. The Tribulation will be a time of great suffering and turmoil in the earth. During this time there will be famine, plagues, economic disaster, natural disasters, and many deaths. But the Bible also teaches that Christ's church will be taken away from the world before that time: *"But I would not have you to be ignorant, brethren, concerning them which are asleep, that ye sorrow not , even as others which have no hope. for if we believe that Jesus died and rose again, even so them also which sleep in Jesus will God bring with him. For this we say unto you by the word of the Lord, that we which are alive and remain unto the coming of the Lord shall not prevent them which are asleep. For the Lord himself shall descend from heaven with a shout, with the voice of the archangel, and with the trump of God: and the dead in Christ shall rise first: then we which are alive and remain shall be caught up together with them in the clouds to meet the Lord in the air: and so shall we ever be with the Lord. Wherefore comfort one another with these words"* (1 Thessalonians 4:13-18).

The tribulation will end with a great battle in the valley of Meggido, often called Armageddon, where all the armies of the world will gather to fight each other, but then unite to fight against Christ as He returns to the earth with His angels and saints. Guess who wins. This is the second coming in which Christ will come to rule and to judge.

The Millennial Reign of Christ

Once Christ has returned, He will establish a kingdom on earth in which He will reign for a thousand years. His co-regents will be the immortal saints of his Church — us. There will be believing Gentiles who have survived the Tribulation living on the earth and a believing nation of Israel, who finally see their Messiah. But it is not a time of perfect peace, because there are still rebellious and sinful men on the earth. So Christ rules strictly *"with a rod of iron"* (Revelation 19:15). There is a final rebellion at the end of this period after which the stage is set for entering the eternal state.

The Resurrection

Before we can enter the final state, we must be resurrected. In heaven, we do not become angels, as in the cartoons; neither are we disembodied souls floating around. Our bodies are transformed. That's right. The body that we lived in on earth is changed into a new kind of body which we will live in forever. When God first made man, he made him out of dust and breath; Therefore, it should be no surprise that the dust will not go away in eternity. When Christ comes to get us, He "*will transform our lowly body that it may be conformed to His glorious body,*" (Philippians 3:20-21).

What glorious body is that? The one that he showed us after He rose from the dead. It was a real body that had flesh and bones (Luke 24:39, *"So He stood over her and rebuked the fever, and it left her. And immediately she arose and served them"*), that Thomas could feel (John 20:27, *Then He said to Thomas, "Reach your finger here, and look at My hands; and reach your hand here, and put it into My side. Do not be unbelieving, but believing"*), and in which Jesus could prepare a meal and eat (John 21:9, *"Then, as soon as they had come to land, they saw a fire of coals there, and fish laid on it, and bread;"* Luke 24:43, *"And He took it and ate in their presence"*). Jesus made it a point to convince His disciples that His resurrected body was real and not a ghost or a phantom. But it was also a very different kind of body in that Jesus was able to appear in the middle of a locked room (John 20:26, *"And after eight days His disciples were again inside, and Thomas with them. Jesus came, the doors being shut, and stood in the midst, and said, 'Peace to you!'"*) and float straight up to heaven (Acts 1:9, *"Now when He had spoken these things, while they watched, He was taken up, and a cloud received Him out of their sight."*) Paul says that the main difference is that our new body will be incorruptible and immortal (1 Corinthians 15:38-52). This new body is called the resurrection body, which is very different from the ideas of reincarnation (coming back as some other life form), or a spiritual body (a non-material existence). We remain ourselves in a transformed physical existence.

In addition to the physical transformation, there is also a spiritual transformation. To go along with our perfected body, we gain a perfected mind, soul, and spirit. This transformation occurs when we see God for who He really is. We have been changed by the new birth and have some knowledge of God, *"But when that which is perfect has come, then that which is in part will be done away. When I was a child, I spoke as a child, I understood as a child, I thought as a child; but when I became a man,*

I put away childish things. For now we see in a mirror, dimly, but then face to face. Now I know in part, but then I shall know just as I also am known," (1 Corinthians 13:10, 12). Seeing God face to face will have some profound effects on us. We will be confirmed in the choice we have made to love and obey God, so that we can never turn away from it. Once we fully understand God's love and goodness, there is nothing that could possibly seem better that we would choose it. In God, we will find not only the fulfillment of all the longings of our soul, but intellectual and aesthetic satisfaction that is beyond anything we can imagine. In this perfect vision of God, our minds, emotions, and wills are transformed so that nothing could possibly detract us from loving Him with all our heart, soul, mind, and strength.

There are really two resurrections spoken of in Scripture. The first one is a resurrection to life, and the second is a resurrection to death, or the second death. The first resurrection happens in three phases, the first of which was the resurrection of Jesus as the firstfruits (1 Corinthians 15:23, *"But each one in his own order: Christ the firstfruits, afterward those who are Christ's at His coming.")* The second phase is the rapture, of which Paul says, *"Behold, I tell you a mystery: We shall not all sleep, but we shall all be changed—in a moment, in the twinkling of an eye, at the last trumpet. For the trumpet will sound, and the dead will be raised incorruptible, and we shall be changed,"* (1 Corinthians 15:51-52). The rapture is when those who have believed in Christ get their new bodies. The third phase of the first resurrection is for the people who became believers during the Tribulation period and for the Old Testament believers: *"Blessed and holy is he who has part in the first resurrection. Over such the second death has no power, but they shall be priests of God and of Christ, and shall reign with Him a thousand years,"* (Revelation 20:6). This resurrection happens at the beginning of the thousand year reign of Christ.

All Shall Be Judged by Christ

2 Corinthians 5:10, *"For we must all appear before the judgment seat of Christ, that each one may receive the things done in the body, according to what he has done, whether good or bad."*

The second resurrection happens at the end of the thousand years in conjunction with the Great White Throne judgment:

> *Then I saw a great white throne and Him who sat on it, from whose face the earth and the heaven fled away. And there was found no place for them. And I saw the dead, small and great, standing before God, and books were opened. And another book was opened, which is the Book of Life. And the dead were judged according to their works, by the things which were written in the books. The sea gave up the dead who were in it, and Death and Hades delivered up the dead who were in them. And they were judged, each one according to his works. Then Death and Hades were cast into the lake of fire. This is the second death. And anyone not found written in the Book of Life was cast into the lake of fire.* (Revelation 20:11-15)

Before the final state, there will be a reckoning in which all men will be judged. Those who have not believed will be judged by a simple criteria: is their name written in the book of life? While these people may try to argue that they should be saved on the basis of their works, no one can be saved by that standard. Those whose names are not found written in the book of life will be cast into a place, called the lake of fire, prepared for Satan and his angels.

This lake of fire was prepared for the devil and his angels (Matthew 25:41, *"Then He will also say to those on the left hand, 'Depart from Me, you cursed, into the everlasting fire prepared for the devil and his angels.'"*) Hell was not intended that men should ever be there. However, by rejecting the grace God has offered them and by their rebellion, they have chosen to follow Satan. In this way, all evil men and angels will be locked away forever — isolated from God and His people — so that God can finally establish a world in which all people have chosen to love him.

There is no reason for believers to live in fear of judgment, but believers will also be judged, not to see if they should enter heaven, but to see what their rewards will be. This judgment of believers is sometimes called the *bema,* or the judgment seat of Christ. Paul tells us that all of our works will be tested to see what their value is.

> *For no other foundation can anyone lay than that which is laid, which is Jesus Christ. Now if anyone builds on this foundation with gold, silver, precious stones, wood, hay, straw, each one's work will become clear; for the Day will declare it, because it will be revealed by fire; and the fire will test each one's work, of what sort it is. If anyone's work which he has built on it endures, he will receive a reward. If anyone's work is burned, he will suffer loss; but he himself will be saved, yet so as through fire.* (1 Corinthians 3:11-15)

Those of us who have served Christ well, in obedience, and have impacted people's lives will find that those works withstand the fire. To build upon the foundation of Christ means to do things that advance His kingdom. But we will also have works that are merely straw and stubble that burn up immediately. What might those works be? Primarily, they are all the things done for selfish reasons, to look good, to gain personally, to advance ourselves in some way, or to give us prestige. It is very easy for Christians to do the right things for the wrong reasons. The danger is that some Christians might spend their whole life doing only things that will be burnt up - activities that have no value in Christ's kingdom. It is possible that they might receive no reward and may even suffer loss even though they are saved.

The New Heavens and New Earth

When all of God's plan is finished, after all of humanity is judged, then the earth will be completely destroyed by fire (2 Peter 3:10, *"But the day of the Lord will come as a thief in the night, in which the heavens will pass away with a great noise, and the elements will melt with fervent heat; both the earth and the works that are in it will be burned up"*) and a new earth will take its place (Revelation 21:1, *"Now I saw a new heaven and a new earth, for the first heaven and the first earth had passed away. Also there was no more sea."*) All of the effects of Adam's sin will be wiped away and a new and perfect creation will be made for a redeemed humanity to fill.

This new earth will be the home of all redeemed and resurrected humanity from all times, where we will live forever in the presence of the Father. There will be no more sin because we will all know God in a perfected way and will no longer be under the influence of our sin nature. There will be no more death because we will all be immortal and sin can never enter our race again. There will also be no more sorrow and no more pain (Revelation 21:4, *"And God will wipe away every tear from their eyes; there shall be no more death, nor sorrow, nor crying. There shall be no more pain, for the former things have passed away."*)

On this new earth, there will be a new Jerusalem which God will make. It will have walls decorated with precious jewels, streets of gold, and twelve gates each made of a single pearl (Revelation 21:19-23, *"The foundations of the wall of the city were adorned with all kinds of precious stones: the first foundation was jasper, the second sapphire, the third chalcedony, the fourth emerald, the fifth sardonyx, the sixth sardius, the seventh chrysolite, the eighth beryl, the ninth topaz, the tenth chrysoprase, the eleventh jacinth, and the twelfth amethyst. The twelve gates were twelve pearls: each individual gate was of one pearl. And the street of the city was pure gold, like transparent glass. But I saw no temple in it, for the Lord God Almighty and the Lamb are its temple. The city had no need of the sun or of the moon to shine in it, for the glory of God illuminated it. The Lamb is its light."*

The New Jerusalem

This is where we will spend eternity — not in some ethereal realm among the clouds and stars as some movies have portrayed it, but living a very tangible life in a perfected world with perfected people and in the presence and fellowship of a perfect God. This is the blessedness that we know is ours. This is the glorification that was predestined for us when God chose us. This is our home, and we will always be restless until we can go home.

Chapter Seven

A NEW FELLOWSHIP

— The Church —

When you accepted Jesus as your Lord, you assumed some new responsibilities. Jesus said, *"If you love Me, keep My commandments,"* (John 14:15). Jesus also said, *"Therefore whoever hears these sayings of Mine, and does them, I will liken him to a wise man who built his house on the rock,"* (Matthew 7:24). It is your responsibility to find out what Jesus taught and then to do what he said. When Paul met Jesus he asked, *"Lord, what do You want me to do?" And the Lord said to him, "Arise and go into the city, and you will be told what you must do."* (Acts 9:6).

The Church

Being born again means entering into a new family - the family of God. You have been delivered from the kingdom of darkness and translated into the kingdom of God's dear Son (Colossians 1:13, *"He has delivered us from the power of darkness and conveyed us into the kingdom of the Son of His love."*) In this family, we are all brothers and sisters of the same Father. All Christians belong to one body and Jesus is the head. (1 Corinthians 12:13, *"For by one Spirit we were all baptized into one body— whether Jews or Greeks, whether slaves or free— and have all been made to drink into one Spirit."*) That body is His church. (Colossians 1:14-19, *"In whom we have redemption through His blood, the forgiveness of sins. He is the image of the invisible God, the firstborn over all creation. For by Him all things were created that are in heaven and that are on earth, visible and invisible, whether thrones or dominions or principalities or powers. All things were created through Him and for*

Him. And He is before all things, and in Him all things consist. And He is the head of the body, the church, who is the beginning, the firstborn from the dead, that in all things He may have the preeminence. For it pleased the Father that in Him all the fullness should dwell.") As a member of His body, which is the church, you need to be a member of a local New Testament church that believes the Word of God and exalts Jesus as the way of salvation. (Acts 4:12, *"Nor is there salvation in any other, for there is no other name under heaven given among men by which we must be saved."*) You need the for your own sake, but the church also needs you.

In the Greek New Testament the word for church is *ecclesia*, which comes from two Greek words with the root meaning of "to call out." In Christ's teaching, we are the sheep whom He called out of the world and heard his voice (John 10:16, *"And other sheep I have which are not of this fold; them also I must bring, and they will hear My voice; and there will be one flock and one shepherd.")* But it also describes the way Paul would start a church. Typically, he would enter a city and go teach in the tabernacle. Once it was clear that he was teaching about Jesus, the people would run him out of the city and stone him. Then Paul would turn around and call for anyone who believed what he said to come out to him. In every city, there were a few who were "called out" in this way and Paul stayed with them and taught them until they were established in their faith.

In usage, the meaning was "assembly," and was adopted in New Testament times to refer to the church in two ways. One refers to the local assembly or congregation of Christians meeting together for worship, Bible study, teaching and service. The other is the universal church composed of every believer in Jesus Christ.

Christ is the head of the church (Colossians 1:18, *"And He is the head of the body, the church, who is the beginning, the firstborn from the dead, that in all things He may have the preeminence."*) As such, He is our leader and the one whom we obey. He is also the unifying point of the body. No matter how different any two parts of the body are, what we have in common is our desire to follow Him. Paul called Christ the chief cornerstone of the church (1 Peter 2:7, *Therefore, to you who believe, He is precious; but to those who are disobedient, "The stone which the builders rejected has become the chief cornerstone"*; Ephesians 2:20, *"Having been built on the foundation of the apostles and prophets, Jesus Christ Himself being the chief corner stone, You are the Christ, the Son of the living God,")* which is the stone that determines the angles at which all the other stones are set. Christ said that He would build His church upon a particular stone, which was the truth that Peter uttered, *"Thou art the Christ, the Son of the living God,"* (Matthew 16:16).

We are the members of Christ's body. As such, we are all different, just as a hand is different from an eye. Yet each one of us plays an important role in the functioning of the whole body (1 Corinthians 12:27, *"Now you are the body of Christ, and members individually."*). Our goal as a body is to *"grow up in all things into Him who is the head— Christ—from whom the whole body, joined and knit together by what every joint supplies, according to the effective working by which every part does its share, causes growth of the body for the edifying of itself in love,"* (Ephesians 4:15-16). The only way that we can be joined together rightly is if every joint — every one of us — supplies the body with our own unique contribution. The whole body needs our strengths to compensate for weaknesses in others, and we need the strength of the other members to compensate for our weaknesses. If we all pull together under Christ's headship, then the whole body can be built up in love.

Your first responsibility as a member of the body of Christ is to make sure you are part of the assembly. *"And let us consider one another in order to stir up love and good works, not forsaking the assembling of ourselves together, as is the manner of some, but exhorting one another, and so much the more as you see the Day approaching,"* (Hebrews 10:24-25). If you are not there, you cannot encourage others and they can't encourage you. Christians who don't fellowship with other Christians tend to fade away, just like a glowing coal taken out of the fire quickly loses its heat.

The second responsibility you have to the church is to use your gift. Every Christian has a spiritual gift (1 Corinthians 12:12, *"For as the body is one and has many members, but all the members of that one body, being many, are one body, so also is Christ,"*) we will talk about those later in the book. For right now, let's just talk about the spiritual leaders that Christ has given the church. *"And He Himself gave some to be apostles, some prophets, some evangelists, and some pastors and teachers,"* (Ephesians 4:11). These four types of leaders use their giftedness in the church for a very specific reason: for the equipping of the saints for the work of ministry and for the edifying of the body of Christ, (Ephesians 4:12). It is not the job of evangelists or pastors to do the work of ministry; it is their job to *equip the saints* to do that work.

Because of their special work on our behalf, we are told to treat our spiritual leaders with respect and appreciation (1 Thessalonians 5:12, *"And we urge you, brethren, to recognize those who labor among you, and are over you in the Lord and admonish you"*; Hebrews 13:7, *"Remember those who rule over you, who have spoken the word of God to you, whose faith follow, considering the outcome of their conduct"*), sharing all good things with them (Galatians 6:6, *"Let him who is taught the word share in all good things with him who teaches."*) They are Christ's gift to you and His body. By contrast, we are told to turn away from false teachers. (2 Timothy 3:5, *"Having a form of godliness but denying its power. And from such people turn away!"*) (2 John 10-11, *"If anyone comes to you and does not bring this doctrine, do not receive him into your house nor greet him; for he who greets him shares in his evil deeds."*) This submission to those who have authority over you is your third responsibility to the church (1 Peter 5:5, *"Likewise you younger people, submit yourselves to your elders. Yes, all of you be submissive to one another, and be clothed with humility, for 'God resists the proud, but gives grace to the humble.'"*

Ordinances of the Church

Ordinances are special rituals or acts of worship which are mandated for all Christian churches. There are two ordinances observed by the Church. Both of them were instituted by Jesus Himself. They are baptism and the Lord's Supper.

Baptism

One of the first responsibilities of a Christian is to confess Jesus publicly and be baptized. There is no reason to be ashamed of your faith in Christ, and Jesus asked us to tell others about becoming a Christian. He said, *"Therefore whoever confesses Me before men, him I will also confess before My Father who is in heaven,"* (Matthew 10:32). Paul also told us, *"That if you confess with your mouth the Lord Jesus and believe in your heart that God has raised Him from the dead, you will be saved,"* (Romans 10:9). So apparently making a public declaration of our faith is a pretty important thing to do.

Some pastors ask new converts to "walk the aisle" or "come forward" during the service as a public confession of their faith, and there is nothing wrong with that; but the New Testament pattern is that water baptism was the outward public expression by which people declared their faith in Christ.

Baptism didn't start with Jesus or John the Baptist. Even before they came along, part of the ritual for a Gentile to become a Jew was that he had to be baptized to take his new identity in the nation of Israel. Therefore, when John came asking Jews to be baptized, as if they were a Gentile who had no part in the promises of God, it took a humble and devout Jew to follow him. But the meaning of baptism was clear to all: it was a sign that you identified yourself with a particular group of people.

The Greek word *baptizo* was originally used to mean dipping a cloth in the dye, so that it took on a new color. It is no wonder that baptism came to mean dipping, or immersing someone in water to indicate a change in his life and a new identity.

The Meaning of Baptism

The apostles taught that baptism was an outward sign of the inward reality of one's new birth. It gave the believer a vivid picture and experience of three important realities about his conversion:

1. That he died with Christ, was buried, and is now raised with Him to walk in a new kind of life (Romans 6:3-4, "*Or do you not know that as many of us as were baptized into Christ Jesus were baptized into His death? Therefore we were buried with Him through baptism into death, that just as Christ was raised from the dead*

by the glory of the Father, even so we also should walk in newness of life"),

2. That he has a new identity and is a new creation in Christ (2 Corinthians 5:17, *Therefore, if anyone is in Christ, he is a new creation; old things have passed away; behold, all things have become new*", and

3. That his sins have been washed away so that he can live a new life of righteousness (Acts 22:16, *"And now why are you waiting? Arise and be baptized, and wash away your sins, calling on the name of the Lord*"; Revelation 7:14, *And I said to him, "Sir, you know." So he said to me, "These are the ones who come out of the great tribulation, and washed their robes and made them white in the blood of the Lamb."*)

Do public confession or baptism save us? No, we are not saved by anything that we do. Does God need us to be baptized or confess before he can save us? No, *we need it.* We need to break through any fears and embarrassment by doing something to proclaim our faith. We need to be able to point to a date and place where we made that public statement. We need to go through some kind of experience to confirm in our own minds that all of the inner changes that happened at the moment we believed are all real.

Baptism is the first step of obedience for a new believer in Christ. We should consider the motive, the method, as well as the meaning of baptism.

The Method of Baptism

As we mentioned earlier, the Greek word for baptism clearly indicated "to dip," "to immerse," "to plunge," or "to submerge." When John the Baptist called people down to the Jordan River, it wasn't to sprinkle them; he intended to dip them. Nowhere in the Bible is there any indication that any other method of baptism was used.

From where did these other methods of baptism come? Within a couple of hundred years after Christ, parents wanted to do something to dedicate their children in the faith, much like circumcision in the Old Testament. Infant baptism became a very popular way to do this, but infants can't be submerged. Therefore, sprinkling and pouring a small amount of water came into use, but the meaning of baptism became unclear as well.

Does that mean other forms of baptism are worthless? Not necessarily. It is a fine idea to consecrate children to the Lord; but it is not the same thing as being baptized as a believer. Being sprinkled and anointed both have symbolic reference in Old Testament ritual which can give them significance; but they are not the same as going into the grave (the water) with Christ and rising from it.

However, much more important than the method of baptism used is the motive behind it. Why are you being baptized? We are to be baptized after we have believed as an expression of our obedience to our Lord, our love for God, and our joy over the grace that has been given us. To experience baptism in the right context for the right reasons is uniquely special for believers.

The Motive for Baptism

Our first motive for baptism should be obedience. It is not something that makes a lot of sense to do. You don't have to do it to be saved, and in some ways it seems kind of silly. But the main reason to do it is that Jesus said you should. One of the last things He told His disciples was, *"Go therefore and make disciples of all the nations, baptizing them in the name of the Father and of the Son and of the Holy Spirit, teaching them to observe all things that I have commanded you,"* (Matthew 28:19-20). Their assignment was clear:

1. Make disciples (another translation of this word for "teach") in all nations
2. Baptize them, and
3. Teach them to obey

Jesus clearly expected us to be baptized as a sign that we are His disciple. In fact, it is almost like a test to see if you will be obedient to Him in other things.

Our second motive should be love. If we understand what Jesus has done for us because of His love for us, then it is reasonable to respond to that love with love. *"We love Him because He first loved us,"* (1 John 4:19). But how can we show love for Jesus? We can't give Him a hug or bake Him a cake. He said, *"If you love Me, keep My commandments,"* (John 14:15). The first thing that he has commanded a new believer to do is to be baptized. If you understand what Jesus has done for you, then being baptized for Him is no problem.

The third motive for baptism is joy. In Acts 8:26-40, we find a story about a royal official from Ethiopia who becomes a believer. He was traveling along reading chapter 53 of Isaiah (which is about the Messiah) and wondering what it meant, when a deacon from the church in Jerusalem named Philip was led to be in his path. Philip answered his questions by telling him all about Jesus and the Ethiopian believed. Here was a man who came to Jerusalem to worship even though he was not a Jew. He was a Gentile who loved to read God's word. He was seeking, but very much aware that he was lost. He was so excited to learn that the Messiah had come and purchased his forgiveness, that he stopped the coach as soon as he saw water and asked to be baptized! When Philip left him, "He went on his way rejoicing."

Joy is one of the fruits of the Spirit (Galatians 5:22, *"But the fruit of the Spirit is love, joy, peace, longsuffering, kindness, goodness, faithfulness."*) John said that fellowship with God causes joy (1 John 1:4, *"And these things we write to you that your joy may be full"*) When you are relieved of the burden of your sins and realize that you have just become a son of God, what is the natural response? Joy! (1 Pet 1:8, *"Whom having not seen you love. Though now you do not see Him, yet believing, you rejoice with joy inexpressible and full of glory.")* Baptism is not a burden; it is an exciting experience in which you both express and realize that your life has begun anew because of your new identity in Christ's body.

The Lord's Supper

While baptism celebrates our new birth, the Lord's Supper commemorates Christ's death. Paul gives us a clear explanation of this ordinance referring to the supper that Christ shared with His disciples on the night He was betrayed (1 Corinthians 11:23-26).

The observance is also called communion in some churches, because in it we share in the benefits of Christ's death. Some churches refer to it as the eucharist, which is a reference to the Greek word for thanksgiving and focuses on the first words of Paul's account *"...that the Lord Jesus on the same night in which He was betrayed took bread; and when He had given thanks, He broke it and said, 'Take, eat; this is My body which is broken for you; do this in remembrance of Me.'"* (1 Corinthians 11:23-24).

The bread symbolizes the body of Christ, which was broken for our sakes. The wine represents His blood. As we take the Lord's Supper, we symbolically take the body and blood of Christ into our own bodies. It is a picture of each of us as individuals assimilating our portion of the benefit of Christ's death. In the Lord's Supper, we take the forgiveness found in His body and blood and make it our own. It is an expression of how we have received grace from Him. Paul says that we are to do this to "shew" or proclaim the Lord's death until he comes. It is to be a permanent part of our worship together.

This ritual is meant to be observed by all believers, but Paul adds a warning. *"Therefore whoever eats this bread or drinks this cup of the Lord in an unworthy manner will be guilty of the body and blood of the Lord,"* (1 Corinthians 11:27). The context of the letter explains that some were coming to the "love feasts" for the food, but were not living lifestyles that reflected Christ's righteousness. So he advised, *"But let a man examine himself, and so let him eat of the bread and drink of the cup. For he who eats and drinks in an unworthy manner eats and drinks judgment to himself, not discerning the Lord's body,"* (11:28-29). We should approach this table with introspection and reverence. How can we meditate on the words, *"This is my body which is broken for you,"* and not consider the sin of which we are forgiven by it? The best preparation for this meal is reflection on our present life, confession of any sin which is evident to us, and thanksgiving for the gift of Christ's body and blood.

The Example of the Early Church

Many of the patterns which we practice today were started in the earliest days of the Church. Even on the day of Pentecost when the apostles received the Holy Spirit and the church began, *"then those who gladly received his word were baptized; and that day about three thousand souls were added to them,"* (Acts 2:41). That must have been some baptismal service! But the point is that the early church began baptizing people from the very beginning.

They also established the basic elements of our worship in Acts 2:42, *"And they continued steadfastly in the apostles' doctrine and fellowship, in the breaking of bread, and in prayers."* These four elements — teaching, fellowship, the Lord's Supper, and prayer — are still the staples of worship around which all services are built. They represent each of the activities with which the church needs to be concerned: education about the Word of God, sharing personal needs and encouragement, proclamation of the Lord's death and forgiveness, and supplication to the Father for our needs.

Another pattern the early church set for us was to proclaim the Word of God. When Peter and John had been arrested and threatened if they continued to preach the gospel, they prayed, *"Now, Lord, look on their threats, and grant to Your servants that with all boldness they may speak Your word,"* (Acts 4:29). Preaching the word was more important to them than their personal safety. The results of that prayer were startling: *"And when they had prayed, the place where they were assembled together was shaken; and they were all filled with the Holy Spirit, and they spoke the word of God with boldness,"* (4:31). Almost thirty years later, the priority had not changed when Paul wrote, *"Being greatly disturbed that they taught the people and preached in Jesus the resurrection from the dead. And they laid hands on them, and put them in custody until the next day, for it was already evening. However, many of those who heard the word believed; and the number of the men came to be about five thousand,"* (4:2-4).

The early church also set a pattern for being persecuted. Jesus had said, *"If the world hates you, you know that it hated Me before it hated you,"* (John 15:30). When Peter and John were arrested a second time and beaten, *"They departed from the presence of the council, rejoicing that they were counted worthy to suffer shame for His name,"* (Acts 5:41). If they were getting the same response Jesus had gotten, they must be doing something right! We can rejoice in persecution knowing that men who hate the truth will hate us, but those who hear us and believe will be saved.

Finally, we find that the early church set a pattern for dealing with false teachers. Amazingly early in the history of the church the truth of the gospel was being distorted by some. The first distortion and controversy concerned whether or not the new Gentile believers needed to be circumcised and follow the Mosaic Law (Acts 15:1, *"And certain men came down from Judea and taught the brethren, 'Unless you are circumcised according to the custom of Moses, you cannot be saved.'"*) The solution of the early church was to call together a council of all the leaders of churches and the apostles to discuss the question (15:6, *"Now the apostles and elders came together to consider this matter."*) They weighed the testimony on both sides of the issue, compared it with Scripture, and made a decision that was to be final for all churches (Acts 15:14-17, "*Simon has declared how God at the first visited the Gentiles to take out of them a people for His name. And with this the words of the prophets agree, just as it is written: 'After this I will return and will rebuild the tabernacle of David, which has fallen down; I will rebuild its ruins, and I will set it up; So that the rest of mankind may seek the Lord, even all the Gentiles who are called by My name, says the Lord who does all these things.'"*) The decision of this council was then circulated among the churches so that everyone knew to reject these false teachers and not prolong the controversy (15:19-20), *"Therefore I judge that we should not trouble those from among the Gentiles who are turning to God, but that we write to them to abstain from things polluted by idols, from sexual immorality, from things strangled, and from blood."* Almost every book in the New Testament deals with the subject of false teachers and warns that we must be careful not to allow them to corrupt our teaching (1 John 4:1-3, *"Beloved, do not believe every spirit, but test the spirits, whether they are of God; because many false prophets have gone out into the* *world. By this you know the Spirit of God: Every spirit that confesses that Jesus Christ has come in the flesh is of God, and every spirit that does not confess that Jesus Christ has come in the flesh is not of God. And this is the spirit of the Antichrist, which you have heard was coming, and is now already in the world";*2 Peter 2:1, *"But there were also false prophets among the people, even as there will be false teachers among you, who will secretly bring in destructive heresies, even denying the Lord who bought them, and bring on themselves swift destruction.")*

We still have false teachers in the world today, mostly spreading the same heresies that Paul and John encountered. When seeking a doctrinally sound, biblically based church, it is important to avoid false churches and teachers that look Christian but are actually false prophets (Matthew 7:13-15, *"Enter by the narrow gate; for wide is the gate and broad is the way that leads to destruction, and there are many who go in by it. Because narrow is the gate and difficult is the way which leads to life, and there are few who find it. Beware of false prophets, who come to you in sheep's clothing, but inwardly they are ravenous wolves."*) In the section "A New Mission Field," we will discuss how to identify pseudo-Christian churches and cults.

Your Participation in the Local Church

A local New Testament church is a group of baptized believers who have voluntarily joined themselves together to carry out the commands of Christ. Jesus gave us a mission that requires us to act as His body, and not as self-sufficient individuals. We need each other, therefore, we must come together to fulfill our commission from Christ. The early Christians joined the church in the city where they lived.

Only those who are truly saved should be a member of a local New Testament church (Acts 2:47, *And the Lord added to the church daily those who were being saved.*) Since salvation is the only requirement to be a member of Christ's body, then salvation should be the only requirement for membership in a local church. While there are always visitors in our churches and many can sit in the pews for years without being saved, a person should experience the new birth before becoming a member of a local group of believers.

You should join a local church that honors and teaches the Bible. The Bible should be the focus of any church's ministry. It doesn't make sense to come to church and discuss an article in *Reader's Digest.* Nor does it make any sense to go to a church where you are taught that the Bible is wrong, that it is only a book of fables, or that some parts of the Bible should be ignored. Insist on choosing a church where the Bible is held up as the Word of God. Take your Bible to church with you and follow the preacher and teacher as they explain its truths.

You should attend faithfully the church you join. You will receive encouragement from other Christians (Hebrews 10:25, *"Not forsaking the assembling of ourselves together, as is the manner of some, but exhorting one another, and so much the more as you see the Day approaching"*), as well an increased faith from learning God's Word (Romans 10:17, *"So then faith comes by hearing, and hearing by the word of God.")* It takes time to develop relationships with people in a church, and it doesn't happen automatically. You have to work at it. Attending every Sunday possible is only a beginning of what it means to be a member of the body.

If you are not already a member of a local church, prayerfully list two or three you will visit in the next month, with the purpose of seeking God's will on which church He would have you join. Watching a service on television on Sunday morning is not the same as going to church. Listening to Christian radio is good, but it is not a substitute for fellowship with other Christians. Odds are that you won't find a perfect church; you'll only find ones that are filled with imperfect saints. But don't let that be an excuse. Find a place where you can grow and serve, then dedicate yourself to doing that.

Consider the following suggestions for making your church worship more meaningful.

> Bow for silent prayer before the service begins. Pray for yourself, for the minister, for those taking part in the service, and for those worshipping. Pray that Christ will be very real to all and that those who do not know Christ may come to know Him.
>
> Always take your Bible. Underline portions that are made

especially meaningful by the sermons. Meditate upon the words of the hymns. Take notes on the sermon and apply them to your life.

If you are a part of a local church, ask God to show you ways in which you can be more used by Him by being of service in the church. God uses the New Testament church to organize and utilize members for specific duties and responsibilities so that each member may have a part in building up His Kingdom. Some of those opportunities include teaching a Sunday School class and working with children in the nursery. Don't assume that any ministry is either beyond or beneath your ability. Just make yourself available for God to use in whatever way He will.

Chapter Eight

A NEW RESPONSIBILITIES

Quiet Time
Stewardship
Obedience

A New Purpose

What is God's purpose for you now that you are His child? It is simple, and we have mentioned it several times already. He wants to conform you to the image of His Son. (Romans 8:28-29, "*And we know that all things work together for good to those who love God, to those who are the called according to His purpose. For whom He foreknew, He also predestined to be conformed to the image of His Son, that He might be the firstborn among many brethren.*") That doesn't mean we all need to start wearing long robes, long hair, and a beard. It doesn't even mean that we have to adopt Jesus' personality. God wants to conform us to His righteousness, His moral character, and His selfless devotion to obeying God.

Before we go any further, we need to make something clear. There is a difference between becoming a Christian and growing as a Christian. We become a Christian by grace through faith. We don't do anything to deserve it; we just believe — we just say yes to God when He offers us the present of salvation. (John 1:12, *"But as many as received Him, to them He gave the right to become children of God, to those who believe in His name*.") When we do, He justifies us automatically, right then and there. That is, He makes us right with Himself, gives us Christ's righteousness, and takes away the judgment of sin against us. Because God has done this when we didn't do anything to deserve it, we know we can't do anything to lose it. We are secure in our salvation because it depends entirely on God's faithfulness, not our own. Receiving Christ is a one time event with profound and lasting consequences.

That is how we become a Christian. But growing in Christ is different. It doesn't happen automatically or instantly. It takes time and it takes work. Growing in Christ requires that you be *"transformed by the renewing of your mind"* (Romans 12:2). Renewing your mind means learning to think about things the way God does; and to do that, you have to study His word. Growing in Christ also means growing in faith and learning to trust God more and more. That will require walking with God and seeing Him answer your prayers, provide for you, rescue you from trouble, and transform disasters in your life into blessings. Growing in Christ also requires growing obedience to God's commands, especially that hard one about loving one another. That all takes time and deliberate effort to learn about God and to follow Him. Paul even says, *"Work out your own salvation with fear and trembling,"* (Philippians 2:12).

Philippians 2:12 doesn't teach that sanctification is all up to you. The rest of that sentence says, *"For it is God who works in you both to will and to do for His good pleasure,"* (Philippians 2:13). Being transformed is no easy task. In fact, it is impossible without God's help. It doesn't make sense to be saved by grace but expect to grow in Christ by our own efforts. *"Are you so foolish? Having begun in the Spirit, are you now being made perfect by the flesh?"* (Galatians 3:3). All of the disciplines of Christian growth — prayer, Bible study, giving, etc. — are simply ways for us to open ourselves up to the way God wants to transform us. To discipline yourself to do these things, you will have to develop some new habits. Yes, we have to walk in those habits day by day, but we are to walk in the Spirit, not in the flesh. God has given us His Spirit to guide us in our growing knowledge of God and to transform us. *"But we all, with unveiled face, beholding as in a mirror the glory of the Lord, are being transformed into the same image from glory to glory, just as by the Spirit of the Lord,"* (2 Corinthians 3:18). And we have the promise of God, *"Being confident of this very thing, that He who has begun a good work in you will complete it until the day of Jesus Christ,"* (Philippians 1:6).

The things that we are talking about in this chapter are some of the disciplines required for growth. These things are not required to be a "real Christian." There are lots of real Christians that struggle with these things. They are the steps of obedience that lead to growth as you learn more about God and learn to trust Him more. You don't have to do any of these things to be saved, but you do have to do them if you want to grow in your faith, knowing that God will bless your obedience and do His part to change your life. 1 Peter 3:18, *"For Christ also suffered once for sins, the just for the unjust, that He might bring us to God, being put to death in the flesh but made alive by the Spirit."*

We have talked about the body of Christ and how he gave spiritually gifted men to lead the Church. In Ephesians 4:14-15 the reason for that is given: *"That we should no longer be children, tossed to and fro and carried about with every wind of doctrine, by the trickery of men, in the cunning craftiness of deceitful plotting, but, speaking the truth in love, may grow up in all things into Him who is the head— Christ."* God doesn't want us to remain immature children in the faith, but to "grow up" and be like Christ in all things. We do this by speaking the truth in love. What truth? God's truth — His Word. Not beating each other over the head with it, but lovingly confronting those whose lives are not conformed to the Word so that God may change their hearts.

What if we don't want to grow? Or don't want to put in the time and the work to grow? Paul says that we remain "babies" who have to be fed spiritual pabulum, because we can't handle solid food (1 Corinthians 3:1-2, *"And I, brethren, could not speak to you as to spiritual people but as to carnal, as to babes in Christ. I fed you with milk and not with solid food; for until now you were not able to receive it, and even now you are still not able"*). He also says that such believers are "carnal", or fleshly. If we don't grow in the Spirit, then our flesh (sin) remains our master, and nothing about our life changes even though we are saved.

The solution is simple enough. *"As newborn babes, desire the pure milk of the word, that you may grow thereby,"* (1 Peter 2:2). There is nothing wrong with being a baby and needing milk. But if you want to stay a baby, then something is wrong. God's Word is the key to growth in knowledge and in grace. *"All Scripture is given by inspiration of God, and is profitable for doctrine, for reproof, for correction, for instruction in righteousness,"* (2 Timothy 3:16). God inspired the Bible (literally, "God-breathed") so that it would be useful to us in four ways:

doctrine — What's right: teaching; the facts about the faith; adds to our understanding of who God is and how He deals with us

reproof — What's not right: confronting a person about his sin

correction — How to get right: explaining to a person about his errors in thinking or doctrine

instruction in righteousness — How to stay right: teaching someone to obey God and develop a Christian lifestyle and character

The first and last uses deal with teaching and the middle two deal with confronting. Each pair has one that talks about our knowledge of the truth, but the other addresses the practical matters of how we live. We should expect the Bible to both teach us and confront us about our lifestyle and our understanding. The ultimate reason for giving us the word and using it in this way is "*that the man of God may be complete, thoroughly equipped for every good work,*" (3:17).

How often should you study the Bible? How often does a baby need milk? There is no command in Scripture that tells us we have to spend from 6:23 to 6:57 every morning in Bible study, but there are examples. In one of the cities where Paul started a church, *"These were more fair-minded than those in Thessalonica, in that they received the word with all readiness, and searched the Scriptures daily to find out whether these things were so,"* (Acts 17:11). David said, *"Oh, how I love Your law! It is my meditation all the day,"* (Psalm 119:97). Daily Bible study and meditation give you the opportunity to keep your mind focussed on what God is doing in your life each day and keeps you constantly in the learning mode. If you are to be transformed, it will happen little by little as your thoughts are confronted by the Word of God. This is not a sprint; it is a marathon. Slow and steady progress is the best way to go.

Once you begin studying the Word, you will find that there are all kinds of benefits that you never would have expected. The reason for studying the Bible is not what we get out of it, but what we become through it. Paul told his young protege Timothy, "*Be diligent to present yourself approved to God, a worker who does not need to be ashamed, rightly dividing the word of truth,*" (2 Timothy 2:15). Your ultimate goal is to be useful to God, knowing His Word, and letting that have its natural effect by transforming your mind and your life.

An effective prayer life is also necessary for Christian growth. One of the main reasons many people feel that they fail in the Christian life is that they have failed to pray. Jesus said, "*...that men always ought to pray and not lose heart,*" Luke 18.1. We may not get an answer to our prayers exactly when we want it, but prayer is our communication with God and the heart of our relationship with Him.

God as your Father wants you to have many things, "*yet you do not have because you do not ask,*" (James 4:2). As his sons, we have open access to the Father, and may approach Him with boldness and full confidence that He is willing and able to do whatever we ask. Jesus reminded us of God's goodness and love towards us.

> *Therefore, brethren, having boldness to enter the Holiest by the blood of Jesus, by a new and living way which He consecrated for us, through the veil, that is, His flesh, and having a High Priest over the house of God, let us draw near with a true heart in full assurance of faith, having our hearts sprinkled from an evil conscience and our bodies washed with pure water.* (Hebrews 10:19-22).

But Jesus also taught us that for prayer to be answered, there are certain "if's" that we must meet. "*If you abide in Me, and My words abide in you, you will ask what you desire, and it shall be done for you,*" (John 15:7). Jesus expects those who will ask the Father for things to be those who have trusted in Christ and are resting in Him, fellowshipping with Him daily, and studying His Word consistently.

Jesus also expects us to recognize that we only have access to the Father through Him, so He said, *"Until now you have asked nothing in My name. Ask, and you will receive, that your joy may be full,"* (John 16:24). Asking in Jesus name means to ask with His authority, but it also implies that you are asking something that He would approve.

We must also believe when we ask. *"But let him ask in faith, with no doubting, for he who doubts is like a wave of the sea driven and tossed by the wind. For let not that man suppose that he will receive anything from the Lord,"* (James 1:6-7). It is not a question of, "Do I have enough faith?" Either you have faith concerning the thing you ask or you don't. Your faith may grow to include more and more areas of your life, but about any given thing, you either believe or you don't. If you don't, you need to ask yourself why not? Do you think God doesn't love you enough to do that? Or are you just fearful about what might happen if God does not come through? Or do you know deep down that you shouldn't be asking for it? There are answers in the Word that can help you overcome your doubts, which brings us to the final "if."

"Now this is the confidence that we have in Him, that if we ask anything according to His will, He hears us. And if we know that He hears us, whatever we ask, we know that we have the petitions that we have asked of Him," (1 John 5:14-15). How can we know what the will of God is so that we can ask according to it? We may not always know, but the Word of God will give us a great many statements to tell us what God wills. It tells us of His character so that we know what kind of things He wills. Ultimately, it is walking with Him, coming to know God Himself and not just about Him, and learning to accept His answers to our prayers that will teach us how to ask according to His will.

There are also some things which can build a wall between us and God so that our prayers are hindered. Unconfessed sin (Psalm 66:18, *"If I regard iniquity in my heart, the Lord will not hear"*), doubt (James 1:6-8, *"But let him ask in faith, with no doubting, for he who doubts is like a wave of the sea driven and tossed by the wind. For let not that man suppose that he will receive anything from the Lord; he is a double-minded man, unstable in all his ways"*), asking with self-indulgent motives (James 4:2-3, *"You lust and do not have. You murder and covet and cannot obtain. You fight and war. Yet you do not have because you do not ask. You ask and do not receive, because you ask amiss, that you may spend it on your pleasures"*), and disrespect for your spouse (1 Peter 3:7, *"Husbands, likewise, dwell with them with understanding, giving honor to the wife, as to the weaker vessel, and as being heirs together of the grace of life, that your prayers may not be hindered"*) can all be roadblocks to having your prayers answered. We cannot use the privilege of prayer like wishes in Aladdin's lamp. Prayer is not a magical formula by which we can make God do what we want. It is God's tool to change us. We must approach God on His terms, rest in His goodness and grace, and receive the answer from His hand with thanksgiving.

There are significant promises made to all who are willing to follow the path of prayer and humble themselves before the Father. *"And my God shall supply all your need according to His riches in glory by Christ Jesus,"* (Philippians 4:19). *"Let us therefore come boldly to the throne of grace, that we may obtain mercy and find grace to help in time of need,"* (Hebrews 4:16).

A New Habit - Quiet Time With God

Spending time each day with God will mean that you have to develop a new habit. That habit is often called a quiet time. It is your time to be quiet with God, to read His Word, to pray, and to develop your relationship with Him.

There is no right way or wrong way to have a quiet time except that not doing it is not the right way to do it. However, there are some ideas in Scripture that can help you find the best way for you to spend effective time with God.

Those ideas begin with the proper attitudes. First, we need to be aware that we really need to be there. *"As the deer pants for the water brooks, so pants my soul for You, O God,"* (Psalm 42:1). *As* We should have a longing to spend time with God and an expectancy that we will go away refreshed. We should also have an attitude of reverence, or fear, toward God. That does not mean that we should be afraid of our Father who loves us, but that we should have complete reverence for His authority, His holiness, His power, and His grace by which we can come before Him. (Psalm 89:7, *"God is greatly to be feared in the assembly of the saints, and to be held in reverence by all those around Him"*; Habakkuk 2:20, *"But the LORD is in His holy temple. Let all the earth keep silence before Him."*) There should also be an attitude of repentance from our sin and a willingness to confess and be cleansed of our sin. (1 Corinthians 15:34, *"Awake to righteousness, and do not sin; for some do not have the knowledge of God. I speak this to your shame."*) Also included must be an attitude of willingness to obey whatever God shows us that day. (John 7:17, *"If anyone wants to do His will, he shall know concerning the doctrine, whether it is from God or whether I speak on My own authority"*; 14:15, *"If you love Me, keep My commandments"*; *vs.* 23, *"Jesus answered and said to him, 'If anyone loves Me, he will keep My word; and My Father will love him, and We will come to him and make Our home with him.'"*)

While no Scripture commands it, many people find that the morning is the best time for them to spend time with God (Proverbs 8:17, *"I love those who love me, and those who seek me diligently will find me"*; Mark 1:35, *"Now in the morning, having risen a long while before daylight, He went out and departed to a solitary place; and there He prayed."*) Morning may be the only time of the day that you are not likely to be distracted or interrupted. It also gives you the opportunity to start your day with a fresh perspective and a renewed commitment to be of service to God that day. The amount of time you spend is up to you. You might want to start with longer time than you really expect to use and grow into it. That way you don't have to readjust your schedule later. But your emphasis should be on quality, not on quantity. You could waste three hours a day without ever really getting anything from your quiet time, but it would be better to spend a very well focussed five minutes in which you truly meet God and walk away changed.

The place where you go to meet God could be almost anywhere, but it should be a quiet place where you will not be interrupted. (Luke 5:15-16, *"However, the report went around concerning Him all the more; and great multitudes came together to hear, and to be healed by Him of their infirmities. So He Himself often withdrew into the wilderness and prayed.*") You may have to isolate yourself somewhat or go to a place where no one else will go. One student found that he never had to worry about distractions if he had his quiet time in the graveyard that was adjacent to his campus. You will find that wherever you choose, no matter how elaborate or plain the decor, it will become a holy place to you because it is the place that you go to meet God. (Genesis 19:27, *"And Abraham went early in the morning to the place where he had stood before the LORD."*)

You can organize your time in whatever way is beneficial for you. Here is a really simple plan to follow:

Relax: wait on God (Psalm 46:10, *"Be still, and know that I am God; I will be exalted among the nations, I will be exalted in the earth!"*; Isaiah 30:15, *"For thus says the Lord GOD, the Holy One of Israel: In returning and rest you shall be saved; in quietness and confidence shall be your strength. But you would not";* 40:31, *"But those who wait on the LORD shall renew their strength; they shall mount up with wings like eagles, they shall run and not be weary, they shall walk and not faint."*) Just take a few minutes to set aside all the other cares and focus your energies on listening to God. Of course, God is always ready; what we are really doing is waiting on ourselves to be ready to receive what God has for us.

Request: pray briefly (Psalm 119:18, *"Open my eyes, that I may see wondrous things from Your law";* 139:23-24, *"Search me, O God, and know my heart; try me, and know my anxieties; And see if there is any wicked way in me, and lead me in the way everlasting."*) Ask God to meet you in your time there, to open your eyes to the truth in His Word, and to give you the strength to put into practice whatever He shows you.

Read: select a portion of God's Word. It is always best to have a program that you are working on so that you don't have to think too much about this. You can study the passage that last Sunday's sermon was about. You can work your way through a specific book or you can study a specific topic and find all the Scriptures that relate to it. If you aren't sure where to start, Proverbs has thirty-one chapters — one for each day of the month — and you can read the chapter that matches that day's date. A Proverb a day keeps the Devil away.

Reflect & Remember: meditate on the passage you have studied and memorize a verse. (Joshua 1:8, *"This Book of the Law shall not depart from your mouth, but you shall meditate in it day and night, that you may observe to do according to all that is written in it. For then you will make your way prosperous, and then you will have good success."*) Whatever you have studied, take some extra time to think about it. What does it mean? How does that relate to other things you know? How does this passage fit with what comes before it and after it? What are some ways you can apply this passage to your life? This is a great time to keep your Scripture memory program on track.

Record: write down what God has given you. The best way to lock up the treasures you discover is to write them down. That helps you to understand better and gives you a way to remind yourself of the ground you have covered. Was it a command you need to obey? A promise you should claim? A new truth you have learned? Sins to avoid? An example to follow? A service to perform? A prayer to echo? Whatever it is, write it down and record what you learned and how you plan to apply this nugget.

Request: enjoy a time of prayer with God. Now is the time to do your serious praying. This may be a totally new experience for you. It may not feel comfortable at first to address God, and you may even feel silly. But soon you will realize that He really is there, and He really is listening. Eventually you will spend more and more time in prayer. To get you started, here is a pattern for your prayers.

1. **Praise God** (Psalm 50:23, *"Whoever offers praise glorifies Me; and to him who orders his conduct aright I will show the salvation of God."*) Tell God that you appreciate how awesome He is and all that He has done for you.

2. **Repent of your sins** (Psalm 32:1-5, *"Blessed is he whose transgression is forgiven, whose sin is covered. Blessed is the man to whom the LORD does not impute iniquity, and in whose spirit there is no deceit. When I kept silent, my bones grew old through my groaning all the day long. For day and night Your hand was*

heavy upon me; my vitality was turned into the drought of summer. I acknowledged my sin to You, and my iniquity I have not hidden. I said, 'I will confess my transgressions to the LORD, and You forgave the iniquity of my sin.'"; Psalms 51:1-13, *"Have mercy upon me, O God, according to Your lovingkindness; according to the multitude of Your tender mercies, blot out my transgressions. Wash me thoroughly from my iniquity, and cleanse me from my sin. For I acknowledge my transgressions, and my sin is always before me. Against You, You only, have I sinned, and done this evil in Your sight— that You may be found just when You speak, and blameless when You judge. Behold, I was brought forth in iniquity, and in sin my mother conceived me. Behold, You desire truth in the inward parts, and in the hidden part You will make me to know wisdom. Purge me with hyssop, and I shall be clean; wash me, and I shall be whiter than snow. Make me to hear joy and gladness, that the bones You have broken may rejoice. Hide Your face from my sins, and blot out all my iniquities. Create in me a clean heart, O God, and renew a steadfast spirit within me. Do not cast me away from Your presence, and do not take Your Holy Spirit from me. Restore to me the joy of Your salvation, and uphold me by Your generous Spirit. Then I will teach transgressors Your ways, and sinners shall be converted to You."*; Proverbs 28:9, 13, *"One who turns away his ear from hearing the law, even his prayer is an abomination. He who covers his sins will not prosper, but whoever confesses and forsakes them will have mercy.")* Admit your shortcomings to God and humbly ask for forgiveness.

3. **Ask for yourself and others** (Matthew 7:7-9, *"Ask, and it will be given to you; seek, and you will find; knock, and it will be opened to you. For everyone who asks receives, and he who seeks finds, and to him who knocks it will be opened. Or what man is there among you who, if his son asks for bread, will give him a stone?"*; Hebrews 4:16, *"Let us therefore come boldly to the throne of grace, that we may obtain mercy and find grace to help in time of need."* Make your requests to God believing in Jesus'

name that He will hear your prayer.

4. **Yield yourself to God and His will** (Psalm 143:10, *"Teach me to do Your will, for You are my God; your Spirit is good. Lead me in the land of uprightness.";* Romans 12:1-2, *"I beseech you therefore, brethren, by the mercies of God, that you present your bodies a living sacrifice, holy, acceptable to God, which is your reasonable service. And do not be conformed to this world, but be transformed by the renewing of your mind, that you may prove what is that good and acceptable and perfect will of God.")* In humility, after you have made your requests known to God, recognize your submission to Him and be willing to accept whatever answer He gives.

From time to time, it is a good idea to change things. Give yourself a chance to try new things and avoid the trap of just going through the motions and becoming stale. Remember that your main purpose is to meet with God and to know Him better. Get focused as you begin and avoid distractions. You have work to do, and this is the only time today you have to do it. You can expect Satan to resist your plans for this meeting. He will get in your way in any way he can, because he doesn't want you to grow. But don't let him stop you. If you miss a day, don't quit; just decide to meet with God the next day!

If you want to make a commitment to begin having regular quiet times, you can pray this prayer: "Lord, I desire to meet with You every day in Your Word. I need Your power in order to consistently accomplish this goal. Please help me in this endeavor! Lord, today I commit myself. Thank you for helping me!"

How to Study the Bible

Study Tools

There are certain tools you will want if your are going to get serious about Bible study. The Bible can be hard to understand, and we often need help to find out what it means. It can be very helpful to get advice from men who have spent years studying the Scriptures. That help is available in books. Here are a few suggestions about the basics you may want to have.

A good study Bible: This is a Bible that has notes introducing each book, cross-references in the margins, and explanatory notes where they are needed. There will probably be maps and helpful lists and essays in the back. Some of the best study Bibles are *Scofield*, *Ryrie*, and the *Thompson Chain Bible*.

A Bible concordance: A concordance is list of every word found in the Bible and verses where the words occurs. A concordance can be helpful if you are looking up every verse about a certain topic like "money." Just look up the word "money" and you will see every verse in the Bible that has that word. It can also help you look up a verse of which you may remember a word or two of, but you don't remember the reference. The classic concordance that all others refer to is *Strong's*. Make sure the concordance you use is for the translation that you use most often.

A Bible dictionary: There are words, people, and places in the Bible that may be hard to find in a regular dictionary. Even if you find them, the meaning in an English dictionary may not tell you much that helps you understand how it is used in the Bible or the significance of it. *Unger's* and *Zondervan's* are great Bible dictionaries.

A Bible Handbook: A handy reference for the historical background of each book of the Bible and some helpful insights for interpretation can be found in a Bible Handbook. Halley's and Unger's are old standards, but the new handbook by Wilmington is a wonderful resource.

A one-volume Bible commentary: There are hundreds of commentaries on each book of the Bible and you could spend a fortune trying to collect them all; however, a good one volume commentary will usually answer your questions and doesn't take much shelf space. A commentary is a set of explanatory notes that walk you through a book of the Bible verse by verse and often contains insights from the original languages. Matthew Henry, Wycliffe, and Liberty are the best choices here. The *Bible*

Knowledge Commentary is a two volume set that is also good.
A one-volume Bible doctrine book: Sometimes you need information on Bible doctrines to make sense of a passage. For instance, if you are studying Romans 4, you might want more information on the doctrine of salvation by faith. When you get to Romans 5, you will want to clarify what imputed sin is. Having a book that outlines and explains the major doctrines of the Bible can be invaluable. Charles Ryrie's *Basic Theology* or *Major Bible Themes* by Chafer and Walvoord (a condensation of Chafer's nine-volume set) are good choices.

A question and answer book: There are some passages that need special explanations that commentaries don't have space to give and that may require some special knowledge of history, archaeology, or science. For those passages, there are books that just handle those commonly asked questions with answers that are hard to find. We suggest *The Bible Has the Answer* by Henry Morris, *Dr. Rice, Here is my Question* by John R. Rice, or *Encyclopedia of Bible Difficulties* by Gleason Archer.

Rules for Understanding the Bible

There are also certain rules for Bible study that will help you find the meaning of the Scriptures and answer some of your own questions. If following these four principles doesn't give you an answer to your question, then you need special information from one of the reference books mentioned above.

1. Take the Bible literally!
   It is a common error to assume that all of the Bible is poetry so that we don't take it literally. It is easy to explain away a passage you don't understand or don't want to believe if you just interpret it metaphorically. Unless there is a compelling reason to do so, the plain, normal interpretation should always be followed. You should interpret the Bible the same way you would any other book. There are clearly poetic statements that cannot be true literally, i.e., "as far as the east is from the west" or to say that God, who is Spirit, has body parts. As Dr. David L. Cooper says, "When the plain sense of Scripture makes common sense, seek no other sense."

2. Keep it in the proper context!
You have probably heard people use the saying, *"Am I my brother's keeper?"* (Genesis 4:9) to indicate that they are not. But taken in context, this statement was made by a man who had just killed his brother and was trying to cover it up! In the same way, some people have taken Jesus' statement that in the resurrection people are "like the angels in heaven" (Matthew 22:30) to mean that we have no physical bodies and are given wings. In the context, Jesus was asked about marriage in the resurrection, and His answer referred only to the issues of marriage and procreation. The statement really means that we will only be like the angels in that we won't be getting married or having babies. It is always important to make sure you understand how every statement fits into its context. It will also enrich your understanding of every verse.

3. Be alert to the figurative use of language!
While the Bible should be interpreted literally as much as possible, figures of speech and poetic expressions are used. When Jesus said, *"You are the salt of the earth,"* (Matthew 5:13), he didn't mean that we are salt in any literal sense. He meant that we are to the world around us like salt is to meat - a preservative and a flavor enhancer. We preserve moral goodness in those around us, and we enrich the lives of all around us. Some of the keys to recognizing when figurative language is being used are the words *like* or *as*, which signal a metaphor or analogy. Any statement that is impossible to understand literally is probably figurative, like "you are salt" and "you are light." Sometimes you just have to look at the context. When Jesus said, "The harvest truly is plenteous, but the laborers are few," (Matthew 9:37) He wasn't talking about wheat. The context makes it clear that He was talking about people.

4. Compare Scripture with Scripture!
The best commentary on the Bible is the Bible itself. It is amazing how one verse explains or clarifies another. Sometimes the authors of Scripture assume that you already know what is taught elsewhere and make a statement that must be taken in that light. For instance, James says, *"What doth it profit, my brethren,*

though a man say he hath faith, and have not works? can faith save him? ... Ye see then how that by works a man is justified, and not by faith only," (James 2:14, 24). These verses make it sound like salvation is by works, not by faith. When we look at Paul's writings, we see statements that seem just the opposite: *"Therefore we conclude that a man is justified by faith without the deeds of the law,"* (Romans 3:28). Do we conclude that they disagree? No, we see them agree on the content of the Gospel in Acts 15. As we compare the passages, we find that they are talking about two different things. Paul is talking about salvation and uses the example of Abraham when he first believed (Romans 4 and Genesis 15), but James is talking about sanctification and the testing of Abraham's faith in sacrificing Isaac (Genesis 22).

Sometimes one verse will add to the meaning of another verse. For instance, Paul mentions *"our light affliction, which is but for a moment,"* in 2 Corinthians 4:17. But later in the book, he tells us what he considers "light affliction":

> *From the Jews five times I received forty stripes minus one. Three times I was beaten with rods; once I was stoned; three times I was shipwrecked; a night and a day I have been in the deep; in journeys often, in perils of waters, in perils of robbers, in perils of my own countrymen, in perils of the Gentiles, in perils in the city, in perils in the wilderness, in perils in the sea, in perils among false brethren; in weariness and toil, in sleeplessness often, in hunger and thirst, in fastings often, in cold and nakedness—* (2 Corinthians 11:24-27)

That information sheds a whole new light on the first passage.

Chapter Study

One of the best ways to study Scripture is to study a chapter at a time. You might study a chapter in a day or you may take a week to study it.

No matter how long you take or how deep you dig in your study, taking a whole chapter gives you a clear idea of the context for every statement and teaches you to see the relationships between all the ideas in the chapter. Select a chapter to study and follow the process we will go through here. A suggested list of chapters to start with are in the workbook. We will use Psalm 112 for our study here.

As we approach the chapter, we want to make observations and analyze the information in the chapter by asking a series of basic questions:

1. What is the main subject? - This may be a difficult question and you may have to put it off until you have observed more, but you need to identify the central theme or issue that is covered in the passage. In Psalm 112, the main idea is "God blesses the righteous man."

2. Who are the main characters? - Who is mentioned in this passage and what role do they play? What do they do? Our psalm has the righteous man, his descendants, God, and, at the end, the wicked.

3. What has been said about Jesus Christ? - In the New Testament, the name of Christ appears every few verses. But what about the Old Testament? There are a lot of passages that are about the Messiah who is to come, but there are also a lot of places where Christ is hidden in the Old Testament. He may be foreshadowed in a person like Joseph or David, or he may appear as the Angel of the Lord. What does Psalm 112 say about Jesus? Nothing directly, but we know that Jesus is the door through which all blessing comes, and we could read Jesus into the description of the righteous man.

4. What is the main verse? - Is there one verse that seems to sum it all up? Is there one verse the whole chapter either leads up to or flows out of? In the case of our sample chapter, it looks as if verse one is that verse. Everything else just adds detail to the statement *"Blessed is the man that feareth the LORD, that delighteth greatly in his commandments"* (v.1).

5. What are the main promises? - There are not always promises to be found, but there is usually some sign of hope given. Also, be careful not to take general statements of outcomes as promises. Much of the book of Proverbs tells how things usually work, but there are very few actual promises there like Jesus' *"Lo, I am with you alway, even unto the end of the age"* (Matthew 28:20). In our passage, the righteous man is promised blessings on his descendants (v. 2), wealth (v. 3), good fortune (v. 4-5), and security (v. 6), both in his circumstances and emotionally (v. 7).

6. What are the main commands? - There are some commands given in almost every chapter of the Bible except in the historical books. Where there are not direct commands, marked by the imperative voice grammatically, there may be implied commands when someone is praised for a certain act or scorned for another. That is the case in our chapter. The psalmist does not tell us we should give to the poor, but he says that the righteous man does (vv. 4, 9). Likewise, he does not say "Don't worry," but he does lift up the example of the righteous: *"He shall not be afraid of evil tidings: his heart is fixed, trusting in the LORD. His heart is established, he shall not be afraid, until he see his desire upon his enemies"* (vv. 7-8).

7. Are there any specific sins mentioned? - While some chapters will have lists of sins (Galatians 5:19-21), there will be others that do not mention sin. In those chapters, you might need to think of what sin is the opposite of the behaviors presented as good. The chapter we have chosen does not address any sin specifically; however, it exalts some behaviors and we could identify their opposites as sin. Generosity is praised (v. 4, 5, 9), so we can see that miserliness and stinginess are sins to be avoided. Oddly enough, generosity is the only specific righteous deed that is mentioned. Is it possible that the message of the psalm is that this one trait is what qualified this man for the blessing he received?

8. What have I learned from this chapter? - The most important part of this process is to capsulize what you have learned. You can't do this before you have gone through the other observations, but you

must do it too for the rest of the process to be of any value. In Psalm 112, you might have learned that God blesses the righteous in lots of different ways, that a big part of righteousness is generosity in giving, that those who give generously will receive wealth, that the righteous are secure, and that they don't worry, but trust in the Lord. You might also have learned that the wicked hate to see the righteous blessed and become really angry and resentful about it.

Once you have done all that, you should outline the chapter. You can have a written outline with main divisions, subpoints, and sub-sub points; or you can do a chart that shows main divisions. The point is that you take all this information about specifics and, from that, create a picture of the whole chapter. Outlining gives you the chance to see how each section fits with the other sections, and you may start seeing the central message of the passage more clearly by doing this. If you are not sure where the main divisions of the passage are, it is usually best to follow the paragraph divisions. Even in Bibles where the text is divided by verses, paragraphs are usually indicated by the verse number being in bold type whenever a new paragraph begins. Occasionally, you may decide that the subject changes in a place where there is no paragraph break. As long as you are sure of it, it is your outline so you can do what you want.

If we did a written outline of Psalm 112, it would look like this:

I. Introduction: God Blesses Righteous Men (v. 1) *"Praise the LORD! Blessed is the man who fears the LORD, who delights greatly in His commandments."*

  A. God's blessing is on the righteous.

  B. The righteous are described as those who fear God and love His commandments.

II. The Blessings of the Righteous (v. 2-6) *"His descendants will be mighty on earth; the generation of the upright will be blessed. Wealth and riches will be in his house, and his righteousness endures forever. Unto the upright there arises light in the darkness;*

he is gracious, and full of compassion, and righteous. A good man deals graciously and lends; he will guide his affairs with discretion. Surely he will never be shaken; the righteous will be in everlasting remembrance."

A. The children of the righteous will be blessed. (v. 2) *"His descendants will be mighty on earth; the generation of the upright will be blessed."*

B. The righteous will have wealth and honor. (v. 3) *"Wealth and riches will be in his house, and his righteousness endures forever."*

C. The righteous will be delivered from trouble because of his generosity. (v 4-5a) *"Unto the upright there arises light in the darkness; he is gracious, and full of compassion, and righteous. A good man deals graciously and lends."*

D. The righteous will be established securely and will be remembered. (v. 5b & 6) *"A good man deals graciously and lends; he will guide his affairs with discretion. Surely he will never be shaken; the righteous will be in everlasting remembrance."*

III. The Responses of the Righteous (v. 7-9) *"He will not be afraid of evil tidings; his heart is steadfast, trusting in the LORD. His heart is established; he will not be afraid, until he sees his desire upon his enemies. He has dispersed abroad, he has given to the poor; his righteousness endures forever; his horn will be exalted with honor."*

A. The righteous does not fear, but trusts in God. (v. 7) *"He will not be afraid of evil tidings; his heart is steadfast, trusting in the LORD."*

B. The righteous overcomes his adversaries without fear. (v. 8) *"His heart is established; he will not be afraid, until he sees his desire upon his enemies."*

C. The righteous is praised for his generosity. (v. 9) *"He has dispersed abroad, he has given to the poor; his righteousness endures forever; his horn will be exalted with honor."*

IV. The Response of the Wicked (v. 10) *"The wicked will see it and be grieved; he will gnash his teeth and melt away; the desire of the wicked shall perish."*

A. They express their anger and resentment over the blessing of the righteous (v. 10).

B. But their desire (to have the blessing of the righteous for themselves) will not happen (v. 10).

A more graphic way of presenting the same outline might be as follows:

God Blesses the Righteous	The Blessings of the Righteous	The Responses of the Righteous	The Response of the Wicked
= fear God + love commands	Children Wealth and honor Delivered Established	Trust, not fear Overcomes, not fearful Generous	Anger Frustrated desires

The same kind of outlining can be done for paragraphs and for whole books. Outlining can be a very useful tool in helping you to understand what you have studied, and, if you ever become involved in teaching, these become good lesson plans.

A New Master

"Believe on the Lord Jesus Christ, and you will be saved, you and your household," (Acts 16:31)

1. To believe in Jesus as Lord means to trust in, surrender to, and

rely upon Him as Savior from sin and as the master, ruler, and leader of your life. Before receiving Christ, you were your own ruler, making all decisions according to your own wisdom and emotions. Now that Jesus is Lord, you must moment by moment allow Him to control your life.

What is the role Jesus should take in your life? Let's look at the titles given to Jesus in the Bible and see what we can learn about his authority. Jesus Christ is Lord. (Philippians 2:11, *"...that every tongue should confess that Jesus Christ is Lord, to the glory of God the Father."*) That means that He is the One to Whom all creation is subject. He is sovereign over all the universe. Jesus is called King of Kings and Lord of Lords (Revelation 19:16, *"And He has on His robe and on His thigh a name written: KING OF KINGS AND LORD OF LORDS"),* indicating that no other King or Lord takes precedence over Him. Acts 2:36 says, *"Therefore let all the house of Israel know assuredly that God has made this Jesus, whom you crucified, both Lord and Christ."* The addition of the title "Christ" means that Jesus is God's anointed One, the Savior, and the fulfillment of God's promises to us. Jesus also asked us to question what we meant by the titles we gave Him saying, *"You call me Teacher and Lord, and you say well, for so I am. If I then, your Lord and Teacher, have washed your feet, you also ought to wash one another's feet,"* (John 13:13). Isn't our Master the One Whom we follow and obey?

2. We have all lived most of our lives for ourselves, seeking only to satisfy our own desires. (2 Corinthians 5:15, *"And He died for all, that those who live should live no longer for themselves, but for Him who died for them and rose again."*) Now that we have a new master, things have changed. *"I beseech you therefore, brethren, by the mercies of God, that you present your bodies a living sacrifice, holy, acceptable to God, which is your reasonable service,"* (Romans 12:1). It is only reasonable, in light of the mercies God has shown us, that we give back to him a total commitment of our lives. Jesus should now have preeminence in our lives, just as He has preeminence in all creation. (Colossians 1:18, *"And He is the head of the body, the church, who is the beginning, the firstborn*

from the dead, that in all things He may have the preeminence.") Our first priority will always be to please our master.

We have already seen the verse that tells us how to show that we love God; we are to obey His commandments. (John 14:21, *"He who has My commandments and keeps them, it is he who loves Me. And he who loves Me will be loved by My Father, and I will love him and manifest Myself to him.")* But we haven't looked at the promise that accompanies that statement: "and he that loveth me shall be loved of my Father, and I will love him, and will manifest myself to him." Our expression of love is returned by the manifestation of His love.

We can't just pretend to be His disciples. Paying lipservice to His commands or putting on a front for others does not please Him. Jesus warned us not to be men like that:

> *And why call ye me, Lord, Lord, and do not the things which I say? Whosoever cometh to me, and heareth my sayings, and doeth them, I will shew you to whom he is like: He is like a man which built an house, and digged deep, and laid the foundation on a rock: and when the flood arose, the stream beat vehemently upon that house, and could not shake it: for it was founded upon a rock. But he that heareth, and doeth not, is like a man that without a foundation built an house upon the earth; against which the stream did beat vehemently, and immediately it fell; and the ruin of that house was great* (Luke 6:46-49).

If we are to call Him Lord, then He must truly be Lord to us. We must be sincerely intent on doing His will in His power. (Philippians 2:13, *"For it is God who works in you both to will and to do for His good pleasure, for without Him we can do nothing");* (John 15:5, *"I am the vine, you are the branches. He who abides in Me, and I in him, bears much fruit; for without Me you can do nothing*.")

Does it sound as if we are being overly dramatic about this? Then maybe you are taking it too lightly. Make no mistake about it; becoming a disciple of Christ has its price. In fact, one day when the crowd seemed to be too full of people who were not sincere, Jesus stopped in His tracks, turned to all those who were following Him, and said, *"If anyone comes to Me and does not hate his father and mother, wife and children, brothers and sisters, yes, and his own life also, he cannot be My disciple. And whoever does not bear his cross and come after Me cannot be My disciple. For which of you, intending to build a tower, does not sit down first and count the cost, whether he has enough to finish it—"* (Luke 14:26-28). Can you pay the price? Are you willing to sacrifice your family relationships if necessary? Are you willing to put your selfish desires to death? Jesus was very clear that we can't serve two masters. (Matthew 6:24, *"No one can serve two masters; for either he will hate the one and love the other, or else he will be loyal to the one and despise the other. You cannot serve God and mammon."*) But that is what the first commandment is all about anyway. It says, *"You shall love the Lord your God with all your heart, with all your soul, and with all your mind,"* (Matthew 22:37). To be a disciple of Jesus demands forsaking all (Luke 14:33, *"So likewise, whoever of you does not forsake all that he has cannot be My disciple.")*. There were many in the crowd that followed Jesus who were not willing to pay the price. (John 6:66, *"From that time many of His disciples went back and walked with Him no more."*)

When Jesus first started teaching the disciples that He was going to have to suffer and die, they didn't like it much. It didn't fit their idea of what the Messiah should do and it put them in danger. So Jesus made it clearer for them. He laid out a plan for discipleship. *"If anyone desires to come after Me, let him deny himself, and take up his cross daily, and follow Me,"* (Luke 9:23). Three not-so-simple steps is all that it takes be His disciple.

Denying self means to set aside your personal ambitions and the control over your life and ask the question, "Lord, what do you want me to do, and how do you want me to do it?" Isaiah 6:8, *"Also I heard the voice of the Lord, saying: 'Whom shall I send, and who will go for Us?' Then I said, 'Here am I! Send me.' "*

Taking up your cross had a really clear meaning to the people in Jesus' day. The only reason to take up a cross was to die. Jesus said we need to die daily, but it's funny how we keep getting off that cross trying to take control again.

The third step is to **follow**. When Abraham was called by God, all he was told is that God would show him the land that would be his inheritance. All Abraham could do was to follow until he got there. That's the kind of faith we have to have: let God lead and we just follow. Psalm 32:8, *"I will instruct you and teach you in the way you should go; I will guide you with My eye."*

This job description may not be what you thought it was. But like any job, you might be able to live with it if the benefits are good. What will be the reward for following Jesus in this world? *"So Jesus answered and said, 'Assuredly, I say to you, there is no one who has left house or brothers or sisters or father or mother or wife or children or lands, for My sake and the gospel's, who shall not receive a hundredfold now in this time— houses and brothers and sisters and mothers and children and lands, with persecutions— and in the age to come, eternal life,'"* (Mark 10:29-30). No matter what you give up for the sake of following Christ, you will be rewarded with an abundance of the same things. That's not some spiritualized by-and-by promise; that's for now in this world. You don't lose by following Christ; you gain a hundred fold. Oh, by the way there was one more thing on that list of benefits: "with persecutions." Yes, you get all the good stuff, but you will also be persecuted. God will bless you, but the world will still hate you. 2 Timothy 3:2, *"For men will be lovers of themselves, lovers of money, boasters, proud, blasphemers, disobedient to parents, unthankful, unholy"*; 2 Timothy 3:12, *"Yes, and all who desire to live godly in Christ Jesus will suffer persecution."* Then again, trials produce character, which is the real reward. Wait until you hear about the retirement plan: "and in the world to come eternal life." Can you set a price on that?

Now you may be thinking, "Well, I could just believe in Christ, but not really follow him. That way, I still get the eternal life stuff, but I don't have to do all that self-denial part." That's true! But then you face another problem. *"For we must all appear before the judgment seat of Christ, that each one may receive the things done in the body, according to what he has done, whether good or bad,"* (2 Corinthians 5:10). We all, meaning Christians, will be held accountable for what we have done with our lives since the new birth. As we said in chapter 6, this is not to see if we will be saved, but whether we will have rewards in Christ's kingdom. *"For other foundations can no man lay than that is laid, which is Jesus christ. Now if any man build upon this foundation gold, silver, precious stones, wood, hay, stubble; every man's work shall be made manifest: for the day shall declare it, because it shall be revealed by fire; and the fire shall try every man's work of what sort it is. If any man's work abide which he hath built thereupon, he shall receive a reward. If any man's work shall be burned, he shall suffer loss: but he himself shall be saved; yet so as by fire"* (1 Corinthians 3:11-15). It is entirely possible for a person to be saved, but to have no reward from his Master.

A New Stewardship

If God is our Master, what does that make us? Servants? In some places Paul and Peter call themselves servants. (Romans 1:1, *"Paul, a bondservant of Jesus Christ, called to be an apostle, separated to the gospel of God";* 2 Peter 1:1, *"Simon Peter, a bondservant and apostle of Jesus Christ.")* But we are also sons! When a son is given responsibility by the father, he is not acting as a servant, but as a steward - one given authority to oversee something and to manage it. Therefore, we still have to answer to the Master for how we have handled that responsibility.

In the New Testament, the Greek word for *stewardship* is the same word from which we get our word *economy*. Stewardship referred to the servant who was in charge of the house. It was his job to govern the other servants, manage the household finances, and see to it that everything in the house was in order. He was given a budget, a schedule, and free reign to deal with everything else. It was a position of great authority and great trust, but if the steward proved unfaithful, he faced grave consequences.

One of Jesus' parables explains the idea of stewardship well.

> *"For the kingdom of heaven is like a man traveling to a far country, who called his own servants and delivered his goods to them. And to one he gave five talents, to another two, and to another one, to each according to his own ability; and immediately he went on a journey. Then he who had received the five talents went and traded with them, and made another five talents. And likewise he who had received two gained two more also. But he who had received one went and dug in the ground, and hid his lord's money.*
>
> *"After a long time the lord of those servants came and settled accounts with them. So he who had received five talents came and brought five other talents, saying, 'Lord, you delivered to me five talents; look, I have gained five more talents besides them.' His lord said to him, 'Well done, good and faithful servant; you were faithful over a few things, I will make you ruler over many things. Enter into the joy of your lord.' He also who had received two talents came and said, 'Lord, you delivered to me two talents; look, I have gained two more talents besides them.' His lord said to him, 'Well done, good and faithful servant; you have been faithful over a few things, I will make you ruler over many things. Enter into the joy of your lord.' Then he who had received the one talent came and said, 'Lord, I knew you to be a hard man, reaping where you have not sown, and gathering where you have not scattered seed. And I was afraid, and went and hid your talent in the ground. Look, there you have what is yours.*

> *"But his lord answered and said to him, 'You wicked and lazy servant, you knew that I reap where I have not sown, and gather where I have not scattered seed. So you ought to have deposited my money with the bankers, and at my coming I would have received back my own with interest. Therefore take the talent from him, and give it to him who has ten talents,'"* Matthew 25:14-28.

The point of the parable is clear. God expects us to use the resources that He has given us in such a way that we are profitable to Him. Those who were given less but were profitable received the same commendation as the one who was given more. They were invited to "enter thou into the joy of thy Lord." Only the one servant who buried his gifts was chastised. He proved himself unfaithful. He did not steal or squander his Master's possessions; he just did nothing.

As Christians, we also are given stewardship over God's possessions. Each of us is given twenty-four hours each day in which we may serve Him. Each of us is given a body through which we accomplish our work for Him. Each of us is given both natural and spiritual abilities for His use. And each of us is given an amount of money which He has entrusted to our care. Some are given a better body than others; some are given greater abilities; some are given more money, but that is not the issue. It doesn't matter what someone else has. What are you going to do with what He has given you?

Stewardship of Time

"So teach us to number our days, that we may gain a heart of wisdom," (Psalm 90:12).

There are three constants about time: 1) It comes one day at a time, 2) Each day has only twenty-four hours, and 3) It passes whether we use it consciously or not. If we are to be good stewards of this asset, we must use it wisely and carefully. Paul tells us to "redeem the time," meaning to give value to something that would otherwise be worthless (Ephesians 5:16).

1. Your Attitude toward Time

a. Contrary to the popular phrase that time is money, the truth is that the two are very different. Time is infinitely more precious and cannot be saved or collected for later use. Time is spent automatically, whether you decide to spend it in a particular way or not. Once spent, it cannot be returned, refunded, traded, or exchanged.

b. The value of each moment is determined once and for all by the way in which it is spent. While you know in specific terms how much money you have left and when you will get more, your time may run out at any moment. Should you run out of money, you can always get more; but if you run out of time, it is gone forever. *"For what is your life? It is even a vapor that appears for a little time and then vanishes away"* (James 4:14).

The only way for you to decide how much your time is worth is to redeem it from the fate of being wasted and give it value by doing something valuable in it. Time is both a gift and a responsibility, for we will be called into account for the way in which we have used it.

> *Take heed, watch and pray; for you do not know when the time is. It is like a man going to a far country, who left his house and gave authority to his servants, and to each his work, and commanded the doorkeeper to watch. Watch therefore, for you do not know when the master of the house is coming— in the evening, at midnight, at the crowing of the rooster, or in the morning—"lest, coming suddenly, he find you sleeping* (Mark 13:33-37).

In order to use your time wisely, you have to understand what the will of God is, both in general and for you.

(Ephesians 5:17, *"Therefore do not be unwise, but understand what the will of the Lord is."*) If you understand that, all priorities will fall into place, your activities will become productive, and you will not find yourself wasting time. If you understand God's will, you will have a purpose driving your life which will not allow you to let time pass. Ultimately, the wisdom required to redeem your time will come as you are filled with the Holy Spirit. (Ephesians 5:18, *"And do not be drunk with wine, in which is dissipation; but be filled with the Spirit."*)

2. The Most Important Use of Time

What do you think is the most important thing you can do with your time from God's perspective? What is God's will? He desires all men to be saved and come to a knowledge of the truth. (1 Timothy 2:4, *"Who desires all men to be saved and to come to the knowledge of the truth."*) There is no more important thing you can do to add value to your time than to work toward that end. (Mark 16:15, *"And He said to them, 'Go into all the world and preach the gospel to every creature.'"*) *"The fruit of the righteous is a tree of life; and he that winneth souls is wise,"* (Proverbs 11:30). What more important thing could there be than to lead another to eternal life? It shares with them the most valuable treasure you have and has eternal significance. It is wise to invest your time to sharpen your skills to learn how to share your testimony and your faith in Christ.

Does that mean that the value of your life is measured by the notches on your Bible, indicating how many people you have led to Christ? Not at all! God only asks you to be faithful in sharing the gospel and leave the results to Him. There are also many things you can do which will plant a seed in the life of an unbeliever. Simple kindnesses, providing transportation, spreading the Word in subtle ways, doing good for others — all these things have effects in the hearts of people you may never see. Your focus must be on loving people, knowing that God can use you as a light in their lives.

When someone does believe, "*...there will be more joy in heaven over one sinner who repents than over ninety-nine just persons who need no repentance,*" (Luke 15:7). God's greatest joy is in seeing salvation come to mankind. God sings. (Zephaniah 3:17, *"The LORD your God in your midst, the Mighty One, will save; he will rejoice over you with gladness, he will quiet you with His love, he will rejoice over you with singing.")* That is why Christ was willing to suffer; *"who for the joy that was set before Him endured the cross, despising the shame, and has sat down at the right hand of the throne of God,"* (Hebrews 12:2). We are the joy set before him — we who have believed in Him for our Life. Paul says that his greatest joy was in those who were led to Christ and established in the faith through the work of his team. *"For what is our hope, or joy, or crown of rejoicing? Is it not even you in the presence of our Lord Jesus Christ at His coming? For you are our glory and joy,"* (1 Thessalonians 2:19-20).

3. Your Use of Time

No matter who you are, how important you are, how rich you are, you only get 168 hours each week. No matter who you are, you will spend about 50 hours of that time sleeping and 15-20 hours eating. You can't stop doing those things. But some people seem to be able to accomplish more with the time that is left than others do. Why is that?

Invariably, it has to do with two critical factors: planning and discipline. Those who are most effective know in advance exactly how they will spend their time. That does not mean that they have to be rigid about sticking to their schedule, but they have set priorities and allotted the time required to accomplish the things that need to be done. If something unexpected comes up, they can deal with it by adjusting their schedule, but the point is that they have a schedule to adjust. However, all the planning in the world won't do a bit of good if you don't follow through with your plan. That is where discipline comes in. Discipline is the ability to carry out your plan even in the face of obstacles.

Time	Monday	Tuesday	Wednesday	Thursday	Friday	Saturday	Sunday
6:00							
7:00							
8:00							
9:00							
10:00							
11:00							
12:00							
1:00							
2:00							
3:00							
4:00							
5:00							
6:00							
7:00							
8:00							
9:00							
10:00							
11:00							
12:00							

1. Study and class __________
2. Devotional life __________
3. Activities & athletics __________
4. Commuting __________
5. Christian service __________
6. Rest __________
7. Recreation __________
8. Employment __________
9. Laundry and cleanup __________
10. Miscellaneous __________

> One of the best places to start is to see where your time is going right now. What is happening to it? You can find out if you will track yourself and see what happens. The chart on the previous page can be helpful in finding out just how many hours you really are spending in sleep, work, quiet time, Christian service, relaxation, etc. Once you know where your time is going, you will be able to see more clearly what you need to adjust so that your use of time more closely reflects the priorities of your life.

After you have tracked yourself for a week, don't just forget about it. Now is your chance to take control and be a good steward of your time. That doesn't mean you have to spend all of your time in Christian service. If you aren't getting the rest and exercise you need, spending time in the word, and taking care of your financial and family responsibilities, you cannot be effective in ministry. Your goal must be to find a balance in which you can be effective in doing the most important things that must be done. Redeem as much time as possible, but remember that time spent refreshing yourself makes the work more effective.

Stewardship of Your Temple

Your body is the temple of God. It houses the Holy Spirit. (1 Corinthians 6:19, *"Or do you not know that your body is the temple of the Holy Spirit who is in you, whom you have from God, and you are not your own?")* Part of your stewardship before God is to care for this temple so that it can be used for God's purposes. Paul says that those who live simply in the flesh cannot please God. Our flesh is the home of our sin nature, which drives us to disobedience when we obey its lusts. Christians are to live in the Spirit, not in the flesh, by recognizing that we have a new nature which is driven by a passion to fulfill the desires of God. (Romans 8:8-9, *"So then, those who are in the flesh cannot please God. But you are not in the flesh but in the Spirit, if indeed the Spirit of God dwells in you. Now if anyone does not have the Spirit of Christ, he is not His."; "Present your bodies a living sacrifice, holy, acceptable to God, which is your reasonable service,"* Romans 12:1, *"For you were bought at a price; therefore glorify God in your body and in your spirit, which are God's,"* 1 Corinthians 6:20.) Your body must be used for God's purposes. You are the steward to whom the responsibility is given to make sure that your body is fit for God's use and that you are doing those things which will glorify him. Three areas will require special attention for you to be a good steward: your tongue, your heart, and your lusts.

Controlling the Tongue

"For we all stumble in many things. If anyone does not stumble in word, he is a perfect man, able also to bridle the whole body. But no man can tame the tongue. It is an unruly evil, full of deadly poison," (James 3:2, 8). Being able to control your tongue is central to controlling the rest of your life, just as a horse is controlled by the bit in his mouth or a rudder controls a ship (James 3:3-6, *"Indeed, we put bits in horses' mouths that they may obey us, and we turn their whole body. Look also at ships: although they are so large and are driven by fierce winds, they are turned by a very small rudder wherever the pilot desires. Even so the tongue is a little member and boasts great things. See how great a forest a little fire kindles! And the tongue is a fire, a world of iniquity. The tongue is so set among our members that it defiles the whole body, and sets on fire the course of nature; and it is set on fire by hell.")* When it is used destructively, the tongue causes anger, contention, bitterness, jealousy, hatred, envy, and all kinds of trouble. *"Death and life are in the power of the tongue, and those who love it will eat its fruit,"* (Proverbs 18:21).The impact of what we say to others can be devastating or can give life. It is all in how we choose to use our tongue.

The real problem of why the tongue is so full of poison is that the tongue shows us what is in a man's heart. *"Brood of vipers! How can you, being evil, speak good things? For out of the abundance of the heart the mouth speaks. A good man out of the good treasure of his heart brings forth good things, and an evil man out of the evil treasure brings forth evil things. But I say to you that for every idle word men may speak, they will give account of it in the day of judgment,"* (Matthew 12:34-36). The reason that our tongue is so hard to control is that our heart has evil hidden in it which comes out when we speak, especially in saying the things we think we don't really mean (idle words).

Controlling the Heart

It is so important to be a good steward of your heart. Proverbs 23:7, *"For as he thinks in his heart, so is he. Eat and drink! he says to you, but his heart is not with you."* The heart of man, in the Bible, is the seat of his thoughts, desires, and emotions. While we tend to think that these things are not physical, the fact is that all emotional responses happen in the body. If you are frightened, there is an adrenaline rush, your pulse races, and your hands shake. If you are worried, your stomach ties up in knots, your muscles tense, and you bite your fingernails. Emotions are bodily reactions to mental or spiritual perceptions.

There are two great dangers in the stewardship of our emotions. One is that emotions are not always right. They deal with perceptions of reality, not reality itself, and our perceptions can be clouded by all kinds of things. Our past experiences, not knowing the whole truth about something, prejudices, and miscommunication all distort our perceptions of reality. On top of that, the heart will rationalize and justify itself to us in order to get what it wants. That is why Jeremiah warns us that, "*The heart is deceitful above all things, and desperately wicked,*" (Jeremiah 17:9). You cannot simply trust your heart or your feelings in all things. Neither can you disregard them or you will not be able to act on anything. Rather, your prayer should always be, *"Search me, O God, and know my heart; try me, and know my anxieties; and see if there is any wicked way in me, and lead me in the way everlasting,"* (Psalm 139:23-24).

What God wants from us is to put our hearts, our emotions, and desires on the altar before Him, just as we have done with every part of our life, so that he may change them to conform to His will. *"The sacrifices of God are a broken spirit, a broken and a contrite heart— these, O God, You will not despise,"* (Psalm 51:17). *"For the eyes of the LORD run to and fro throughout the whole earth, to show Himself strong on behalf of those whose heart is loyal to Him,"* (2 Chronicles 16:9). So we must strive to have the mind of Christ. Philippians 2:5-8, *"Let this mind be in you which was also in Christ Jesus, who, being in the form of God, did not consider it robbery to be equal with God, but made Himself of no reputation, taking the form of a bondservant, and coming in the likeness of men. And being found in appearance as a man, He humbled Himself and became obedient to the point of death, even the death of the cross."* We must gird up the loins of our mind with the Word of God. (1 Peter 1:13, *"Therefore gird up the loins of your mind, be sober, and rest your hope fully upon the grace that is to be brought to you at the revelation of Jesus Christ.";* Philippians 4:6-7, *"Be anxious for nothing, but in everything by prayer and supplication, with thanksgiving, let your requests be made known to God; and the peace of God, which surpasses all understanding, will guard your hearts and minds through Christ Jesus, which gives us peace of mind."* Isaiah 26:3, *"You will keep him in perfect peace, whose mind is stayed on You, because he trusts in You."* Proverbs 4:20, *"My son, give attention to my words; incline your ear to my sayings. Do not let them depart from your eyes; keep them in the midst of your heart; For they are life to those who find them, and health to all their flesh."*)

Controlling the Lusts

Finally, the stewardship of your body means to control your lusts. Sexual sin is the most common, the most powerful, and the most destructive of all sins. It is sexual sin that Paul is specifically addressing in 1 Corinthians 6 when he brings up the issue of your body as the temple of God. It is the one way in which we sin against ourselves — it hurts us as much as anyone. No one is above falling into this type of sin. Even David, the man after God's own heart, fell into sexual sin; and his desire was so strong that he justified murder in order to fulfill it (2 Samuel 11:14-27).

But God takes sexual sin very seriously. Jesus warned that to even allow our thoughts to dwell on sexual desire is to have the sin of adultery in our hearts. (Matthew 5:28, *"But I say to you that whoever looks at a woman to lust for her has already committed adultery with her in his heart.")* There is even the warning that those who live in sins of a sexual nature will not inherit the kingdom of God. (1 Corinthians 6:9-11, *"Do you not know that the unrighteous will not inherit the kingdom of God? Do not be deceived. Neither fornicators, nor idolaters, nor adulterers, nor homosexuals, nor sodomites, nor thieves, nor covetous, nor drunkards, nor revilers, nor extortioners will inherit the kingdom of God. And such were some of you. But you were washed, but you were sanctified, but you were justified in the name of the Lord Jesus and by the Spirit of our*

God.") But clearly sexual sin is inappropriate for someone whose body belongs to Christ. (1 Corinthians 6:13-18, *"Know ye not that your bodies are the members of Christ? shall I then take the members of Christ, and make them the members of an harlot? God forbid. What? know ye not that he which is joined to an harlot is one body? for two, saith he, shall be one flesh. But he that is joined unto the Lord is one spirit. Flee fornication. Every sin that a man doeth is without the body; but he that committeth fornication sinneth against his own body.")*

Being a Christian does not mean being a prude. It means that you recognize the sanctity of sex (Hebrews 13:4, *"Marriage is honorable among all, and the bed undefiled; but fornicators and adulterers God will judge"*) and its proper place in marriage. In fact, the Song of Solomon is a whole book of the Bible dedicated to celebrating the beauty of sex within marriage. It is sex outside of the marriage relationship that is condemned in such strong terms. The purpose of sex is to unite two people making them one flesh, as Paul referred to, and sex where this purpose is frustrated causes only pain and degradation.

There are ways to overcome the power of your lusts. One is to not allow your mind to dwell on thoughts that drag you into depravity. *"Finally, brethren, whatever things are true, whatever things are noble, whatever things are just, whatever things are pure, whatever things are lovely, whatever things are of good report, if there is any virtue and if there is anything praiseworthy— meditate on these things,"* (Philippians 4:8). Scripture memorization will also help to control your lusts. *"Your word I have hidden in my heart, that I might not sin against You!"* (Psalm 119:11). And even if you should find yourself in a difficult situation in which temptation seems too strong to avoid, *"No temptation has overtaken you except such as is common to man; but God is faithful, who will not allow you to be tempted beyond what you are able, but with the temptation will also make the way of escape, that you may be able to bear it,"* (1 Corinthians 10:13). Finally, there is the simple and direct reminder to you that the power of sin is broken so that you do not have to obey it. "*For sin shall not have dominion over you: for ye are not under the law, but under grace,*" (Romans 6:14). You have a new Master, and His grace controls your life.

Stewardship of Your Talents

God created man with a great variety of talents. Some have organizational talents, others are better at relationships, still others have creative abilities. The Christian church is composed of people endowed with different gifts and abilities. It is this diversity existing within the unity of the faith that makes the Church attractive to those outside. All that the Christian possesses should be dedicated fully to God to be used as He directs; and so our talents are another area of stewardship for the believer.

The Scriptures refer to the church as the body of Christ. Christ is its Head. (1 Corinthians 12:27, *"Now you are the body of Christ, and members individually."*; Ephesians 5:23, *"For the husband is head of the wife, as also Christ is head of the church; and He is the Savior of the body."*) Just as your body has many specialized parts, each having its own function, so the church is composed of many individuals, each with his own special function to perform and contribution to make to the rest of the body. Believers who do not use their talents in the Church are robbing the body of the gift of their uniqueness, and they are robbing themselves of the blessings that come to them from others on the Church.

Every Christian possesses both natural and spiritual gifts. All men have natural gifts (abilities and talents), for they come to us at physical birth or are learned during our lifetime. Spiritual gifts are special abilities imparted by the Holy Spirit to Christians. These enable Christians to minister to others in behalf of Christ.

Your natural abilities are not useless. God can use them in all kinds of practical ways. They may enhance your spiritual gift. For instance, if you have the spiritual gift of helps, your natural ability to fix cars can be used in His service. If your spiritual gift is exhortation, your musical talents can be put to good use. But you do need to heed the warning not to let yourself become proud or boastful about your natural abilities, for they come from God and not from yourself. 1 Corinthians 4:6-7, *"Now these things, brethren, I have figuratively transferred to myself and Apollos for your sakes, that you may learn in us not to think beyond what is written, that none of you may be puffed up on behalf of one against the other. For who makes you differ from another? And what do you have that you did not receive? Now if you did indeed receive it, why do you boast as if you had not received it?"* Rather, in humility thank God that He has prepared you for ministry by giving you those abilities. "*And whatsoever ye do in word or deed, do all in the name of the Lord Jesus, giving thanks to God and the Father by him,*" (Colossians 3:17).

There are five passages about spiritual gifts found in the New Testament. None of these lists are complete; they are all organized differently, and none of them come with definitions of the gifts or instructions on how to find your gift. The list in Romans paints in broad strokes the gifts necessary in a local church body, while the list in Corinthians is more specific. The second list in 1 Corinthians specifically is said to be in order of importance. The short list in Ephesians really only speaks about the gifted men God gives to lead the Church, and Peter only gives principles for the use of gifts. That should probably suggest that we approach the topic with a fairly high degree of flexibility and not try to force a more rigid structure on this teaching than the Scriptures give them. The lists are found in the following places:

> **Romans 12:3-8** - *For I say, through the grace given to me, to everyone who is among you, not to think of himself more highly than he ought to think, but to think soberly, as God has dealt to each one a measure of faith. For as we have many members in one body, but all the members do not have the same function, so we, being many, are one body in Christ, and individually members of one another. Having then gifts differing according to the grace that is given to us, let us use them: if prophecy, let us prophesy in proportion to our faith; or ministry, let us use it in our ministering; he who teaches, in teaching; he who exhorts, in exhortation; he who gives, with liberality; he who leads, with diligence; he who shows mercy, with cheerfulness.*
>
> **1 Corinthians 12:8-9** - *For to one is given the word of wisdom through the Spirit, to another the word of knowledge through the same Spirit, to another faith by the same Spirit, to another gifts of healings by the same Spirit.*
>
> **1 Corinthians 12:28-31** - *And God has appointed these in*

the church: first apostles, second prophets, third teachers, after that miracles, then gifts of healings, helps, administrations, varieties of tongues. Are all apostles? Are all prophets? Are all teachers? Are all workers of miracles? Do all have gifts of healings? Do all speak with tongues? Do all interpret? But earnestly desire the best gifts. And yet I show you a more excellent way.

Ephesians 4:4-16 - *There is one body and one Spirit, just as you were called in one hope of your calling; one Lord, one faith, one baptism; one God and Father of all, who is above all, and through all, and in you all. But to each one of us grace was given according to the measure of Christ's gift. Therefore He says: "When He ascended on high, he led captivity captive, and gave gifts to men." (Now this, "He ascended"— what does it mean but that He also first descended into the lower parts of the earth? He who descended is also the One who ascended far above all the heavens, that He might fill all things.) And He Himself gave some to be apostles, some prophets, some evangelists, and some pastors and teachers, for the equipping of the saints for the work of ministry, for the edifying of the body of Christ, till we all come to the unity of the faith and of the knowledge of the Son of God, to a perfect man, to the measure of the stature of the fullness of Christ; that we should no longer be children, tossed to and fro and carried about with every wind of doctrine, by the trickery of men, in the cunning craftiness of deceitful plotting, but, speaking the truth in love, may grow up in all things into Him who is the head— Christ—from whom the whole body, joined and knit together by what every joint supplies, according to the effective working by which every part does its share, causes growth of the body for the edifying of itself in love.*

1 Peter 4:10-11 - *As each one has received a gift, minister it to one another, as good stewards of the manifold grace of God. If anyone speaks, let him speak as the oracles of God.*

> *If anyone ministers, let him do it as with the ability which God supplies, that in all things God may be glorified through Jesus Christ, to whom belong the glory and the dominion forever and ever.* Amen.

From these passages we can make a composite list of the spiritual gifts (combining any two that might be identical). Then you can look up the words in a Bible dictionary and see what it might mean to have that gift. We could give you all of the answers here, but it is better for you to discover them for yourself.

Are all of the spiritual gifts listed in the Bible? Since we know that no list is complete, it is possible that other gifts exist which are not mentioned. On the other hand, we need to be careful not to add to what Scripture says. While there is probably not a spiritual gift of basket-weaving, we should be open to the possibility that other gifts may exist.

Even though some gifts may be more important than others (1 Corinthians 12:28-31), there is no basis for pride because of your gift or office. The consistent message of Scripture is that we all need one another, regardless of our gifts, for the unity of the body. *"For as we have many members in one body, but all the members do not have the same function, so we, being many, are one body in Christ, and individually members of one another,"* (Romans 12:4-5). Without all the members working together, the body is weak and immature (Ephesians 4:11-16). The pastor needs the member with the gift of mercy just as much as any other member of the body. Those with the gift of administration may hold an office in the church, but they still rely on those with the gift of giving to provide funds for all that they envision. We must relate to each other in mutual interdependence, knowing that this is God's plan for meeting the needs of all.

Every Christian is given at least one spiritual gift and often more. (1 Corinthians 12:11, *"But one and the same Spirit works all these things, distributing to each one individually as He wills."*; Romans 12:3, *"For I say, through the grace given to me, to everyone who is among you, not to think of himself more highly than he ought to think, but to think soberly, as God has dealt to each one a measure of faith.")* How can you know what your gift is? The best way is to simply follow Christ and not worry about it. When you see what you are doing, how God uses you, and what activities God blesses, it will be clear what your gift is. You can always pray that God will clarify to you what ways He wants to use you, and you can ask the opinions of mature Christians who know you well. Ultimately, however, it is more important that you are obedient to Christ in using whatever abilities you have for His glory, even if no one has identified that as a spiritual gift.

Stewardship of Your Treasure

*"And you shall remember the LORD your God, for it is He who gives you power to get wealth, that He may establish His covenant which He swore to your fathers, as it is this day" (*Deuteronomy 8:18).

Along with the stewardship of your time, your body, and your talents, you are also given stewardship over your money. As with the other areas we have discussed, money is not given to you to do with as you please but is given as a means for you to glorify God. Ultimately, it is not really your money, but God's; and you are given stewardship over it. The way that you handle your financial stewardship will determine over how much you will be given responsibility. 2 Corinthians 9:6, *"But this I say: He who sows sparingly will also reap sparingly, and he who sows bountifully will also reap bountifully."* The first and most important responsibility you have as a steward of God's money is to give back to Him a portion of what He has given you.

Before the Law, even before there was a nation, there was Abraham giving a tenth (a tithe) of the spoils of battle to Melchizedek, a priest of God (Genesis 14:17-20).

The nation of Israel never did very well in obedience to this command: therefore, God chastised them in the last book of the Old Testament. He reminded Israel that the tithe which He commanded belonged to Him. By not giving it to Him, they were robbing God and bringing a curse on themselves. (Malachi 3:8-9, *"Will a man rob God? Yet you have robbed Me! But you say, 'In what way have we robbed You?' In tithes and offerings. You are cursed with a curse, for you have robbed Me, even this whole nation.'")* But God promised them that if they would test Him in this one thing, they would see that He is faithful to bless them with abundance. *"And try Me now in this, says the LORD of hosts, If I will not open for you the windows of heaven and pour out for you such blessing that there will not be room enough to receive it"* (Malachi 3:10).

We no longer live under the Law, but under grace. While we are no longer bound by the Old Testament Law to tithe, we do give out of gratitude for what God has done for us and out of love for God and His church. (2 Corinthians 8:24, *"Therefore show to them, and before the churches the proof of your love and of our boasting on your behalf."*) The New Testament commands to give do not specify an amount, but simply say *"as God hath prospered him."* (1 Corinthians 16:2, *"On the first day of the week let each one of you lay something aside, storing up as he may prosper, that there be no collections when I come."*) Does this mean you don't have to give a tithe? No, it means you don't have to feel like you should stop at a tithe. Give graciously in proportion to the grace you have received.

There are several principles of giving seen in the New Testament, most of which are mentioned in 2 Corinthians chapters 8 and 9, where Paul is talking about a special offering being made by the Gentile churches for the impoverished saints in Jerusalem. Let's look at some of these principles:

1. Plan your giving. Don't do it on the spur of the moment. The Corinthian church collected offerings on the first day of the week. (1 Corinthians 16:1-2, *"Now concerning the collection for the saints, as I have given orders to the churches of Galatia, so you must do also: On the first day of the week let each one of you lay something aside, storing up as he may prosper, that there be no collections when I come,")* and Paul told them to avoid a last minute collection when he got there.

2. Before you give your money to God, give your heart and yourself to Him. (2 Corinthians 8:5, *"And not only as we had hoped, but they first gave themselves to the Lord, and then to us by the will of God.")* To obey is better than sacrifice. (1 Samuel 15:22, *"Then Samuel said: 'Has the LORD as great delight in burnt offerings*

and sacrifices, as in obeying the voice of the LORD? Behold, to obey is better than sacrifice, and to heed than the fat of rams.'")

3. Give freely, not under compulsion. (2 Corinthians 9:7, *"So let each one give as he purposes in his heart, not grudgingly or of necessity; for God loves a cheerful giver."*)

4. You will reap what you sow. (Galatians 6:7-8, *"Do not be deceived, God is not mocked; for whatever a man sows, that he will also reap. For he who sows to his flesh will of the flesh reap corruption, but he who sows to the Spirit will of the Spirit reap everlasting life."* (2 Corinthians 9:6, *"But this I say: He who sows sparingly will also reap sparingly, and he who sows bountifully will also reap bountifully."*) The more you give, the more God will bless you. (2 Corinthians 9:8, *"And God is able to make all grace abound toward you, that you, always having all sufficiency in all things, may have an abundance for every good work.")* In Jesus' own words, *"Give, and it will be given to you: good measure, pressed down, shaken together, and running over will be put into your bosom. For with the same measure that you use, it will be measured back to you."* (Luke 6:38).

5. Give by faith, not by sight. If you calculate what you can afford to give, you probably won't ever give, and then you won't have an abundance from which to give. If you decide what you will give by faith, *"My God shall supply all your need according to his riches in glory by Christ Jesus,"* (Philippians 419).

Giving has always been a matter of obedience and faith. It is a statement of gratitude and thanksgiving for all that God has given us. Ultimately, you and all your possessions belong to Him (1 Corinthians 6:19-20, *"Or do you not know that your body is the temple of the Holy Spirit who is in you, whom you have from God, and you are not your own? For you were bought at a price; therefore glorify God in your body and in your spirit, which are God's")*; but at the same time, it is an act of faith showing our utter dependence on Him to supply all that we need. The only motive for giving that will ever make any sense is to let God be glorified, first through what you give to Him and then through what He will give back to you.

Chapter Nine

A NEW STANDARD OF LIVING

By becoming a Christian you have accepted a new standard of living. Christ called it the abundant life. Before receiving Jesus into *your* life as your Savior and Lord, your main criteria for your actions were, "What is in it for me? What will I enjoy? What will my friends think?" After becoming a Christian, your questions should be, "What would honor the Lord most? What would Jesus want me to do? How would this action affect my Christian testimony? Will this action help me to grow to be more like Jesus?"

Becoming a Christian is putting off the old man and putting on the new man. (Ephesians 4:22-24, *"That you put off, concerning your former conduct, the old man which grows corrupt according to the deceitful lusts, and be renewed in the spirit of your mind, and that you put on the new man which was created according to God, in true righteousness and holiness."*) It means you stop doing certain things, and you begin doing other things. It means dying to the old life of sin and living a new life with the resurrected Christ in control. (Galatians 2:20, *"I have been crucified with Christ; it is no longer I who live, but Christ lives in me; and the life which I now live in the flesh I live by faith in the Son of God, who loved me and gave Himself for me.")*

The Blessed Life

The teachings of Jesus are not easy. He taught that we should love our enemies. (Matthew 5:44, *"But I say to you, love your enemies, bless those who curse you, do good to those who hate you, and pray for those who spitefully use you and persecute you."*) He taught that if we are struck on the cheek, we should offer the other cheek as well. (Matthew 5:39, *"But I tell you not to resist an evil person. But whoever slaps you on your right cheek, turn the other to him also."*) He even said, *"Be ye therefore perfect, even as your Father which is in heaven is perfect."* (Matthew 5:48). Jesus came that we might have life and have it more abundantly. (John 10:10b, *"The thief does not come except to steal, and to kill, and to destroy. I have come that they may have life, and that they may have it more abundantly."*) If we are to experience the abundant life, we need to take seriously the teachings of Jesus.

In Matthew 5:3-12, he taught that there were nine character traits which lead to blessing and are keys to having the abundant life. Each trait is introduced by the phrase, *"Blessed are the...."* and followed by the type of blessing one will receive. If you picked up any dozen modern self-improvement books, they would say something like, "Blessed are the strong **...** Blessed are the disciplined **...** Blessed are the organized **...** Blessed are the independent **...**," but Christ's ideas are a little different from that.

Blessed are...	
the poor in spirit:	for theirs is the kingdom of heaven.
they that mourn:	for they shall be comforted.
the meek:	for they shall inherit the earth.
they which do hunger and thirst after righteousness:	for they shall be filled.
the merciful:	for they shall obtain mercy.
the pure in heart:	for they shall see God.
the peacemakers:	for they shall be called the children of God.
they which are persecuted for righteousness' sake:	for theirs is the kingdom of heaven.
ye, when men shall revile you, and persecute you, and shall say all manner of evil against you falsely for my sake:	Rejoice, and be exceeding glad: for great is your reward in heaven: for so persecuted they the prophets which were before you.

If we translate those into character traits, what would we call them? *"Poor in spirit"* would be those devoid of pride — humility. *"They that mourn"* — would be those grieving over sin and compassion for others. "The meek" must mean gentleness. *"To hunger for righteousness"* you must be a person who really desires to be better than he is — we could call that goodness. Purity or sincerity would be the hallmark of the pure in heart. Being a peacemaker requires sobriety — the ability to keep a level head and not react to others. But wait a minute! — What does it take to be persecuted? It takes the courage to stand for something that others don't like. Though it may sound like the last one is just more persecution, to withstand that kind of extended assault demands a high level of integrity, a commitment to your values, so that you will not waver. These are the kind of people who will inherit the kingdom of heaven, who will be filled with righteousness, who will see God, who will be called the children of God, and whose reward will be great. Matthew 5:12, *"Rejoice and be exceedingly glad, for great is your reward in heaven, for so they persecuted the prophets who were before you."*

There are a lot of specific things that the Christian is called to do which will set him apart from others. We are called to be the light of the world, the ones who people look to for goodness and enlightenment. But we are not to attract attention to ourselves or do good to impress others. Rather, Matthew 5:16, *"Let your light so shine before men, that they may see your good works and glorify your Father in heaven."*

The way we deal with conflict should be different, too. Rather than anger, retaliation, bickering, and waiting for the other person to apologize, Jesus told us of a different way to handle conflict. (Matthew 5:23-24, *"Therefore if you bring your gift to the altar, and there remember that your brother has something against you, leave your gift there before the altar, and go your way. First be reconciled to your brother, and then come and offer your gift.")* We are called to initiate reconciliation and make amends if necessary so that nothing in our conscience stands between us and God.

Is it ever right to swear? Matthew 5:34, *"But I say to you, do not swear at all: neither by heaven, for it is God's throne,"* that is, to take a vow to insure your promise? Jesus taught that we should never have to do that.

The fact is that we don't have authority over any of those things we might swear by, like heaven or the earth. Even if you swear by your own head, you can't stop a single hair from turning gray. Jesus said, Matthew 5:37, *"But let your 'Yes' be 'Yes,' and your 'No,' 'No.' For whatever is more than these is from the evil one."* In other words, be good for your word and you don't have to swear by anything. If your yes means yes and your no means no, there is no reason to add anything to them.

Jesus had a strange idea about how we should treat people who are out to get us, too. He said, *"You have heard that it was said, 'You shall love your neighbor and hate your enemy.' But I say to you, love your enemies, bless those who curse you, do good to those who hate you, and pray for those who spitefully use you and persecute you,"* (Matthew 5:43-44). The Old Testament had taught that you should love your neighbor, but the popular interpretation of that was that your enemy was not your neighbor, so you can hate him. Jesus rejected that idea. Why do we have to love them, bless them, do good for them, and pray for them? Can't we just ignore them? Jesus' whole point is that we should be different. We should love our enemies. (Matthew 5:45-46, *"That you may be sons of your Father in heaven; for He makes His sun rise on the evil and on the good, and sends rain on the just and on the unjust. For if you love those who love you, what reward have you? Do not even the tax collectors do the same?")*. God does not withhold His goodness from those who hate Him. If we are to be His ambassadors, we have to act like He does.

But Jesus also warned us against something that can destroy our effectiveness and our relationship with God — spiritual pride. It is very easy to start thinking that you are better than everyone else and make a big show about how spiritual you are. The moment you start doing that — living your religious life for others to *see* — you quit being spiritual. *"Take heed that you do not do your charitable deeds before men, to be seen by them. Otherwise you have no reward from your Father in heaven. Therefore, when you do a charitable deed, do not sound a trumpet before you as the hypocrites do in the synagogues and in the streets, that they may have glory from men. Assuredly, I say to you, they have their reward. But when you do a charitable deed, do not let your left hand know what your right hand is doing, that your charitable deed may be in secret; and your Father who sees in secret will Himself reward you openly. And when you pray, you shall not be like the hypocrites. For they love to pray standing in the synagogues and on the corners of the streets, that they may be seen by men. Assuredly, I say to you, they have their reward,"* (Matthew 6:1,5). If you are praying, or giving, or going to church, or teaching, just to be seen by other people, then you already have what you wanted. There is no other reward. *"But when you do a charitable deed, do not let your left hand know what your right hand is doing, that your charitable deed may be in secret; and your Father who sees in secret will Himself reward you openly. But you, when you pray, go into your room, and when you have shut your door, pray to your Father who is in the secret place; and your Father who sees in secret will reward you openly,"* (Matthew 6:3-4,6). Make sure you catch that: what is done in secret is rewarded openly.

While saving is taught as a wisdom principle in the Old Testament, Jesus also warned us not to cling to material possessions as if our security was in them. *"Do not lay up for yourselves treasures on earth, where moth and rust destroy and where thieves break in and steal; but lay up for yourselves treasures in heaven, where neither moth nor rust destroys and where thieves do not break in and steal. For where your treasure is, there your heart will be also,"* (Matthew 6:19-21). If you are too focussed on getting stuff in this world, your heart will never be set on your true home in heaven.

Jesus also taught us to be different in the way we deal with everyday problems. While most of the world consumes themselves in worry, Jesus said, *"Which of you by worrying can add one cubit to his stature?"* (Matthew 6:27). What *good* does it do to worry? His solution was to trust that God would provide for you. Doesn't He provide for everything else in creation?

> *Look at the birds of the air, for they neither sow nor reap nor gather into barns; yet your heavenly Father feeds them. Are you not of more value than they? So why do you worry about clothing? Consider the lilies of the field, how they grow: they neither toil nor spin; and yet I say to you that even Solomon in all his glory was not arrayed like one of these. Now if God so clothes the grass of the field, which today is, and tomorrow is thrown into the oven, will*

He not much more clothe you, O you of little faith (Matthew 6:26, 28-30)?

Jesus' perspective makes it really clear: does God love you more than He loves a flower or a bird? Aren't you more important to God than they are? So, why worry? *"Therefore do not worry, saying, 'What shall we eat?' or 'What shall we drink?' or 'What shall we wear? For after all these things the Gentiles seek. For your heavenly Father knows that you need all these things,"* (Matthew 6:31-32).

The underlying principle of all this advice is simple: *"But seek first the kingdom of God and His righteousness, and all these things shall be added to you,"* (Matthew 6:33). If we seek His kingdom and His righteousness, we are not putting on a show for others; and we act towards others in the way God would act, loving our enemies and reconciling conflicts. All the things — earthly treasures, food, clothing, housing — will be given to you, not because you sought these things, but because you sought righteousness.

The Cleansed Life

We all want to live up to this new standard of life. But most of us see that there is a gap between where we are and where we need to be. What do we need to do to become more like the people Jesus wants us to be? The first step that we need to take is to take a good look at ourselves and see what we might need to clean up in our lives.

God does not fill a dirty vessel with His power and love. Cleansing precedes filling. Is that because God is so holy that He can't dwell in the presence of our sin? Habakkuk 1:13, *"You are of purer eyes than to behold evil, and cannot look on wickedness. Why do You look on those who deal treacherously, and hold Your tongue when the wicked devours a person more righteous than he?"* Maybe, but when we have sin that we cling to, we usually shut God out so that He doesn't have a chance to see if He might fill our lives. We often yearn for spiritual power and do not have it because of impure motives, double-mindedness, or unconfessed sin. To be filled vessels, we must be cleansed vessels. 1 Peter 1:15-16,

"But as He who called you is holy, you also be holy in all your conduct, because it is written, 'Be holy, for I am holy.'"

Just so that there is no misunderstanding, we are talking about your daily walk with Christ here, not your salvation. You can be saved, but sinning. In fact, as long as you are in this life, there will be some degree of sin. But the sins that you hang on to and refuse to let go of create a roadblock between you and God. It does not change the fact of your salvation, but you will not be able to enjoy your relationship with God or the benefits of that relationship while that roadblock is there.

It is the same in earthly families. A teenage son who is disobedient to his father does not cease to be the father's son, but he doesn't get the keys to the car either. More importantly, his father is displeased with him, and they don't share the same joy in their relationship that was once there. Their relationship becomes confrontational and guarded. In the same way, a Christian may do things that displease the Father and strain their relationship, but that does not mean he is no longer a son of God. It is a relationship that has conflict which needs resolution. Isaiah said, *"But your iniquities have separated you from your God; and your sins have hidden His face from you, so that He will not hear"* (Isaiah 59:2). *"If I regard iniquity in my heart, the Lord will not hear"* (Psalm 66:18).

This state of having a roadblock in our relationship is often called being "out of fellowship" with God. One thing that characterizes a person who is not in fellowship with God is double-mindedness. (James 1:8, *"He is a double-minded man, unstable in all his ways."*) This person wants to be seen as a Christian, probably goes to Church and has some Christian friends, but still clings to some of the people and values of the world, too. So they are in the pew Sunday morning after being in the bar Saturday night. They are trying to resolve two sets of values that really do contradict each other, so that they are of two minds about everything. In every decision they make, you never know which way they will go.

How to Be Cleansed

How can cleansing occur in the life of a person who is out of fellowship with God? The solution is found in 1 John 1:9, *"If we confess our sins, He is faithful* and *just to forgive us our sins and to cleanse us from all unrighteousness*."

The word ***confess*** means to "say the same thing as another" — to agree with God. When God brings to your attention the fact that something you have done is sin, you are to confess — agree with God — say the same thing that God says about it. Do not just say, "I have sinned," but state what the sin was and agree with God, looking at it from His viewpoint. When you see your sin as God sees it, it is not possible for you to continue in it.

The results of confession are dramatic. *"God is faithful..."* — that means He is going to do the same thing every time; you can count on Him to always react the same way. *"... to forgive us our sins ..."* The Bible teaches over and over that when God forgives, the matter is completely done away with. God forgets it. (Isaiah 43:25, *"I, even I, am He who* blots *out your transgressions for My own sake; and I will not remember your sins."*) (Psalm 103:12, *"As far as the east is from the west, so far has He removed our transgressions from us."*) You can't get much farther than that. That sin becomes a dead issue in God's mind and it is no longer in the way of your relationship — unless you decide to bring it back up by feeling guilty over something God has forgotten.

But the other result is the amazing part. God doesn't just forgive; He also cleanses. That means he cleans out the garbage in our soul that drove us to that sin and that was created by the sin. He gives us a chance to start all over again, not with just a clean slate, but with the knowledge of how wicked that sin really is. Once you have confessed your sin, you have the power to overcome it and never have to return to it. God is faithful to do that for you every time.

So why do some people fall back into the same sin? There could be many reasons, but it usually boils down to one of three things. Some people don't really confess. They say the words, but they don't really see their sin as God sees it. They may be sorry for the consequences they are facing, but they are not really sorry for the sin. Another reason is that they still cling to their feelings of guilt and refuse to accept God's forgiveness.

They still see themselves as guilty of that sin, so that they end up doing it to fulfill that self-image. That is a refusal to believe what God says. The other reason is that they don't even realize that they have been cleansed. If you don't know it has happened, you can't call on God to fulfill His promise the next time temptation comes. Your cleansing is a fact that you must accept by faith and cling to that faith, hanging on to God's faithfulness and His power, to overcome that sin day by day. I John 4:4, *"You are of God, little children, and have overcome them, because He who is in you is greater than he who is in the world."*

Ask anyone who has worked through a twelve-step program, like Alcoholics Anonymous, Overeaters Anonymous, or Alanon (not the ones who showed up at meetings, but the ones who worked the steps). The power of that program and the reason for its success lies in the fifth step, where we "admit to ourselves, to God, and to another human being the exact nature of our wrongs." That truth, that honesty and openness, breaks the power of the disease. The disease of addiction and the sins that it leads to are all wrapped up in deception and delusion — lies which come from the Father of lies. When we tell the truth about our sin and confess — when we quit lying to ourselves and get honest with God — He is faithful to forgive and to cleanse us. Then He comes back into our lives in a dynamic way, and we can walk in fellowship with him.

According to Proverbs 28:13, *"He who covers his sins will not prosper, but whoever confesses and forsakes them will have mercy."* Psalm 32:5, *"I acknowledged my sin to You, and my iniquity I have not hidden. I said, 'I will confess my transgressions to* the *LORD,' and You forgave the iniquity of my sin."* Remember Adam in the Garden? As soon as he sinned, what did he do? He hid. He was afraid God would find out that he was naked. It had never been a problem before, but now he was ashamed because of his sin, so he hid himself and tried to cover his shame with a fig leaf. When we cover our sin, we have to hide ourselves, and we become afraid that we will be found out. Nothing in our lives can prosper in that state. We shut people out, we put up a front, we lie and rationalize, we blame everyone else, and we become fearful and suspicious. Rather than reaching out and expanding ourselves, we shrink into a shell. Prosperity only comes when we can be honest and open, when we can take responsibility and act, and when we can live in faith knowing that we don't deserve God's goodness and mercy.

Living "in fellowship" with God

When we confess our sins, our fellowship with God is restored. Walking in fellowship with the Father and the Son is referred to as "walking in the light". Two things happen when we are walking in the light: *"But if we walk in the light as He is in the light, we have fellowship with one another, and the blood of Jesus Christ His Son cleanses us* from *all sin,"* (1 John 1:7). Not only is our fellowship with God restored, but so is our fellowship with other believers, through whom we experience God's love. The second result is that word again ***cleanse***. This time it is in the present tense, indicating that it is a continual type of thing, it keeps on happening and is on-going. Once we have confessed, Jesus would love to keep walking with us and showing us His light to keep us from falling back into sin. The more we walk in the light, the less likely we are to return to the darkness of hiding in our sin. John 8:32, *"And you shall know the truth, and the truth shall make you free."*

There are other changes going on inside of us. A new power enters our life. God goes to work in us, *"for it is God who works in you both to will and to do for His good pleasure,"* (Philippians 2:13). His good pleasure is to conform us to the image of His Son. As we learn to rely on God the way Jesus did, we learn that *"I can do all things through Christ who strengthens me,"* (Philippians 4:13). While we can't live a cleansed life by ourselves, we can rely on God's power to strengthen us and to transform us into the people he wants us to be. What is this power within us? It is the power of the Holy Spirit who indwells us. Paul summarizes the argument he made in chapters 6 and 7 of Romans saying,

> *But you are not in the flesh but in the Spirit, if indeed the Spirit of God dwells in you. Now if Christ is in you, the body is dead because of sin, but the Spirit is life because of righteousness. But if the Spirit of Him who raised Jesus from the dead dwells in you, He who raised Christ from the dead will also give life to your mortal bodies through His Spirit who dwells in you* (Romans 8:9-11).

Every Christian receives the indwelling of the Spirit when he believes, because we are baptized by the Spirit and sealed by the Spirit at that time. 1 Corinthians 12:13, *"For by one Spirit we were all baptized into one body— whether Jews or Greeks, whether slaves or free— and have all been made to drink into one Spirit."* Ephesians 4:30, *"And do not grieve the Holy Spirit of God, by whom you were sealed for the day of redemption."* We no longer have to live life in the flesh — in the power of our sinful nature — because the power of the Spirit which raised Christ from the dead has given us a new life. If you are walking in the light, you are walking in the Spirit.

Paul describes that more in Galatians. *"I say then: Walk in the Spirit, and you shall not fulfill the lust of the flesh,"* (5:16). Doesn't that mean the same thing as being cleansed from sin? You bet it does! And while walking in the flesh leads to all kinds of sin, walking in the Spirit bears its own fruit in your life. *"But the fruit of the Spirit is love, joy, peace, longsuffering, kindness, goodness, faithfulness, gentleness, self-control. Against such there is no law,"* (5:22-23). Isn't it amazing how similar that list is to the list of character traits Jesus talked about in Matthew 5? Could it be that we could become the kind of people Jesus wants us to be by walking in the Spirit?

If we have confidence in the power of the Spirit and walk in it, when temptation comes, we can say, "Sin, you are not my master any more and you can't reign over me. I am dead to sin because I died with Christ. And I am alive to God because of the Spirit in me, so I can do the right thing right now." Don't take my word for it. Look at what Paul says:

> *Likewise you also, reckon yourselves to be dead indeed to sin, but alive to God in Christ Jesus our Lord. Therefore do not let sin reign in your mortal body, that you should obey it in its lusts. And do not present your members as instruments of unrighteousness to sin, but present yourselves to God as being alive from the dead, and your members as instruments of righteousness to God.* (Romans 6:11-13).

The power of this presence in our lives changes everything. Living a righteous life is no longer an impossible burden to bear; it is absolutely possible to avoid sin. It is absolutely possible to obey God and to become that person God wants me to be. It is only a matter of remembering, *"For you died, and your life is hidden with Christ in God,"* (Colossians 3:3). If that is where my life is hidden, then that is where I will look for it. To find it, all I have to do is walk in the light and in the Spirit.

The Separated Life

Do you know what the word ***holy*** meant before it became a religious word? It meant "set apart", as in setting something apart for a special purpose, like the china your mother only used at Thanksgiving. God wants us to be "holy," too. He wants us to be set apart from the rest of the world. That doesn't mean isolated so that we only talk to Christians, but He wants us to be noticeably different because we are fulfilling the special purpose He has for us. 1 Peter 1:15-16, *"But as He who called you is holy, you also be holy in all your conduct, because it is written, 'Be holy, for I am holy.'"*

Put Off the Old ... Put On the New

Paul tells us that to make our new identity in Christ evident, we need to *"put off, concerning your former conduct, the old man which grows corrupt according to the deceitful lusts,"* (Ephesians 4:20-32). By that he means to renew our minds so that we think differently. Then we will quit doing the same old things and start doing new things that fit our new identity, and he gives some specific examples. He says to quit lying and start speaking the truth; quit burying your anger and be honest so you can resolve the situation; quit stealing and start working for a living; quit tearing people down and start building them up; quit grieving the Spirit and walk in the Spirit; quit harboring bitterness and wrath and start being kind and forgiving. These are the kinds of changes that will set you apart from the people around you.

But there is a deeper meaning to Paul's words. In Ephesians 2:15 he defines the "new man" as the Church - a body made up of Jews and

Gentiles which was not spoken of in the Old Testament, *"Having abolished in His flesh the enmity, that is, the law of commandments contained in ordinances, so as to create in Himself one* new *man from the two, thus making peace and that He might reconcile them both to God in one body through the cross, thereby putting to death the enmity. And He came and preached peace to you who were afar off and to those who were near. For through Him we both have access by one Spirit to the Father,"* (Ephesians 2:15-18). Using this understanding of the term, to put on the new man would mean to identify yourself with the Church and other believers. If you become intimately related to Christ's Church, your sense of who you are and your behaviors will change. 2 Corinthians 5:17, *"Therefore, if anyone is in Christ, he is a new creation; old things have passed away; behold, all things have become new."*

Seek Christian Fellowship

The first step in identifying yourself with the body of Christ is to become a part of a Bible-believing church and serve through the opportunities given you. Find a church where the focus is on teaching the Word of God and where you feel that you can fit in. Just start going and building relationships. You will be amazed at how important those relationships will become. The next step is to see if there is something you can do to serve. It might be as simple as setting up chairs or helping to make coffee. However, as you become more involved, you will find yourself becoming more deeply attached to the church because you have invested part of yourself there.

Second, ask God to give you wisdom and discernment in the friends you choose. If you spend 90% of your time with non-Christians and 10% with Christians, which group will have the greater influence on your life? It does no good to go to church on Sunday and spend the rest of the week with friends who drag you back into the world's ways. There are not many forces more powerful than the power of association. Seek to be with those who inspire you to be more effective as a Christian. Sunday School and Bible studies are a great place to meet people with whom you can develop friendships. Psalm 119:63, *"I am a companion of all who fear You, and of those who keep Your precepts."*

Serve with other Christians in bringing the gospel to others in ways which would be impossible to do alone. When we work as a team, Christ puts our strengths together in a special way to make an impact on unbelievers. Your role on the team doesn't have to put you in the spotlight, but no matter where you serve, your contribution will make a difference in the success of the whole. One of the most important roles in an evangelism team is to be praying for the team.

Be available to all who need your service and spiritual counsel. It is amazing what God will do if you just make yourself available. All of a sudden, unbelievers will cross your path who need to hear the gospel; believers who need someone to talk to will call; and you will bump into people who will encourage you, too. Even if you don't know a lot about the Bible, God will use what you do know in mighty ways if you will open yourself up to letting Him use you.

God's Children Should Be Different from the World.

How will the world know that you are a disciple of Jesus? Jesus said, *"By this all will know that you are My disciples, if you have love for one another."* (John 13:35). Love is to be the hallmark of the Christian. Genuine caring and concern, being excited to see each other, and doing things beyond the call of duty for one another are important parts of our fellowship. John even says that you can have assurance that you are born again because you love the brethren. (1 John 3:14, *"We know that we have passed from death to life, because we love the brethren. He who does not love his brother abides in death.")*

Christians aren't perfect. Sometimes a Christian may fall into a sinful pattern and not do anything to change it, even though he knows it's not right. Should you still hang around that person? Should you still let him come to Bible studies? Galatians 6:1-2 says, *"Brethren, if a man is overtaken in any trespass, you who are spiritual restore such a one in a spirit of gentleness, considering yourself lest you also be tempted. Bear one another's burdens, and so fulfill the law of Christ."* The loving thing to do is to go to your brother and try to bring him back into the fellowship. But first, make sure that your own spiritual foundation is secure and watch that you aren't tempted to join him. The whole principle is that, in love, we bear one another's burdens — no one has to face his struggles alone.

Should you keep company or have close fellowship with a Christian that is living in sin? If you tried to avoid everyone who sins, you'd have to go to heaven to find anyone to talk to. But if there is someone who has made a choice to keep on in a sin that is really serious, even after he has been confronted about it, then it is best to stay away from him. (1 Corinthians 5:9-11, *"I wrote to you in my epistle not to keep company with sexually immoral people. Yet I certainly did not mean with the sexually immoral people of this world, or with the covetous, or extortioners, or idolaters, since then you would need to go out of the world. But now I have written to you not to keep company with anyone named a brother, who is sexually immoral, or covetous, or an idolater, or a reviler, or a drunkard, or an extortioner— not even to eat with such a person.")* There are two reasons for that. The first is that it protects you from being either corrupted by his moral failings or attacked for your moral standards. Second, it is best for him to be cut off from the fellowship of believers so that he can clearly see the sinful world he has chosen live in. If he has cut himself off from fellowship with God, then the loving thing for God's people to do is to cut him off from their fellowship. *"And have no fellowship with the unfruitful works of darkness, but rather expose them"* (Ephesians 5:11). *"But we command you, brethren, in the name of our Lord Jesus Christ, that you withdraw from every brother who walks disorderly and not according to the tradition which he received from us. "And if anyone does not obey our word in this epistle, note that person and do not keep company with him, that he may be ashamed"* (II Thessalonians 3:14). When his sin has run its course and he has to pay the consequences, we pray that he will repent and come back to the Church.

What about those who teach things a little differently than what you hear at church? Should I have fellowship with them? If their teaching is only a little different, but they still hold firmly to the same Gospel you heard and aren't trying to cause a division in your church, then you can have fellowship with them in everything where there is agreement. If, however, they teach a different Gospel, a different Christ, a different God, and are trying to lure people away from the teaching of the Church, have nothing to do with them. *"Now I urge you, brethren, note those who cause divisions and offenses, contrary to the doctrine which you learned, and avoid them. For those who are such do not serve our Lord Jesus Christ, but their own belly, and by smooth words and flattering speech deceive the hearts of the simple,"* (Romans 16:17-18). These are false teachers who are not Christians, though they may use the name of Christ. Their motive is personal gain, either in terms of profit, power, or prestige. They have no fellowship with the Father, so they should have no fellowship with you.

The next question is what your relationship should be to unbelievers. Can you maintain the close friendships you had before you became a Christian? To some extent you can. But as you change, the nature of that relationship changes. You will find distance developing in those relationship rather quickly. You may still be friends, but not as close. Paul warns about being in a relationship of mutual dependence with a non-believer.

> *Do not be unequally yoked together with unbelievers. For what fellowship has righteousness with lawlessness? And what communion has light with darkness? And what accord has Christ with Belial? Or what part has a believer with an unbeliever? And what agreement has the temple of God with idols? For you are the temple of the living God. As God has said: "I will dwell in them and walk among them. I will be their God, and they shall be My people." Therefore "Come out from among them and be separate," says the Lord. "Do not touch what is unclean, and I will receive you. I will be a Father to you, and you shall be My sons and daughters," says the Lord Almighty* (2 Corinthians 6:14-18).

What does He mean "unequally yoked"? A yoke is a wooden harness that two oxen pull against when pulling a wagon. If one ox is considerably bigger or stronger than the other, then they don't pull together very well. They go in circles; the weaker one gets tired from trying to keep up; the stronger resents doing all the work — it just doesn't work. But they are yoked together and can't separate themselves. Paul is warning to avoid those kinds of relationships with unbelievers where you have to count on each other, and you can't separate easily. That would include relationships such as marriage or business partners. Even a roommate relationship with an unbeliever can be difficult. Paul's reasoning is simply that you should not be in a committed relationship with someone with whom you cannot have fellowship. Proverbs 4:14, *"Do not enter the path of the wicked, and do not walk in the way of evil."*

On the night before His death, Jesus prayed for the people who would become His Church. He said, *"I do not pray that You should take them out of the world, but that You should keep them from the evil one. They are not of the world, just as I am not of the world. Sanctify them by Your truth. Your word is truth."* (John 17:15-17). We cannot leave the world; there are people here who need to hear our message and only we can deliver it. But we do not need to be involved in the evil that is in the world. Jesus asked the Father to sanctify (set apart) us through His Word. If we stay focussed on the truth of God's word, we walk in the light of that truth, we are cleansed, and we are sanctified to be his people.

Jesus was sent into the world by His Father, and Jesus, in turn, sent us into the world to complete the task. (John 17:18, *"Were there not any found who returned to give glory to God except this foreigner?")*; *"For the Son of Man has come to seek and to save that which was lost,"* (Luke 19:10). We are now his ambassadors, to whom He gave the message of reconciliation, so that we could reach out to a dying humanity and offer them the hope of salvation. (2 Corinthians 5:18-21, *"Now all things are of God, who has reconciled us to Himself through Jesus Christ, and has given us the ministry of reconciliation, that God was in Christ reconciling the world to Himself, not imputing their trespasses to them, and has committed to us the word of reconciliation. Now then, we are ambassadors for Christ, as though God were pleading through us: we implore you on Christ's behalf, be reconciled to God. For He made Him who knew no sin to be sin for us, that we might become the righteousness of God in Him.")* That task has taken a long time, but, 2 Peter 3:9, *"The Lord is not slack concerning His promise, as some count slackness, but is longsuffering toward us, not willing that any should perish but that all should come to repentance."* God is giving every man all the time He needs to decide his fate and is not in a rush to judge the world. Unless the men hear our message, they cannot believe and be saved. (Romans 10:14,

"How then shall they call on Him in whom they have not believed? And how shall they believe in Him of whom they have not heard? And how shall they hear without a preacher?")

The Directed Life

In addition to being blessed, cleansed and separated, we can now live a directed life. God can and will lead us and show us the directions in which He wants us to go so that we may best be used by Him. Often the way in which He wants us to go is easy to see, but sometimes it is not. However, you will never see God's guidance if you are on the throne of your life and not looking for it. God will only steer the ship if you give Him the helm.

How do you know that God will guide you? He has said that He would. *"The steps of a good man are ordered by the LORD, and He delights in his way,"* (Psalm 37:23). *"Trust in the LORD with all your heart, and lean not on your own understanding; In all your ways acknowledge Him, and He shall direct your paths,"* (Proverbs 3:5-6).

Guidance is primarily a result of living an obedient life. More often than we like to admit, God has already revealed what he wants us to do in His word. Rather than looking for some new truth, we just need to obey the old truths we already have, and God will show us the next step. But there are times when we need to look for more specific guidance.

Seek God's Guidance

> *But know that the LORD has set apart for Himself him who is godly; the LORD will hear when I call to Him. Be angry, and do not sin. Meditate within your heart on your bed, and be still. Offer the sacrifices of righteousness, and put your trust in the LORD. There are many who say, "Who will show us any good?" LORD, lift up the light of Your countenance upon us. You have put gladness in my heart, more than in the season that their grain and wine*

> *increased. I will both lie down in peace, and sleep; for You alone, O LORD, make me dwell in safety* (Psalm 4:3-8).

How do we get His guidance? The same way you cross a street: Stop, Look, and Listen.

> *Stop* - be still. It is so easy to have all the other voices in our lives cover up the voice of God. We get wrapped up in all the perceived pressure from others, but the one force we need to be concerned with is the gentle pressure of His hand. *"Be still, and know that I am God; I will be exalted among the nations, I will be exalted in the earth!"* (Psalm 46:10). God doesn't speak in the raging wind or the earthquake, but in a still small voice, *"Then He said, 'Go out, and stand on the mountain before the LORD.' And behold, the LORD passed by, and a great and strong wind tore into the mountains and broke the rocks in pieces before the LORD, but the LORD was not in the wind; and after the wind an earthquake, but the LORD was not in the earthquake; and after the earthquake a fire, but the LORD was not in the fire; and after the fire a still small voice,"* (1 Kings 19:11-12) which created the universe.
>
> *Look* - study His Word. Most of the time, the answer is right there. It may not be as specific as you like, but the principles God's Word gives often tell you exactly what you need to know. For instance, it won't tell you the name of the person you should marry, but it will tell you what kind of person it is best to marry.
>
> > *Blessed is the man who walks not in the counsel of the ungodly, nor stands in the path of sinners, nor sits in the seat of the scornful; But his delight is in the law of the LORD, and in His law he meditates day and night. He shall be like a tree planted by the rivers of water, that brings forth its fruit in its season, whose leaf also shall not wither; and whatever he does shall prosper* (Psalm 1:1-3).

> *Listen* - meditate on the teachings of God's Word in light of your problem or situation. Answers to the tough ones may not jump off the page at you. You may have to weigh your options, discern which principles apply and which don't, and analyze the situation from a different perspective. And you may need time to be convinced that following God's way is right. Sometimes following Him can cost us relationships, money, status, and possessions. But you have to be convinced that you are following God and that He will reward your faithfulness later. When you act, whatever you do, do it from faith. (Romans 14:23, *"But he who doubts is condemned if he eats, because he does not eat from faith; for whatever is not from faith is sin."*)

Obey His revealed will. There must be a conscious yielding to and dependence upon Him for His Work. That is why we must consciously seek His will. If you constantly reject His leadings, why should you expect Him to keep giving you guidance? Step by step obedience the is key to receiving God's direction. Isaiah 1:19-20, *"If you are willing and obedient, you shall eat the good of the land; But if you refuse and rebel, you shall be devoured by the sword."*

But remember that God's guidance will always be from His viewpoint and will usually conflict with the normal pattern of the world. It may not make any sense at all. It may be totally contrary to what you want to do. So what? If God is leading, it is your job to obey. Trust Him to guide wisely; and when you sense He is leading, obey immediately.

> *Trust in the LORD, and do good; dwell in the land, and feed on His faithfulness. Delight yourself also in the LORD, and He shall give you the desires of your heart. Commit your way to the LORD, trust also in Him, and He shall bring it to pass* (Psalm 37:3-5).

Make Wise Decisions

The ruling principle in Biblical decision making is wisdom. God wants us to know Him well enough that we make decisions using His wisdom every day. That means we have to be concerned about the things God is concerned with, not what the world says. When faced with a problem, a Christian can come to know the answer by asking some questions.

A. *How will this affect me?* - My spiritual growth? - My testimony? - My being used of God? Is this a step forward in my obedience to God, or a step backward? (2 Peter 3:17-18, *"You therefore, beloved, since you know this beforehand, beware lest you also fall from your own steadfastness, being led away with the error of the wicked; but grow in the grace and knowledge of our Lord and Savior Jesus Christ. To Him be the glory both now and forever. Amen."*) Don't evaluate decisions on the basis of what it may cost you, but on the basis of whether it will help your growth and conform you to the image of His Son.

B. *How will this affect others?* - Strong Christians? - Weak Christians? - Lost people? Will the action cause them to stumble? Or will it encourage them to greater obedience? (1 Corinthians 8:9-13, *"But beware lest somehow this liberty of yours become a stumbling block to those who are weak. For if anyone sees you who have knowledge eating in an idol's temple, will not the conscience of him who is weak be emboldened to eat those things offered to idols? And because of your knowledge shall the weak brother perish, for whom Christ died? But when you thus sin against the brethren, and wound their weak conscience, you sin against Christ. Therefore, if food makes my brother stumble, I will never again eat meat, lest I make my brother stumble";* 10:32-33, *"Give no offense, either to the Jews or to the Greeks or to the church of God, just as I also please all men in all things, not seeking my own profit, but the profit of many, that they may be saved.")* You can't control or predict the responses of others, but just ask yourself what you would think if you saw a Christian doing it.

C. *How will this affect God?* Will it dishonor Him, grieve Him, or harden others against Him? Will God be glorified? Will this please Him because I have acted in obedience? Our chief concerns should be the concerns of the kingdom of God. (1 Corinthians 10:31, *"Therefore, whether you eat or drink, or whatever you do, do all to the glory of God.")*

D. *Is this a good use of my time?* Is this profitable? Are there other things I could do that would be a better use of my time? (Ephesians 5:16, *"Redeeming the time, because the days are evil.")*

E. *Can I do this in Jesus' name and be thankful for it?* Is this fitting for an ambassador of Christ? Can I experience His joy in doing it? (Colossians 3:17, *"And whatever you do in word or deed, do all in the name of the Lord Jesus, giving thanks to God the Father through Him."*)

F. *Does this have the appearance of evil?* Does it even look like it might be bad? Could someone draw the wrong conclusions about it easily? All of a Christian's dealings should be completely above board and not require explanation. (1 Thessalonians 5:22, *"Abstain from every form of evil."* Romans 15:16, *"That I might be a minister of Jesus Christ to the Gentiles, ministering the gospel of God, that the offering of the Gentiles might be acceptable, sanctified by the Holy Spirit.")*

G. *Do I have any doubt?* Am I certain that this is God's path for me? Or am I rationalizing to do what I wanted in the first place? This doesn't mean you understand why God told you to do it or how it will all work out. It means that you are sure this is God's direction you are following. (Romans 14:23, *"But he who doubts is condemned if he eats, because he does not eat from faith; for whatever is not from faith is sin.")*

Answering these questions should clarify most of the issues involved. Not everything in your life will fit into nice, neat, black and white categories. But God will direct your paths if you will seek His guidance, yield to Him, trust Him, and commit yourself to following His way.

Chapter Ten

A NEW RESOURCE

FOR TEMPTATIONS AND TRIALS

When you decided to receive Jesus into your life to be Savior and Lord, the devil became your enemy. Before, Satan was controlling your life (Ephesians 2:2-3, *"In which you once walked according to the course of this world, according to the prince of the power of the air, the spirit who now works in the sons of disobedience, among whom also we all once conducted ourselves in the lusts of our flesh, fulfilling the desires of the flesh and of the mind, and were by nature children of wrath, just as the others")* but now, you are God's child, and Satan will put many obstacles in your way to keep you from experiencing the victories Christ has for you. It is important for you to know your position in Christ, and the power you have in His name. As a Christian you can resist the devil, because God will give you a way out. At times you will sin, but you can repent, confess immediately, and continue in sweet fellowship with the Lord. (1 John 1:7-9, *"But if we walk in the light as He is in the light, we have fellowship with one another, and the blood of Jesus Christ His Son cleanses us from all sin. If we say that we have no sin, we deceive ourselves, and the truth is not in us. If we confess our sins, He is faithful and just to forgive us our sins and to cleanse us from all unrighteousness.")*

The Devil

Who tempted Jesus in the wilderness? The devil. (Matthew 4:1, *"Then*

Jesus was led up by the Spirit into the wilderness to be tempted by the devil.") So guess what he wants to do to you? The Bible warns us, *"Be sober, be vigilant; because your adversary the devil walks about like a roaring lion, seeking whom he may devour,"* (1 Peter 5:8). Peter wrote that, and Jesus had told him, *"Simon, Simon! Indeed, Satan has asked for you, that he may sift you as wheat. But I have prayed for you, that your faith should not fail; and when you have returned to Me, strengthen your brethren,"* (Luke 22:31-32). Peter knew how it felt to be devoured by the devil, but he also knew that it was possible to stand firm against the devil and win the battle. How do we do that? *"Therefore submit to God. Resist the devil and he will flee from you."* (James 4:7). That is exactly what Peter had to do, too. He had to give up his pride and boasting in his own faithfulness and start trusting God's faithfulness to deliver him. Then, when Satan tried to lure him into fear or disobedience, he said just what Jesus had said to him once, "*Get behind Me, Satan*!" (Matthew 16:23). And the Devil fled. He will do the same if you resist him too. He cannot stand against the Spirit within you. 1 Peter 5:9, *"Resist him, steadfast in the faith, knowing that the same sufferings are experienced by your brotherhood in the world."* Romans 10:17, *"So then faith comes by hearing, and hearing by the word of God."*

The Flesh

Before experiencing the new birth, you were dead in trespasses and sins. (Ephesians 2:1, *"And you He made alive, who were dead in trespasses and sins."*) You had no spiritual life. You were simply a slave to sin. You were controlled by the lusts of the flesh, fulfilling the desires of your sinful nature and of your natural minds. (Ephesians 2:3, *"Among whom also we all once conducted ourselves in the lusts of our flesh, fulfilling the desires of the flesh and of the mind, and were by nature children of wrath, just as the others.")* You didn't know any other way to live and had no reason to do anything else.

When you repented of your sins and called upon Jesus to be your Savior and Lord, the Holy Spirit came to live in you. (1 Corinthians 6:19, *"Do you not know that the unrighteous will not inherit the kingdom of God? Do not be deceived. Neither fornicators, nor idolaters, nor adulterers, nor homosexuals, nor sodomites.")* Jesus had told his disciples to expect a new relationship to the Spirit, *"the Spirit of truth, whom the world cannot receive, because it neither sees Him nor knows Him; but you know Him, for He dwells with you and will be in you,"* (John 14:17). The disciples knew the Spirit's presence in their ministries, but this was to be a more intimate, personal, and intense relationship than they had experienced before. For each of them, it was indeed a transforming experience, and so it is for us.

Living in your old flesh with the new Spirit brought on a new set of conflicts. The two natures seemed to be at war with one another so that we could not do what we wanted to do. (Galatians 5:17, *"For the flesh lusts against the Spirit, and the Spirit against the flesh; and these are contrary to one another, so that you do not do the things that you wish.")* When we tried to follow the Spirit, our flesh stopped us. The only way to have victory was to put our flesh to death and walk by the Spirit. (Galatians 5:16, *"I say then: Walk in the Spirit, and you shall not fulfill the lust of the flesh.")* When we did that, when we walked by the Spirit, the flesh did not get in the way, and we didn't do those things that it desired.

Instead, a different kind of fruit appeared in our lives — the fruit that comes from the life of the Spirit. (Galatians 5:22-23, *"But the fruit of the Spirit is love, joy, peace, longsuffering, kindness, goodness, faithfulness, gentleness, self-control. Against such there is no law.")* Instead of immorality, we found love. Instead of strife, we found joy. Instead of enmities, we found peace. Instead of anger, we found patience. Everything in our life changed when we became dedicated to walking by the Spirit and putting to death the flesh.

Paul said, *"I have been crucified with Christ; it is no longer I who live, but Christ lives in me; and the life which I now live in the flesh I live by faith in the Son of God, who loved me and gave Himself for me,"* (Galatians 2:20).

Temptation

Who is to blame when you are tempted? Is God tempting you? Is Satan tempting you? The Bible says it is YOU that tempts you. *"Let no one say when he is tempted, 'I am tempted by God'; for God cannot be tempted by evil, nor does He Himself tempt anyone. But each one is tempted when he is drawn away by his own desires and enticed,"* (James 1:13-14). In other words, God doesn't tempt anybody. You are tempted when your flesh sees something that it wants. It is your own lust that draws you away from righteousness. Doesn't Satan fit in there somewhere? All he does is present you with the opportunity for your lust to be aroused. You are the one who responds to what he presents.

Now comes the hard part. Which way do you go? Do you follow your lust, or do you follow the Spirit? *"Then, when desire has conceived, it gives birth to sin; and sin, when it is full-grown, brings forth death,"* (James 1:15). Is that what you want? What is the alternative? Do you have a choice?

God does not leave you hanging out to dry. He promises three things for you in 1 Corinthians 10:13, First, you are not alone. *"No temptation has overtaken you except such as is common to man."* If you wanted to, you could get support from someone else who has had victory over the same kind of temptation. Second, *"God is faithful, who will not allow you to be tempted beyond what you are able."* He promises that you can handle whatever comes your way. You may not feel like it, but God knows you can make it. And finally, *"But with the temptation will also make the way of escape, that you may be able to bear it."* He does not put you in any situation where you are forced to sin. There is always a choice. There is always a way out. When Potiphar's wife grabbed Joseph, he found the way out by slipping out of his clothes and running out of the house naked. (Genesis 39:12, *"...she caught him by his garment, saying, 'Lie with me.' But he left his garment in her hand, and fled and ran outside.")* That was better than adultery. When Daniel was told that he couldn't pray any longer, he chose to do it anyway and was thrown in prison. (Daniel 6:10, *"Now when Daniel knew that the writing was signed, he went home. And in his upper room, with his windows open toward Jerusalem, he knelt down on his knees three times that day, and prayed and gave thanks before his God, as was his custom since early days.")* That was the way out that God provided for him. You may not like the way out that God gives you, but God never puts you in a position where you are forced to sin.

That's what God does for you. But there are things you can do for yourself, too. Sometimes we set ourselves up for a fall and there are ways to avoid that. You can memorize Scripture. *"Your word I have hidden in my heart, that I might not sin against You!"* (Psalm 119:11). That does more than remind you not to sin. It restrains your lusts from taking over so that you are not tempted in the first place. Another thing you can do is to be mindful of your weakness and pray for yourself. *"Watch and pray, lest you enter into temptation. The spirit indeed is willing, but the flesh is weak,"* (Matthew 26:41). The third thing you can do is to avoid situations where you are likely to be tempted. *"Abstain from every form of evil,"* (1 Thessalonians 5:22). It is really hard for an alcoholic to stay sober if he keeps going back to the same bar and hanging out with the same buddies; but if he learns to stay away from the situations where temptations abound, it is a whole lot easier.

You may not feel like you are strong enough to deal with your temptation. That's okay. It is not your feelings that will give you victory. It is your faith. *"For whatever is born of God overcomes the world. And this is the victory that has overcome the world— our faith,"* (1 John 5:4). Why is it that anyone born of God can overcome? How does that work? *"You are of God, little children, and have overcome them, because He who is in you is greater than he who is in the world,"* (1 John 4:4). You don't have to be strong. The Spirit who is in you is greater than any temptation Satan can throw at you.

But how can you resist Satan? Don't assume you can do it by the power of your flesh. You have to take the power of your own lust seriously and you have to hang on to your faith in the new nature. *"Be sober, be vigilant; because your adversary the devil walks about like a roaring lion, seeking whom he may devour. Resist him, steadfast in the faith, knowing that the same sufferings are experienced by your brotherhood in the world,"* (1 Peter 5:8-9). If others can withstand the pressures of Satan, so can you.

Your flesh will be with you as long as you are in this life, but it does not have to rule your life. *"Likewise you also, reckon yourselves to be dead indeed to sin, but alive to God in Christ Jesus our Lord. Therefore do not let sin reign in your mortal body, that you should obey it in its lusts,"*

(Romans 6:11-12). Your flesh may live with you, but it doesn't have to reign. You don't have to obey it because you are dead to it.

The best way to overcome temptation: *"And do not present your members as instruments of unrighteousness to sin, but present yourselves to God as being alive from the dead, and your members as instruments of righteousness to God,"* (Romans 6:13). You can be happy even in the midst of trials and tribulations because Jesus told us, *"In the world you will have tribulation; but be of good cheer, I have overcome the world,"* (John 16:33). Even if you can't overcome the world, He has already done it and your victory is in Him.

Can a Christian live without ever sinning? It is not likely. That would seriously underestimate the tenacity of your sin nature. We cannot deny our sinfulness and be honest with God (1 John 1:8, *"If we say that we have no sin, we deceive ourselves, and the truth is not in us,"; v. 10, "If we say that we have not sinned, we make Him a liar, and His word is not in us."*). On any given occasion it is possible to avoid sin, but what if you do slip into sin? 1 John 1:9, *"If we confess our sins, He is faithful and just to forgive us our sins and to cleanse us from all unrighteousness."* God promises both to forgive us and to cleanse us from our sins.

If God is really in control, why does He even allow us to be tempted? Why does He put us through that? He does it for our own good. *"My brethren, count it all joy when you fall into various trials, knowing that the testing of your faith produces patience. But let patience have its perfect work, that you may be perfect and complete, lacking nothing,"* (James 1:2-4). Testing strengthens our faith and teaches us to wait on God. Testing develops patience, and patience becomes maturity and wholeness.

Peter makes the same point: *"In this you greatly rejoice, though now for a little while, if need be, you have been grieved by various trials, that the genuineness of your faith, being much more precious than gold that perishes, though it is tested by fire, may be found to praise, honor, and glory at the revelation of Jesus Christ,"* (1 Peter 1:6-7). It may not be fun while you are going through it, but your trial — your testing — is really more precious than gold because of the fruit it produces in your life. Peter closes the same book with this statement: *"But may the God of all grace, who called us to His eternal glory by Christ Jesus, after you have suffered a while, perfect, establish, strengthen, and settle you,"* (1 Peter 5:10). In fact, that is the verse that comes right after the one about Satan's wanting to devour you.

The Warfare

We have already talked about the armor that God has provided for our warfare with Satan. But why should we put on that armor? What is the desired result? *"Put on the whole armor of God, that you may be able to stand against the wiles of the devil. For we do not wrestle against flesh and blood, but against principalities, against powers, against the rulers of the darkness of this age, against spiritual hosts of wickedness in the heavenly places. Therefore take up the whole armor of God, that you may be able to withstand in the evil day, and having done all, to stand,"* (Ephesians 6:11-13). The purpose of that armor is to keep us standing, no matter what.

This fight against sin is a real battle. Our warfare is real. Who are the enemies? *"Adulterers and adulteresses! Do you not know that friendship with the world is enmity with God? Whoever therefore wants to be a friend of the world makes himself an enemy of God,"* (James 4:4). *"For the flesh lusts against the Spirit,"* (Galatians 5:17). Those friendly with the world, your own flesh, and *"your adversary the devil"* (I Peter 5:8), all conspire together in this battle. The armor we put on is to protect us from their attacks.

How are we to respond to these enemies who want us to stay in slavery to sin? Rather than letting your worldly friends influence you, *"Do not be conformed to this world, but be transformed by the renewing of your mind, that you may prove what is that good and acceptable and perfect will of God,"* (Romans 12:2). Don't let them drag you back into the darkness of your sin. Be transformed. Rather than allowing your flesh to reign, *"Walk in the Spirit, and you shall not fulfill the lust of the flesh,"* (Galatians 5:16). Rather than give in to the devil, *"Resist the devil and he will flee from you,"* (James 4:7). That is the way to win the battle: be transformed, walk by the Spirit, and resist the devil. That's all it takes to have victory.

Sin doesn't just go away, however. It keeps coming back to haunt us. Therefore, we have to stay on the alert. How do we do that? *"Praying always with all prayer and supplication in the Spirit, being watchful to this end with all perseverance and supplication for all the saints,"* (Ephesians 6:18). And when you think you have prayed enough, *"Continue earnestly in prayer, being vigilant in it with thanksgiving,"* (Colossians 4:2).

Facing Trials

When two Christians face the same tragedy, one may become depressed and defeated while the other bravely presses on and uplifts those around him. One withdraws from the fellowship of the church and becomes bitter, but the other is drawn closer to God. Why should that be? What makes the difference?

Sometimes Christians feel that God has let them down when they find themselves without money, health, prestige, or in severe straits. Such an attitude leads to coldness of heart, prayerlessness, distrust, worry, and selfish living. Attitude makes the difference.

Exodus 14:1-4, *Now the LORD spoke to Moses, saying: "Speak to the children of Israel, that they turn and camp before Pi Hahiroth, between Migdol and the sea, opposite Baal Zephon; you shall camp before it by the sea. For Pharaoh will say of the children of Israel, 'They are bewildered by the land; the wilderness has closed them in. Then I will harden Pharaoh's heart, so that he will pursue them; and I will gain honor over Pharaoh and over all his army, that the Egyptians may know that I am the LORD." And they did so.* The Israelites experienced an unrecognized blessing. God told them to camp at a certain spot where they would be trapped, backed up against the Red Sea. God's plan was to harden Pharaoh's heart so that God could glorify Himself. Moses responded calmly and did what God had commanded. He led the people to the place God had specified.

When the people saw Pharaoh's chariots coming, they panicked. Their immediate reaction was, "We're all gonna die!" They said to Moses, *"Because there were no graves in Egypt, have you taken us away to die in the wilderness? Why have you so dealt with us, to bring us up out of Egypt? Is this not the word that we told you in Egypt, saying, 'Let us alone that we may serve the Egyptians? For it would have been better for us to serve the Egyptians than that we should die in the wilderness,"* (Exodus 14:11-12). They were ready to give up the whole thing. Forget the plagues. Forget Passover. Forget the treasure that the Egyptians gave them when they left. They were convinced that God was going to let them down now. What kind of attitude is that?

Notice how Moses reacted. He told them, *"Do not be afraid. Stand still, and see the salvation of the LORD, which He will accomplish for you today. For the Egyptians whom you see today, you shall see again no more forever. The LORD will fight for you, and you shall hold your peace,"* (Exodus 14:13-14). What a difference! Moses reacted very differently to the same situation because he trusted God to deliver them. He was ready to see what God was going to do to wipe out Pharaoh and his army. He expected God to do what He had promised, and it made all the difference in the world.

But you know what? Moses still missed it. God didn't want them to stand still and hold their peace. God immediately reprimanded Moses for standing around and told him to get the people moving forward. Forward? They were up against the sea. How were they going to move forward? *"But lift up your rod, and stretch out your hand over the sea and divide it. And the children of Israel shall go on dry ground through the midst of the sea,"* (Exodus14:16). Moses' attitude was better than the other children of Israel, but he still didn't understand what God wanted to do. It wasn't enough to stand still in the face of trouble; God wanted them to move forward even though moving forward was impossible. What a difference an attitude of faith can make!

In the end, the children of Israel did reap the blessings from this event. *"Thus Israel saw the great work which the LORD had done in Egypt; so the people feared the LORD, and believed the LORD and His servant Moses,"* (Exodus 14:31). Now that they had seen God work, they had a new reverence for Him. Now that he had delivered them (yet again), they believed Him. I Corinthians 10:13, *"No temptation has overtaken you except such as is common to man; but God is faithful, who will not allow you to be tempted beyond what you are able, but with the temptation will also make the way of escape, that you may be able to bear it."* Also, they learned that they can believe Moses to be God's mouthpiece. After a while, they forgot those lessons and fell back into their attitude of complaining and fear, but for now the lesson was clear.

Why do we become convinced that God has abandoned us? Why do we worry that we will be ruined? Our own attitudes and false beliefs about God and life are the only explanation for this. Those attitudes have to be replaced with attitudes of thankfulness for what we have, faith in a God who loves us, and expectancy that He will complete the work that He has started in us. Look at the promise of Romans 8:28: *"And we know that all things work together for good to those who love God, to those who are the called according to His purpose."* Do you know that? I know you have heard it, but do you KNOW it? It doesn't say that only good things will happen but that all will work together for good in the end. It is not a promise for everyone, only for those who love Him and those whom He has loved. If you know that this is true, why in the world would you cling to the attitude that all is lost?

With the right attitude, we can walk through trials with confidence that God will deliver us on the other side with a richer life. Paul outlines the results of trial for us in Romans 5:3-5: *"And not only that, but we also glory in tribulations, knowing that tribulation produces perseverance; and perseverance, character; and character, hope. Now hope does not disappoint, because the love of God has been poured out in our hearts by the Holy Spirit who was given to us."* Through trials we learn patience, develop experience or character, and become more hopeful, convinced that God loves us all the more. It is in the hardest times of our lives that we will know God's love the most.

Trials are not really hardships; they are blessings that we haven't recognized yet. One of the reasons God gives us unrecognized blessings is so that we can encourage others. *"Blessed be the God and Father of our Lord Jesus Christ, the Father of mercies and God of all comfort, who comforts us in all our tribulation, that we may be able to comfort those who are in any trouble, with the comfort with which we ourselves are comforted by God,"* (2 Corinthians 1:3,4). Sharing the hope you have developed may be the only thing that brings another person through the trial he faces.

The other reason for unrecognized blessings is that you have gotten off-track, and God loves you enough to take a switch to your backside. *"For whom the Lord loves He chastens, and scourges every son whom He receives,"* (Hebrews 12:6). If God is our Father, it is His job to make sure all His sons are disciplined when they need it. While your earthly father may have been wrong or acted out of anger at times, our Heavenly Father only disciplines us to lead us to holiness. *"Now no chastening seems to be joyful for the present, but painful; nevertheless, afterward it yields the peaceable fruit of righteousness to those who have been trained by it,"* (Hebrews 12:11). This blessing is proof of just how much God loves us.

The number one attitude that we have to develop is thanksgiving. We are told to give thanks in all things (1 Thessalonians 5:18, *"In everything give thanks; for this is the will of God in Christ Jesus for you"*) — not FOR all things, but IN all things. Thanksgiving keeps us looking at all of the gifts we have from God rather than what we may have lost. It keeps us focussed on our faith and dependence on Him, rather than fear and isolation from Him. *"Therefore by Him let us continually offer the sacrifice of praise to God, that is, the fruit of our lips, giving thanks to His name,"* (Hebrews 13:15). When we give thanks, we open our hearts to God so that He may add what we need there. But if we fail to give thanks, we shut our hearts off from hearing God's voice or seeing His hand work. The first chapter of Romans contains a long downward spiral that man has taken in his sin from idolatry to debauchery to perversion, but that road to depravity began *"because, although they knew God, they did not glorify Him as God, nor were thankful, but became futile in their thoughts, and their foolish hearts were darkened,"* (Romans 1:21). That is what thanksgiving is all about: recognizing before God, and reminding ourselves that He is God.

The Victory

What we all want is victory over sin, and we can have it! We can resist Satan. We can walk by the Spirit. We can wear that armor. The question is, Are we really the ones winning the battle? Think about the armor for a moment: salvation, righteousness, faith, truth, the gospel, the Word. Is there any thing there that we can take credit for? Perhaps we forgot to notice the phrase that introduces the armor of God to us: *"Finally, my brethren, be strong in the Lord and in the power of His might,"* (Ephesians 6:10). It is just as true for us in fighting sin as it was for David in fighting the Philistines; the battle belongs to the Lord.

If the victory really belongs to Him, what are the odds that He will win? I may not be able to withstand Satan's attacks, but God is bigger than Satan. God *created* Satan. So what are you worried about? *"He who is in you is greater than he who is in the world,"* (1 John 4:4).

"What then shall we say to these things? If God is for us, who can be against us?" (Romans 8:31). No matter how persistent your sin is, no matter what kind of trials you face, no matter how strongly the adversary is opposing you, your confidence is in the God who loves and has committed His Son and His Spirit to you. The battle is already won; Satan's defeat is already accomplished. All that is left is for you to believe.

Chapter Eleven

A NEW POWER

— THE ABIDING LIFE —

The abiding life is one of the most significant phases of the Christian life. To have real abiding joy, we must learn to abide in Christ constantly. Many people never find the secret to a joyous life; consequently, they feel the Lord has let them down. The Christian who is not enjoying his Christian experience has missed the message of God's Word. *"These things have I spoken unto you that My joy might remain in you, and that your joy might be full*" (John 15:11). The abiding life brings lasting joy. Abiding in Christ also makes our lives fruitful. We see our prayers are answered. We are obedient to Him because He lives in and through us.

We don't use the word ***abide*** too much anymore, so you may not really know what it means. The basic meaning is to remain or to stay. The Greek word has the idea of pitching a tent. That is, you have been on a journey and now you found a place that you want to stay for a while. You pitch your tent there, you settle in, you camp out there, you rest there, and you remain there. That is abiding. We abide in Christ when we settle into His life, camp out in His Word, rest in His love, and remain right there. That is our home base, and there is no place we would rather be.

The Abiding Life Explained

To abide in Christ is to live in conscious dependence upon Him, recognizing that it is His life, His power, His wisdom, His resources, His strength, and His ability, operating through you, enabling you to live according to His will. *"I can do all things through Christ who strengthens me"; "For without Me you can do nothing,"* (Philippians 4:13; John 15:5). The Christian relies upon Christ's strength.

Jesus referred to Himself as the vine and Christians as the branches in John 15:5. If a branch is cut off from its vine, it doesn't produce very many grapes. It just withers and dies. The only source of life, of nourishment, of water, or of strength that it has is in its connection to the vine. Jesus told us that if we abide in Him (stay connected to the vine), and He abides in us (the life of the vine flowing through the branch), then we will bear much fruit. If we cut ourselves off from God's Word and Christ's body, then we are fruitless; *"for without me ye can do nothing."* Those dead, dry branches end up being thrown on the fire. They are of no use to anyone.

Jesus carries the analogy a little farther. He says that branches that don't produce fruit even when they are connected to the vine get cut off by the husbandman (God). Unfruitful branches are just draining the plant without contributing. It is all too common today for Christians to come into a church and soak up the teaching and the fellowship, but they never get really connected or involved. Pretty soon, they have jumped to some other church where they do the same thing. Then they wonder why they never really grow or experience the joy of the Christian life.

Also, the branches that do bear fruit get pruned every once in a while so that they can bear more fruit. John 15:2, *"Every branch in Me that does not bear fruit He takes away; and every branch that bears fruit He prunes, that it may bear more fruit."* When you prune a branch, you cut back some of the growth so that it doesn't drain the most productive parts of the branch. You get rid of any growth that is too close together so that it might interfere. Pruning allows the branch to focus its energy in the right direction, and it will produce more fruit than it did before. But when God prunes Christians, He cuts off parts of their life that are distracting them from being productive and fruitful. It may be sin that God prunes away, (and we certainly need to get rid of that entanglement), but it might just be things that drain your energy and keep you from being what you need to be and doing what you need to do. Those things may be relationships, hobbies, habits, or possessions. There can even be attitudes and false beliefs that are holding you back from serving God and loving people.

It is no fun getting pruned. It downright hurts, and a pruned branch looks naked and humiliated. But God prunes for reasons that we never see until after we have gone through the next growth season. It is only in the next growth season that we see how much more fruit we have produced. In the meantime, while the trial is going on, we have to remember that trials produce patience, character, and hope which teach us that God loves us. (Romans 5:3-5, *"And not only that, but we also glory in tribulations, knowing that tribulation produces perseverance; and perseverance, character; and character, hope. Now hope does not disappoint, because the love of God has been poured out in our hearts by the Holy Spirit who was given to us.")* (Hebrews 12:6, *"For whom the Lord loves He chastens, and scourges every son whom He receives.")* Our pruning does hurt; but God is a loving Father who knows what is best for us, and He is helping us to *"...lay aside every weight, and the sin which so easily ensnares us, and let us run with endurance the race that is set before us, looking unto Jesus, the author and finisher of our faith, who for the joy that was set before Him endured the cross, despising the shame, and has sat down at the right hand of the throne of God,"* (Hebrews 12:1-2). Jesus hated the suffering he had to do, too, along with the shame of being hung naked on a pole between two thieves. But the reward was worth it after it was all over. He had joy set before him.

The Results of Abiding in Christ

As Jesus continued in the analogy of the vine, He told us what the result of abiding in Him would be. The first thing He said was that we would see our prayers answered. *"If you abide in Me, and My words abide in you, you will ask what you desire, and it shall be done for you,"* (John 15:7). There are two requirements for having this result. First, we have to remain in Christ. We have to maintain fellowship with Him and His church, even when things get rough. We have to rely on Him as our source of life. And second, His words have to abide in us. We need to be so infiltrated by God's Word — Scriptures we have memorized, new Scriptures we have studied, sermons we have heard — that it becomes a living force in our lives. (Hebrews 4:12, *"For the word of God is living and powerful, and sharper than any two-edged sword, piercing even to the division of soul and spirit, and of joints and marrow, and is a discerner of the thoughts and intents of the heart.")* Having His word abide in us is just like the sap and fluids that the vine gives the branch which abide in it, imparting life and making it fruitful. Then our desires are controlled by His Word, we are submissive to His will, and our loving Father will do anything we ask.

A second result of abiding in Christ is that God is glorified in our lives. *"By this My Father is glorified, that you bear much fruit; so you will be My disciples,"* (John 15:8). We glorify God when we bear the fruit of abiding in Christ. What fruit is that? Our own sanctification, the fruit of the Spirit, the fruit of people saved by our message, the fruits of others who know Christ better because of us, and the results of our righteousness in the world around us. We glorify God when we act like disciples of our Savior and do the kind of things He did. I John 4:17, *"Love has been perfected among us in this: that we may have boldness in the day of judgment; because as He is, so are we in this world."* When we bear that fruit, God is glorified. Another result of abiding in Christ is that our love for God will increase, and we will have joy in our relationship with him.

> *As the Father loved Me, I also have loved you; abide in My love. If you keep My commandments, you will abide in My love, just as I have kept My Father's commandments and abide in His love. These things I have spoken to you, that My joy may remain in you, and that your joy may be full* (John 15:9-11).

Jesus says that He has loved us in the same way that the Father has loved the Son from all eternity. We need to abide — remain, continue, rest, camp — in that love. The number one thing that draws us out of that abiding is when we sin and shut God out of our lives. Jesus reminds us that if we keep his commandments, we will remain in His love. That doesn't mean we have to earn His love. It means that is the way to stay where we can enjoy His love and that is the promise of verse 11, that Christ's joy might abide in us and that we might have it to the fullest possible extent. How do we get that joy? By living in Christ's love, where we will obey His commandments. In the next verse He tells us what His commandment is. *"This is My commandment, that you love one another as I have loved you,"* (John 15:12). We are filled with joy when we love one another because God loves us.

God called us to be His children for a reason. *"You did not choose Me, but I chose you and appointed you that you should go and bear fruit, and that your fruit should remain, that whatever you ask the Father in My name He may give you,"* (John 15:16). Every one of us has been specially chosen by God and ordained to bear fruit. That is our commission from Him. Your fruit will be different than my fruit, but it will all come the same way. We all have to abide in Christ in order to bear fruit, but there is more to the verse: *"...and that your fruit should remain, that whatever you ask the Father in My name He may give you."* The kind of fruit that abiding in Christ produces is not the perishable kind. It is the kind that remains; it is permanent; it is eternal. The only thing that lasts for eternity is the souls of men. Is that the field in which you are working? Are you loving others as Christ has loved you? When our efforts are bearing eternal fruits, then God will gladly grant any request we make.

The Spirit-filled Life

The Person of the Holy Spirit

The Holy Spirit is a person, the third person of the Trinity: Father, Son and Holy Spirit. He is not some vague, ethereal shadow, nor an impersonal force. He is a person and He is equal in every way with the Father and the Son. All of the divine attributes ascribed to the Father and the Son are equally ascribed to the Holy Spirit. They are three persons united in one being called God.

What do we mean that the Holy Spirit is a person? Put it this way: a rock is not a person. It does not think about anything, it only responds to physical forces that move it. It is entirely passive, never intentionally changing anything. Human beings, however, are clearly self-aware and intentionally respond to and act on the things around them. They create, they organize, and they contemplate. Personality is hard to define without getting complicated, but a person can be identified by having intellect, emotions, and will.

The Holy Spirit meets those criteria. In 1 Corinthians 2:11, it is said, *"For what man knows the things of a man except the spirit of the man which is in him? Even so no one knows the things of God except the Spirit of God,"* indicating that He has intelligence. He also has emotions, as evidenced by the fact that He can be grieved. (Ephesians 4:30, *"And do not grieve the Holy Spirit of God, by whom you were sealed for the day of redemption.")* We also see the will of the Holy Spirit exercised as He distributes the gifts in the church. *"But one and the same Spirit works all these things, distributing to each one individually as He wills,"*(1 Corinthians 12:11). We, therefore, can conclude that the Holy Spirit is more than a force; He is a person who thinks, feels, and chooses. He has the ability to knowingly and willingly act on other things.

This person is God. He does things only God can do and fits descriptions only God can fit. For instance, He is active in creation (Genesis 1:2, *"The earth was without form, and void; and darkness was on the face of the deep. And the Spirit of God was hovering over the face of the waters"),* salvation (John 3:6, *"That which is born of the flesh is flesh, and that which is born of the Spirit is spirit"),* revealing God's Word (2 Timothy 3:16, *"All Scripture is given by inspiration of God, and is profitable for doctrine, for reproof, for correction, for instruction in righteousness"),* and in sanctification (2 Thessalonians 2:13, *"But we are bound to give thanks to God always for you, brethren beloved by the Lord, because God from the beginning chose you for salvation through sanctification by the Spirit and belief in the truth").* He is described as having holiness (Luke 11:13, *"If you then, being evil, know how to give good gifts to your children, how much more will your heavenly Father give the Holy Spirit to those who ask Him!"),* eternality (Hebrews 9:14, *"How much more shall the blood of Christ, who through the eternal Spirit offered Himself without spot to God, cleanse your conscience from dead works to serve the living God?"),* omniscience (1 Corinthians 2:10-11, *"But God has revealed them to us through His Spirit. For the Spirit searches all things, yes, the deep things of God. For what man knows the things of a man except the spirit of the man which is in him? Even so no one knows the things of God except the Spirit of God"),* omnipresence (Psalm 139:7, *"Where can I go from Your Spirit? Or where can I flee from Your presence?),* and truth (John 14:17, *"The Spirit of truth, whom the world cannot receive, because it neither sees Him nor knows Him; but you know Him, for He dwells with you and will be in you.")*

The Purpose of the Holy Spirit

The Holy Spirit's function is to be our Comforter, who is sent by the Father and the Son to draw along side us in our distress (John 14:26, *"But the Helper, the Holy Spirit, whom the Father will send in My name, He will teach you all things, and bring to your remembrance all things that I said to you.")* Another role of the Holy Spirit is that He indwells us, enabling us to live the life of Christ (1 Corinthians 3:16, *"Do you not know that you are the temple of God and that the Spirit of God dwells in you?"),* and He is the revealer of God's Word, through whom Christ promised the New Testament with the words, *"However, when He, the Spirit of truth, has come, He will guide you into all truth; for He will not speak on His own authority, but whatever He hears He will speak; and He will tell you things to come,"* (John 16:13).

The primary reason for the Spirit's presence in our lives is found in John 16:14, *"He will glorify Me, for He will take of what is Mine and declare it to you."* He glorifies Christ — to the lost, to the saved, in the church, in the world — He draws attention to and magnifies the glory of Christ. As the One who indwells us, He is our connection to the Vine. He is our source of life and strength. When we abide in Him, we do not obey the flesh, but God. The Spirit bears His fruit in our lives. When the Spirit bears His fruit, we become fruitful and that glorifies God.

The Work of the Holy Spirit

When you become a Christian, the Holy Spirit does a number of things for you and in you. He is the One who gave you a new life in Christ by the new birth. (John 3:5, *"Jesus answered, 'Most assuredly, I say to you, unless one is born of water and the Spirit, he cannot enter the kingdom of God.'")* He baptized you into the body of Christ at the same time. (1 Corinthians 12:13, *"For by one Spirit we were all baptized into one body— whether Jews or Greeks, whether slaves or free— and have all been made to drink into one Spirit.")* From then on, He indwells you, (1 Corinthians 3:16, *"Do you not know that you are the temple of God and that the Spirit of God dwells in you?"),* and you are sealed until Christ comes to get you. (Ephesians 4:30, *"And do not grieve the Holy Spirit of*

God, by whom you were sealed for the day of redemption.") He is the one who brings us the new life and helps us to live that life.

In addition to that, the Spirit bears witness to us that we are children of God (Romans 8:16, *"The Spirit Himself bears witness with our spirit that we are children of God"),* so that we can be convinced of our salvation and of God's love for us (Romans 5:5, *"Now hope does not disappoint, because the love of God has been poured out in our hearts by the Holy Spirit who was given to us.")* When we pray and don't know what to pray for or can't find the words, the Spirit takes over and prays for us in *"groanings which cannot be uttered."* In this way, the Spirit intercedes for us in our prayers and translates the burden of our hearts into a prayer which lines up with the will of God (Romans 8:26-27, *"Likewise the Spirit also helps in our weaknesses. For we do not know what we should pray for as we ought, but the Spirit Himself makes intercession for us with groanings which cannot be uttered. Now He who searches the hearts knows what the mind of the Spirit is, because He makes intercession for the saints according to the will of God.")*

The Results of Being Filled with the Holy Spirit

Every Christian has the Holy Spirit indwelling him, and anyone who doesn't is not a Christian. (Romans 8:9, *"But you are not in the flesh but in the Spirit, if indeed the Spirit of God dwells in you. Now if anyone does not have the Spirit of Christ, he is not His.")* But that doesn't mean that every Christian allows the Holy Spirit to influence his life. It is possible to have the Holy Spirit and still be living in the flesh. On the other hand, once we begin yielding our will to God's will and walking in the power of the Spirit, we can and will be filled with the Spirit.

The words used to describe the filling of the spirit are quite graphic. Luke, the physician, uses a word from which we get our word ***pimple***, indicating something so full it is about to burst because it cannot contain all of its fullness. Paul uses a word which pictures the sails of a ship being filled out and carried along by the wind. The idea is that we can be living so fully under the influence of the Spirit that we are about to burst and are being carried along by His power in all that we do. Galatians

5:25, *"If we live in the Spirit, let us also walk in the Spirit."*

In the Old Testament, certain people were filled with the Spirit to perform certain tasks. For instance, the artisans who worked on the tabernacle were filled with the Spirit. (Exodus 31:3, *"And I have filled him with the Spirit of God, in wisdom, in understanding, in knowledge, and in all manner of workmanship.")* Prophets were filled with the Spirit. (Numbers 11:17, *"Then I will come down and talk with you there. I will take of the Spirit that is upon you and will put the same upon them; and they shall bear the burden of the people with you, that you may not bear it yourself alone.")* Political leaders, such as the Judges over Israel, were filled with the Holy Spirit. (Judges 6:34, *"But the Spirit of the LORD came upon Gideon; then he blew the trumpet, and the Abiezrites gathered behind him.")* Both Saul and David were filled with the Spirit so that they could be kings over Israel. (1 Samuel 10: 9, *"So it was, when he had turned his back to go from Samuel, that God gave him another heart; and all those signs came to pass that day";* 16:13, *"Then Samuel took the horn of oil and anointed him in the midst of his brothers; and the Spirit of the LORD came upon David from that day forward. So Samuel arose and went to Ramah.")* But this filling was the only presence of the Spirit that believers in the Old Testament had. There was no permanent indwelling for Old Testament believers, and when they lost this filling, they were without the Spirit. The Spirit was taken away from Saul because of his disobedience (1 Samuel 16:14, *"But the Spirit of the LORD departed from Saul, and a distressing spirit from the LORD troubled him")*, and David prayed that he might not suffer the same punishment because of His sin. (Psalm 51:11, *"Do not cast me away from Your presence, and do not take Your Holy Spirit from me."*) While the filling of the Spirit in the New Testament is still temporary and subject to our obedience, we do not have to fear the absence of the Spirit because He indwells us as a down payment of the glorification that is to come for us and will not leave us completely. (2 Corinthians 5:5, *"Now He who has prepared us for this very thing is God, who also has given us the Spirit as a guarantee.")*

In the New Testament, the main reason people are filled with the Spirit is to preach the Gospel with boldness. Jesus told his disciples, *"But you shall receive power when the Holy Spirit has come upon you; and you shall be witnesses to Me in Jerusalem, and in all Judea* and *Samaria, and to the end of the earth,"* (Acts 1:8). Being a witness is the natural consequence of receiving this power. Peter was filled with the Spirit when he preached. (Acts 4:8, *"Then Peter, filled with the Holy Spirit, said to them, 'Rulers of the people and elders of Israel...'"*) After facing arrest and threats, the church in Jerusalem prayed that they might keep speaking with the same boldness. (4:29, 31, *"Now, Lord, look on their threats, and grant to Your servants that with all boldness they may speak Your word, And when they had prayed, the place where they were assembled together was shaken; and they were all filled with the Holy Spirit, and they spoke the word of God with boldness.")* There are other results of being filled that we will talk about later.

The biggest difference between the Old and New Testament fillings is that people in the Old Testament were filled as God determined who needed filling. In the New Testament, we are commanded to be filled. Ephesians 5:18 clearly demands, *"And do not be drunk with wine, in which is dissipation; but be filled with the Spirit."* This is not a suggestion or an exhortation; it is a command. If God commands that you do something, that means you have complete control over whether or not it gets done. It is your choice and the ball is in your court. Does God want you to be filled? Of course He does, or He wouldn't have commanded it. The only obstacles to being filled are the ones you put up.

Hindrances to the Spirit's Filling

What do we do to hinder the Spirit from filling us? The Bible warns us of two specific ways that we stop the Spirit from influencing our lives. The Bible calls them grieving the Spirit and quenching the Spirit.

Ephesians 4:30 warns us, *"And do not grieve the Holy Spirit of God, by whom you were* sealed *for the day of redemption."* What is it that would grieve the Spirit of God in us? Sin. Our sin that grieves the Spirit. God knows our weakness, but stubborn sins, the ones we know are wrong but we return to over and over, would especially bring sorrow to the heart of God. The context would suggest that sins in which we tear people down rather than build them up certainly qualify, since these sins destroy the unity of the church, particularly the sins of the tongue.

If we grieve the Holy Spirit, His influence is stifled. However, we may confess our sin and believe God to cleanse us of it so that our fellowship is restored. If it is a sin that keeps recurring, God may choose to chasten you — to prune you — to remove that sin from your life. No matter what it takes for you to have this obstacle removed, it is worth it to be filled with the Spirit and live in His power.

In the midst of a list of closing exhortations to the Thessalonians (rejoice, pray, give thanks, etc.), Paul throws in *"Do not quench the Spirit,"* (1 Thessalonians 5:19). Quenching the Spirit is a second hindrance that may prevent us from being filled. The image is one of pouring water on a fire to extinguish it. One paraphrase even says, "Don't put out the Spirit's fire." If we are constantly putting down the Spirit's promptings, if we discount the work of the Spirit in others, if we dismiss what the Spirit has revealed, we are quenching the Spirit. These are all signs of unbelief. When we refuse to believe that the Spirit can give us life, or that the promises of the Scriptures are ours, or when we refuse to trust God, we are quenching the work of the Spirit. Even when the Spirit reminds us to avoid sin, but we plow ahead into it, we have quenched His work. We cannot be filled if our unbelief will not allow Him to work in our lives.

Asking the Holy Spirit to Fill You

A desire to serve Him and help others should be your motive for being filled with the Holy Spirit. The verb "be filled" in Ephesians 5:18, *"And do not be drunk with wine, in which is dissipation; but be filled with the Spirit,"* is in the present tense which indicates that this command is to be a continual process. Being filled with the Spirit has been likened to breathing. We breathe out our sin by confession and repentance, and we breathe in the Holy Spirit by asking Him to fill us.

We need the Holy Spirit so that the life of Christ will be seen in us through the fruit of the Spirit. It is because the Holy Spirit controls us that we are filled with love, joy, peace, patience, gentleness, goodness, faith, meekness, and self-control. We also need the Holy Spirit's power in our lives to enable us to witness in such a way that people will be convicted of their sin and convinced that Jesus Christ is the only way to

Heaven. The fruit of the Spirit is never an end in itself, but only a means to the end as we win men and women to Christ, which in turn will bring glory and honor to Him.

If you sincerely desire to be filled with the Holy Spirit, you must confess your sins and then present your body to the Lord, yielding your mind, body , and strength to Him. The Holy Spirit wants to control a clean vessel. He is waiting on you. Are you thirsty? Do you yearn to have Him control your life, using you for His own glory? If you do, you might express your desire in a prayer like this.

> *Dear Father, I need You. I acknowledge that I have been in control of my life, and that as a result, I have sinned against You. Forgive me and wash me clean. I thank You that You have forgiven my sins through Christ's death on the cross for me. I now invite Christ to take control of the throne of my life. Fill me with the Holy Spirit as You commanded me to be filled, and as You promised in Your Word that You wold do if I asked in faith. I pray this in the name of Jesus. As an expression of my faith, I now thank You for taking control of my life and for filling me with the Holy Spirit.*

Asking the Holy Spirit to fill you is an exercise of your faith. (Hebrews 11:6, *"But without faith it is impossible to please Him, for he who comes to God must believe that He is, and that He is a rewarder of those who diligently seek Him.")* You cannot see Him; you may not feel Him; but on the basis of His faithfulness to keep His promises, you believe that He will do as you ask. Since He commanded that you be filled by the Holy Spirit, then you can be assured that He wants to fill you. (I John 5:14-15, *"Now this is the confidence that we have in Him, that if we ask anything according to His will, He hears us. And if we know that He hears us, whatever we ask, we know that we have the petitions that we have asked of Him."*) After asking the Holy Spirit to fill you, thank Him. He has heard your prayer and it is God's will that you give thanks. (I Thessalonians 5:18, *"In everything give thanks; for this is the will of God in Christ Jesus for you.")*

Results of the Spirit-Filled Life

If we remove the obstacles of sin and unbelief in our life and ask Him to fill us, He will. As we continue to live in dependence on the Spirit, walking moment by moment in His power, then we will find that the fruit of the Spirit is exhibited in our lives. (Galatians 5:22-23, *"But the fruit of the Spirit is love, joy, peace, longsuffering, kindness, goodness, faithfulness, gentleness, self-control. Against such there is no law.")* That love, joy, peace, patience, gentleness, goodness, faith, humility, and self-control become the basis for your witness to those around you. This fruitfulness in your relationships and your ministry will bring glory to God.

Another result of the Spirit's filling is that your worship will be richer. The very sentence which begins by contrasting being filled with wine with being filled by the Spirit ends by describing Spirit filled worship. *"Speaking to one another in psalms and hymns and spiritual songs, singing and making melody in your heart to the Lord, giving thanks always for all things to God the Father in the name of our Lord Jesus Christ,"* (Ephesians 5:19-20). It is in this way that the joy of the Lord fills our lives and overflows into the lives of others.

The passage continues by saying that Spirit-filled Christians will submit themselves one to another. (Ephesians 5:21, *"Submitting to one another in the fear of God.")* Submission is often misunderstood. It does not mean that the person who submits is of lesser value or inferior. Submission is simply the way that relationships work, but submission is always voluntary and it is always mutual. Even in the Godhead, the Son submits to the Father, and the Spirit submits to both the Father and the Son. (John 15:26, *"But when the Helper comes, whom I shall send to you from the Father, the Spirit of truth who proceeds from the Father, He will testify of Me"*; John 16:14-16, *"He will glorify Me, for He will take of what is Mine and declare it to you. All things that the Father has are Mine. Therefore I said that He will take of Mine and declare it to you. A little while, and you will not see Me; and again a little while, and you will see Me, because I go to the Father.")* In this passage, submission is described in three different types of relationships — marriage, family, and work — and how that submission is expressed by all the parties in those relationships.

A Spirit-filled wife will submit to her husband. (Ephesians 5:22, *"Wives, submit to* your *own husbands, as to the Lord."*) Her submission will be expressed by her subjection to her husband in the same way that she is subject to Christ. This submission would indicate obedience to her husband and a certain amount of respect for him as the one God has ordained to be the head of her family. On the other side of the coin, the Spirit-filled husband is also commanded to submit to his wife as expressed through his love for her. This is not merely the kind of love that gives flowers and candy. It has to do with providing for her, caring for her, and seeing to it that she gets the spiritual training and leadership she needs.

Spirit-filled children are also told to submit to their parents, which is expressed in obedience to them and giving them honor. (Ephesians 6:1-2, *"Children, obey your parents in the Lord, for this is right. Honor your father and mother, which is the first commandment with promise.")* This submission carries its own reward in that they are promised long life. In other words, their fathers won't have to kill them when they are teenagers. The parents, however, also have to submit to their children by exercising discipline without provoking them to anger.

Spirit-filled workers will be submissive and obedient to their employers because as Christians they are honoring the Lord. (Ephesians 6:5-9, *"Bondservants, be obedient to those who are your masters according to the flesh, with fear and trembling, in sincerity of heart, as to Christ; not with eyeservice, as men-pleasers, but as bondservants of Christ, doing the will of God from the heart, with good will doing service, as to the Lord, and not to men, knowing that whatever good anyone does, he will receive the same from the Lord, whether he is a slave or free. And you, masters, do the same things to them, giving up threatening, knowing that your own Master also is in heaven, and there is no partiality with Him."*) Spirit-filled employees will not just go through the motions, nor will they be men pleasers who suck up to the boss and complain behind his back. They will do good work because they are doing it for the Lord. Likewise, the employers also have an obligation to treat their workers with respect and submit to them in this way. Rather than exercising their authority through threats and anger, the Spirit-filled employer realizes that he is no better than his workers and will inspire them to join him in the task.

When you are filled with the Spirit, do you feel any different? You might; but you might not. There is no one feeling that characterizes the Spirit. The point is that you will act differently. Rather than obeying the lusts of the flesh, you will fulfill the law of the Spirit of Love. Do not depend upon feeling. The promise of God's Word, not our feelings, is our authority. The Christian lives by faith in the trustworthiness of God Himself and His Word. This train diagram illustrates the relationship between fact (God and His Word), faith (our trust in God and His Word) and feeling (the result of our faith and obedience.) (John 14:21, *"He who has My commandments and keeps them, it is he who loves Me. And he who loves Me will be loved by My Father, and I will love him and manifest Myself to him."*)

The train will run with or without the caboose. However, it would be futile to attempt to pull the train by the caboose. In the same way, we as Christians, do not depend upon feelings or emotions, but we place our faith (trust) in the trustworthiness of God and the promise of His Word.

Though you may not be aware of change immediately with the passing of time there should be some evidence of your being filled with the Spirit. Ask yourself these questions now and in the future from time to time:

- Do you have a greater love for Christ?
- Do you have a greater love for God's Word?
- Are you more concerned for those who do not know Christ as Savior?
- Are you experiencing a greater boldness, liberty, and power in witnessing?

- Are you seeing the fruit of the Spirit in your life?
- Is your worship richer, free and uninhibited?
- Are you submitting properly in all of your relationships?

The Spirit-filled life is an obedient and abiding life. It can be experienced daily as you

1. Begin each day by asking God to cleanse your life, according to 1 John 1:9, *"If we confess our sins, He is faithful and just to forgive us our sins and to cleanse us from all unrighteousness."*

2. Present your body to the Holy Spirit according to Romans 12:1, 2 , *"I beseech you therefore, brethren, by the mercies of God,* that you present your *bodies a living sacrifice, holy, acceptable to God, which is your reasonable service. And do not be conformed to this world, but be transformed by the renewing of your mind, that you may prove what is that good and acceptable and perfect will of God,"* and ask Him to keep you filled with His power.

3. Ask the Holy Spirit to lead you to men who are lost. Be sensitive to His leading.

4. Expect others to come to Christ through your witness. Do not quench the Spirit by failing to respond.

5. Rejoice in all things, praising God even in adversity. (1 Thessalonians 5:18, *"In everything give thanks; for this is the will of God in Christ Jesus for you";* Romans 8:28, *"And we know that all things work together for good to those who love God, to those who are the called according to His purpose.")*

Chapter Twelve

A NEW MISSION

— Soulwinning —

Therefore whoever confesses Me before men, him I will also confess before My Father who is in heaven. But whoever denies Me before men, him I will also deny before My Father who is in heaven. Matthew 10:32-33

The thing that will bring the most excitement to a Christian is winning others to Christ. Nothing brings more joy than telling others what Christ has done in your life. I am sure you have unsaved friends and perhaps members of your own family who are not saved. What a joy it is to live a changed life before them and witness to them and see that they too can know the joy-filled life that only Jesus Christ can give. You can start by inviting your friends to attend church with you, where they will hear the Gospel.

"But you shall receive power when the Holy Spirit has come upon you; and you shall be witnesses to Me in Jerusalem, and in all Judea and Samaria, and to the end of the earth" (Acts 1:8).

Introduction

The Meaning of a Witness

What is the greatest thing that has ever happened to you? Isn't the most significant thing that ever happened to you what happened when you put your faith in Jesus Christ? Didn't that start a process of change that revolutionized your whole life? Even if you don't realize it yet, it did. So, what is the greatest kindness that you can show to another human being? If you saw a good movie, you'd tell somebody about it. If you ate at a good restaurant, you'd tell somebody about it. If Jesus saved you from your sin, gave you the power to have victory over sin, and guaranteed you eternal life, why wouldn't you tell somebody about it?

The word ***witness*** in the New Testament does not mean "someone who saw something"; it means "someone who testifies about what he saw." You don't become a witness until you get on the stand in court and start telling what you know. *"Let the redeemed of the LORD say so, whom He has redeemed from the hand of the enemy,"* (Psalm 107:2).

The Motivation for Witnessing

Jesus told us we would be His witnesses and testify about what we saw Him do in our lives. (Mark 16:15, *"And He said to* them, *'Go into all the world and preach the gospel to every creature'";* Matthew 28:19, 20, *"Go therefore and make disciples of all the nations, baptizing them in the name of the Father and of the Son and of the Holy Spirit, teaching them to observe all things that I have commanded you; and lo, I am with you always, even to the end of the age.")* If we love Him, we will obey His command. Obedience is one motivation for witnessing.

Paul indicates another motivation. He says, *"For the love of Christ compels us, because we judge thus: that if* One *died for all, then all died; and He died for all, that those who live should live no longer for themselves, but for Him who died for them and rose again,"* (2 Corinthians 5:14-15). If you understand the kind of love that Christ demonstrated for you, you have to tell someone. We are the ones who are alive because He died in our place. How can we help but tell others? We owe him our lives because He gave us life when we were dead. We can't just live for ourselves. The love that Jesus has shown us controls us.

But if we don't witness, the words of Jesus haunt us: *"For whoever is ashamed of Me and My words, of him the Son of Man will be ashamed when He comes in His own glory, and in His Father's, and of the holy angels,"* (Luke 9:26). What a sight! Jesus comes in glory with the glory of the Father and the angels, but all you bring into the scene is shame because you were afraid of what someone might think! If we eliminate that shame, then the glory of Christ is magnified and not diminished.

Perhaps you don't feel as if witnessing fits your personality or that you are not equipped to do it. Have you ever considered who Jesus chose to start His Church? Four of the twelve disciples were fishermen — no formal education and no seminary degrees. They knew how to steer the boat, throw the net, pull it in, and clean it up. That's all! But Jesus walked by them and called, *"Follow Me, and I will make you fishers of men,"* (Matthew 4:19). They didn't know how to be fishers of men, but they trusted that Christ could take the talents and knowledge they had and *make them become* something greater than they had ever been.

The Message

In 2 Corinthians 5:20, we are called ambassadors for Christ. (*"Now then, we are ambassadors for Christ, as though God were pleading through us: we implore you on Christ's behalf, be reconciled to God.")* An ambassador is one who is appointed to interpret the mind of his ruler to those in a foreign land. He is the representative of his government who stands up for the interests of his kingdom and its citizens. Every ambassador is given a foreign policy statement which contains the message that he is to communicate in the land to which he is assigned.

As a representative of Christ, what would be your message to those who do not know Christ personally? Paul says the message we are assigned is reconciliation.

> *Now all things are of God, who has reconciled us to Himself through Jesus Christ, and has given us the ministry of reconciliation, that is, that God was in Christ reconciling the world to Himself, not imputing their trespasses to them, and has committed to us the word of reconciliation. Now then, we are ambassadors for Christ, as though God were pleading through us: we implore you on Christ's behalf, be reconciled to God.* (2 Corinthians 5:18-20)

Jesus said He came into this world to *"seek and to save that which was lost"* (Luke 19:10). *"For even the Son of Man did not come to be served, but to serve, and to give His life a ransom for many"* (Mark 10:45). If we don't continue to do the seeking and proclaiming of our message of salvation, His purpose is frustrated. As His ambassadors, we need to be pleading with men to be reconciled to God.

Paul expresses the message in its most basic elements in 1 Corinthians 15:3-4, *"For I delivered to you first of all that which I also received: that Christ died for our sins according to the Scriptures, and that He was buried, and that He rose again the third day according to the Scriptures."* Christ's death, burial , and resurrection are the heart of the gospel message. Notice that Paul received this, indicating that it was probably the earliest creed formulated in the early church. He died for our sins. His burial was evidence that He really died and His resurrection promises us eternal life.

Motives For Soulwinning

1. When we win souls, we glorify God.

   "Therefore, whether you eat or drink, or whatever you do, do all to the glory of God." (1 Corinthians 10:31). *"Nevertheless He saved them for His name's sake, that He might make His mighty power known."* (Psalm 106:8).

   When we don't win souls,

- God is being disobeyed. *"And He said to them, 'Go into all the world and preach the gospel to every creature (*Mark 16:15).

- Christ's death is being insulted. *"And I, if I am lifted up from the earth, will draw all peoples to Myself" (*John 12:32).

- The Holy Spirit is being ignored. *"And when He has come, He will convict the world of sin, and of righteousness, and of judgment"* (John 16:8).

2. When we win souls, we rescue sinners from hell.

   *"The wicked shall be turned into hell, and all the nations that forget God," (*Ps. 9:17.*) "Let him know that he who turns a sinner from the error of his way will save a soul from death and cover a multitude of sins,"* (James 5:20). *"Then Death and Hades were cast into the lake of fire. This is the second death. And anyone not found written in the Book of Life was cast into the lake of fire,"* (Revelation 20:14-15).

3. When we win souls, we encourage other Christians.

   "For what is our hope, or joy, or crown of rejoicing? Is it not even you in the presence of our Lord Jesus Christ at His coming?" (1 Thessalonians 2:19). *"I say to you that likewise there will be more joy in heaven over one sinner who repents than over ninety-nine just persons who need no repentance... Likewise, I say to you, there is joy in the presence of the angels of God over one sinner who repents,"* (Luke 15:7, 10). *"The LORD your God in your midst, the Mighty One, will save; he will rejoice over you with gladness, he will quiet you with His love, he will rejoice over you with singing,"* (Zephaniah 3:17).

4. When we win souls, we edify the church.

   "And with many other words he testified and exhorted them, saying,

Be saved from this perverse generation. Then those who gladly received his word were baptized; and that day about three thousand souls were added to them. And they continued steadfastly in the apostles' doctrine and fellowship, in the breaking of bread, and in prayers. Then fear came upon every soul, and many wonders and signs were done through the apostles. Now all who believed were together, and had all things in common, and sold their possessions and goods, and divided them among all, as anyone had need" (Acts 2:40-45).

a. Fellowship - *"So continuing daily with one accord in the temple, and breaking bread from house to house, they ate their food with gladness and simplicity of heart"* (Acts 2:46).

b. Teaching - *"And they continued steadfastly in the apostles' doctrine and fellowship, in the breaking of bread, and in prayers"* (Acts 2:42).

c. Unity - *"So continuing daily with one accord in the temple, and breaking bread from house to house, they ate their food with gladness and simplicity of heart, praising God and having favor with all the people. And the Lord added to the church daily those who were being saved"* (Acts 2:46-47).

d. Numerical Growth - *"Praising God and having favor with all the people. And the Lord added to the church daily those who were being saved"* (Acts 2:47).

e. Charity - *"Now all who believed were together, and had all things in common, and sold their possessions and goods, and divided them among all, as anyone had need"* (Acts 2:44-45).

f. Worship - *"Praising God and having favor with all the people. And the Lord added to the church daily those who were being saved"* (Acts 2:47).

g. Adding to the Kingdom - *"Praising God and having favor with all the people. And the Lord added to the church daily those who were being saved*" (Acts 2:47). *And I also say to you that you are Peter, and on this rock I will build My church, and the gates of Hades shall not prevail against it"* (Matthew 16:18).

5. When we win souls, we hasten the return of Christ.

"For I do not desire, brethren, that you should be ignorant of this mystery, lest you should be wise in your own opinion, that blindness in part has happened to Israel until the fullness of the Gentiles has come in" (Romans 11:25). *"For the Lord Himself will descend from heaven with a shout, with the voice of an archangel, and with the trumpet of God. And the dead in Christ will rise first. Then we who are alive and remain shall be caught up together with them in the clouds to meet the Lord in the air. And thus we shall always be with the Lord. Therefore comfort one another with these words"* (1 Thessalonians 4:16-18).

The Difference in Leading a Soul and Winning a Soul to Christ

1. Helping souls to Christ

   a. By giving out tracts, books, tapes, movies.
   b. By supporting radio, TV, and evangelistic projects.
   c. By supporting missions and missionary projects that are giving out the gospel.

2. Bringing souls to Christ

   a. By getting the sinner into the vicinity or atmosphere of the gospel.
   b. By bringing sinners to church and evangelistic meetings.
   c. By bringing sinners to the fellowship or staging a get-together with some friends or the preacher.

3. Leading souls to Christ

   a. By pointing those who are already convicted to Christ.
   b. By praying with those who come forward to receive Christ during in the invitation.
   c. By giving guidance and Scripture to those who are ready to receive Christ.

4. Winning souls to Christ

   a. By persuading those who are not interested.

      "He who WINS souls is wise" (Proverbs 11:30). *"Knowing, therefore, the terror of the Lord, we PERSUADE men; but we are well known to God, and I also trust are well known in your consciences"* (2 Corinthians 5:11). *"And he (Paul) reasoned in the synagogue every Sabbath, and PERSUADED both Jews and Greeks,"* Acts 18:4. *"Then the master said to the servant, 'Go out into the highways and hedges, and COMPEL them to come in, that my house may be filled'"* (Luke 14:23).

   b. By laboring in intercessory prayer for those who are hardened.

      "For as soon as Zion was in LABOR, she gave birth to her children." Isaiah 66:8. "My little children, for whom I LABOR in birth again until Christ is formed in you" (Galatians 4:19).

Scriptural Reasons Every Christian Should Be a Soulwinner

Sinners are perishing.

"The wicked shall be turned into hell, and all the nations that forget God" (Psalm 9:7). *"And anyone not found written in the Book of Life was cast into the lake of fire"* (Revelation 20:15). *"He who*

believes and is baptized will be saved; but he who does not believe will be condemned" (Mark 16:16). *"He who believes in the Son has everlasting life; and he who does not believe the Son shall not see life, but the wrath of God abides on him"* (John 3:36).

Knowing that people without Christ are heading to hell should motivate us to have compassion and show them the way. Not to attempt to help them to Christ is to be guilty of having no compassion toward the damned. It is the sin of not loving our neighbor as ourselves. If we really believed our lost neighbor was heading to hell we would try to rescue him.

2. Love is constraining us.

"For the love of Christ compels us, because we judge thus: that if One died for all, then all died" (2 Corinthians 5:14). *"A new commandment I give to you, that you love one another; as I have loved you, that you also love one another. By this all will know that you are My disciples, if you have love for one another"* (John 13:34-35). "*Look on my right hand and see, for there is no one who acknowledges me; refuge has failed me; no one cares for my soul"* (Psalm 142:4). *"Those who sow in tears shall reap in joy. He who continually goes forth weeping, bearing seed for sowing, shall doubtless come again with rejoicing, bringing his sheaves with him"* (Psalm 126:5-6).

Anyone who has been saved has the indwelling Christ who is compelling every believer to seek out lost souls. Does it concern you that millions are lost and on the road to hell? I believe any person who is really saved will have a desire to see others saved. The indwelling Christ is constraining and compelling us to go into all the world and preach the gospel to everyone.

This working of the Holy Spirit was so great in the Apostle Paul that he said in Romans 9:3, *"For I could wish that I myself were accursed from Christ for my brethren, my countrymen according to the flesh."* Paul also stated in Acts 20:20 that this constraining force was so great that he *"proclaimed it to you, and taught you publicly and from house to house."*

> *I kept back nothing that was helpful, but proclaimed it to you, and taught you publicly and from house to house, testifying to Jews, and also to Greeks, repentance toward God and faith toward our Lord Jesus Christ. And see, now I go bound in the spirit to Jerusalem, not knowing the things that will happen to me there, except that the Holy Spirit testifies in every city, saying that chains and tribulations await me. But none of these things move me; nor do I count my life dear to myself, so that I may finish my race with joy, and the ministry which I received from the Lord Jesus, to testify to the gospel of the grace of God. And indeed, now I know that you all, among whom I have gone preaching the kingdom of God, will see my face no more. Therefore I testify to you this day that I am innocent of the blood of all men. For I have not shunned to declare to you the whole counsel of God. Therefore watch, and remember that for three years I did not cease to warn everyone night and day with tears (*Acts 20:20-27, 31).

It should be noted that in the New Testament each time a person found Christ, this Spirit of wanting to reach others was evident in his life (Philip, Andrew, Samaritan woman). Therefore, not to be winning souls is to be guilty of the sin of quenching the Spirit who is constraining us to go after the lost.

3. God is commanding us.

"And He said to them, 'Go into all the world and preach the gospel to every creature'" (Mark 16:15). *"However, Jesus did not permit him, but said to him, 'Go home to your friends, and tell them what great things the Lord has done for you, and how He has had compassion on you'"* (Mark 5:19). *"Then the master said to the servant, 'Go out into the highways and hedges, and compel them to come in, that my house may be filled'"* (Luke

14:23). *Then He said to them, 'Follow Me, and I will make you fishers of men'"* (Matthew 4:19). *"But you shall receive power when the Holy Spirit has come upon you; and you shall be witnesses to Me in Jerusalem, and in all Judea and Samaria, and to the end of the earth"* (Acts 1:8).

This is God's clear-cut command to every believer to be a soul-winner. Therefore, not to be winning souls is to be guilty of the sin of disobedience of His command.

4. Our position is urging us.

2 Corinthians 5:20, *"Now then, we are ambassadors for Christ, as though God were pleading through us." "Now all things are of God, who has reconciled us to Himself through Jesus Christ, and has given us the ministry of reconciliation"* (2 Corinthians 5:18).

An ambassador is a representative of another. He is an agent or spokesman who has a definite responsibility of speaking for another. This is our position. We are to speak for Christ and in behalf of Christ.

Luke 24:47-48, *"And that repentance and remission of sins should be preached in His name to all nations, beginning at Jerusalem, and you are witnesses of these things."*

The witness is under obligation to tell what he knows. If we know that Christ died for sinners and have experienced Him in our own life, we are responsible to witness this reality to others. We are representing Him. Therefore, not to be winning souls is to be guilty of not fulfilling the ministry God has called us to do.

5. Responsibility is pressing us

Romans 1:14, *"I am a debtor both to Greeks and to barbarians, both to wise and to unwise."* Ezekiel 33:8, *"Let him know that he who turns a sinner from the error of his way will save a soul from death and cover a multitude of sins."* James 5:20, *"Let him know that he who turns a sinner from the error of his way will save a soul from death and cover a multitude of sins." "But none of these things move me; nor do I count my life dear to myself, so that I may finish my race with joy, and the ministry which I received from the Lord Jesus, to testify to the gospel of the grace of God. Therefore I testify to you this day that I am innocent of the blood of all men. For I have not shunned to declare to you the whole counsel of God"* (Acts 20:24,26-27).

We ARE responsible for the lost around us. We ARE our brother's keeper. Paul says, "I am debtor" which means we have a debt (a duty, an obligation) to all classes of people to give them the gospel of Christ. God warns that if we fail to give them the message He will require their blood at our hand. We will answer for it at the judgment.

Therefore, not to be winning souls and carrying out our obligation of sharing the gospel is to be guilty of sending people to hell. Many would be spared from hell if we would only speak out and win them to Christ.

6. The field is calling us.

John 4:35, *"Do you not say, 'There are still four months and then comes the harvest'? Behold, I say to you, lift up your eyes and look at the fields, for they are already white for harvest!"* (Matthew 9:37), *"Then He said to His disciples, 'The harvest truly is plentiful, but the laborers are few.'"*

Yes, the field is calling us to do soulwinning because so many are lost. There are 6 billion people on the earth today and very few of them know the Savior. According to the Interdenominational Foreign Mission Association report, there are 320,000 births every 24 hours and 160,000 deaths every 24 hours. This means a 62 million increase every year. Something like 2 million people are reached with the Gospel each year - only about 1 in 30 - of the world's population increase.

There are approximately 3 million villages in the world without a resident gospel witness. More than half the people in the world do not know the way of salvation. The Bible still waits to be translated into more than 1,500 languages and dialects. At the present rate of progress this would take at least 150 years.

Think of it. 170,000 people die every day on our earth. That is 7,000 per hour or 120 each minute. Probably 90% of these do not know Christ as their Savior. Certainly the field is calling us to win souls. We may say, therefore, not to win souls is to be guilty of indifference. It is being at ease in Zion.

7. Jesus has chosen us.

John 15:8, *"By this My Father is glorified, that you bear much fruit; so you will be My disciples."* John 15:16, *"You did not choose Me, but I CHOSE YOU and appointed you that you should go and bear fruit, and that your fruit should remain, that whatever you ask the Father in My name He may give you."*

Jesus is counting on us to be productive. The fruit spoken of here is referring to other souls won. We understand that a fruitful pear tree is one producing a lot of pears. Likewise a fruitful Christian is one who is producing other Christians.

Do not confuse the **Fruit of the Spirit** with the **Fruit of a Christian**. The former is explained in Galatians 5:22, as being *"love, joy, peace, longsuffering, kindness, goodness, faithfulness,"* which are the nature or attributes of Christ being manifest in us. The fruit of a Christian involves GOING. There is a "Going out" which compares with the "Go" in Psalm 126:6, *"He who continually GOES forth weeping, bearing seed for sowing, shall doubtless come again with rejoicing, bringing his sheaves with him,"* and the "Go" in Luke 14:23, *"Go out into the highways and hedges, and compel them to come in, that my house may be filled."* Notice that Jesus is not only concerned about QUALITY, but also QUANTITY. In John 15:2, *"Every branch in Me that does not bear fruit He takes away; and every branch that* *bears fruit He prunes, that it may bear more fruit,"* He speaks of bringing forth more fruit; and in John 15:5, *"I am the vine, you are the branches. He who abides in Me, and I in him, bears much fruit; for without Me you can do nothing,"* He encourages us to bring forth much fruit. Therefore, not to be winning souls is to be guilty of the sin of lack of love for Jesus who has chosen us to bear fruit.

8. Our salvation experience is compelling us.
2 Corinthians 5:17-18, *"Therefore, if anyone is in Christ, he is a new creation; old things have passed away; behold, all things have become new. Now all things are of God, who has reconciled us to Himself through Jesus Christ, and has given us the ministry of reconciliation."*

A light on a hill cannot be hid and neither can a soul be silent that has experienced the saving grace of God. **Andrew** had to find Peter and tell him. **Philip** had to go tell his brother Nathaniel. The **Samaritan woman** had to tell the whole city. **Paul** could not keep quiet about it. Dear friend, if you really have met Jesus, you will have to tell someone about it. You will have the "can't hep its." *"For we cannot but speak the things which we have seen and heard"* (Acts 4:20).

Romans 1:16, *"For I am not ashamed of the gospel of Christ, for it is the power of God to salvation for everyone who believes."*

The word ***gospel*** means **good news**. It is the good news of salvation from sin through the death, burial, and resurrection of Christ. The Gospel is the "Balm in Gilead." It is the "remedy for the snake bite"; "the cure for sin's cancer"; it is "man's only hope." A lost, sin-sick, hell-bound world must have this message to be saved.

9. Hell is crying out to us.

Luke 16:27, "*Then he said, 'I beg you therefore, father, that you would send him to my father's house.'*" Jude 23, *"But others save with fear, pulling them out of the fire, hating even the garment defiled by the flesh."*

Yes, think about it! Poor, lost, doomed souls in hell are crying and begging us to warn their loved ones not to come there. There is no hope for them, but there might be a little satisfaction in their knowing that a loved one will not follow them to hell.

10. Heaven is encouraging us.

Luke 15:10, *"Likewise, I say to you, there is joy in the presence of the angels of God over one sinner who repents."* Luke 15:7, *"I say to you that likewise there will be more joy in heaven over one sinner who repents than over ninety-nine just persons who need no repentance." "You will show me the path of life; in Your presence is fullness of joy; at Your right hand are pleasures forevermore"* (Psalm 16:11).

A camp meeting breaks out in heaven every time a sinner is won to the Savior. Can you imagine how anxious the saints in heaven, the angels, and even Jesus are for us to win souls? Rejoicing and shouting is taking place among the residents in heaven.

11. Wisdom is compelling us

Proverbs 11:30, *"The fruit of the righteous is a tree of life, and he who wins souls is wise."* Daniel 12:3, *"Those who are wise shall shine like the brightness of the firmament, and those who turn many to righteousness like the stars forever and ever."*

It is a wise and profitable thing to be a soulwinner because the ministry of soulwinning is esteemed so highly in God's evaluation table. It is the dearest thing to the heart of God. Consequently, it pays enormous eternal dividends. A man who turns people to righteousness is wise because he is laying up treasure in heaven. A Christian who is occupied with trivial matters is unwise. Majoring on the minors is foolish.

12. Jesus set the example for us.

Luke 19:10, *"For the Son of Man has come to seek and to save that which was lost."* Luke 4:18, *"The Spirit of the Lord is upon Me, because He has anointed Me to preach the gospel to the poor; he has sent Me to heal the brokenhearted, to proclaim liberty to the captives and recovery of sight to the blind, to set at liberty those who are oppressed."* Mark 2:14, *"As He passed by, He saw Levi the son of Alphaeus sitting at the tax office. And He said to him, 'Follow Me.' So he arose and followed Him."* John 4:4, *"But He needed to go through Samaria,"* (to win the Samaritan woman). Matthew 9:36, *"But when He saw the multitudes, He was moved with compassion for them."*

Jesus, our divine example, led the way in soulwinning. Saving souls was his primary reason for coming to the earth. He was not one who spent his time in his office but was constantly on the field. Soulwinning was the heartthrob of Jesus and should be our heartthrob too.

13. Paul demonstrated it for us.

Acts 20:20-21, *"How I kept back nothing that was helpful, but proclaimed it to you, and taught you publicly and from house to house."* Acts 20:26, 31, *"Therefore I testify to you this day that I am innocent of the blood of all men. Therefore watch, and remember that for three years I did not cease to warn everyone night and day with tears."* 1 Corinthians 2:2, *"For I determined not to know anything among you except Jesus Christ and Him crucified."* 1 Corinthians 3:6, 9, *"I planted, Apollos watered, but God gave the increase. So then neither he who plants is anything, nor he who waters, but God who gives the increase. Now he who plants and he who waters are one, and each one will receive his own reward according to his own labor. For we are God's fellow workers; you are God's field, you are God's building."* 1 Corinthians 9:22, *To the weak I became as weak, that I might win the weak. I have become all things to all men, that I might by all means save some."* Romans 9:2-3, *"That I have great sorrow and continual grief in my heart. For I could wish that I myself were accursed from Christ for my brethren, my countrymen according to the flesh."*

Paul, our human example, demonstrated how Christians should go after the lost. He had a passion for souls. He was going from house to house day and night warning them. Paul talked to everybody he met. He believed that men are lost, he loved them, and he tried to win them. The apostle Paul demonstrated that soulwinning is to be done personally and from house to house.

14. The early Church adopted it.

John 1:45, *"Philip found Nathanael and said to him, 'We have found Him of whom Moses in the law, and also the prophets, wrote— Jesus of Nazareth, the son of Joseph.'"* Romans 8:30, *"Moreover whom He predestined, these He also called; whom He called, these He also justified; and whom He justified, these He also glorified."* John 1:41, *"He first found his own brother Simon, and said to him, 'We have found the Messiah' (which is translated, the Christ)."* John 4:28, *"The woman then left her waterpot, went her way into the city, and said to the men."* Acts 5:42, *"And daily in the temple, and in every house, they did not cease teaching and preaching Jesus as the Christ."* Acts 8:4, *"Therefore those who were scattered went everywhere preaching the word."*

Yes, this was the spirit of the early church, witnessing and preaching the gospel to everyone. Every circumstance became an opportunity to tell the gospel. Persecution was added fuel to their soulwinning fire. They had a message and gave it. They adopted soulwinning as their way of life. Consequently, they were in a continual revival with souls being added to the church daily. May God help us to adopt soulwinning as the theme of our church activities.

The Four Stages of Becoming A Soulwinner

As I look back over my life, it seems that becoming a soulwinner was a gradual and progressive experience. I went through various stages first. I will liken it to a butterfly going through the egg, caterpillar, and cocoon stages before becoming a fully developed butterfly.

1. The egg stage - by example

   The example stage involves living the life before them. We are told in the Scriptures, *"Let no one despise your youth, but be an example to the believers in word, in conduct, in love, in spirit, in faith, in purity"* (1 Timothy 4:12); and in Matthew 5:16, *"Let your light so shine before men, that they may see your good works and glorify your Father in heaven."* 2 Corinthians 3:2, *"You are our epistle written in our hearts, known and read by all men."*

2. The caterpillar stage - passive witnessing

   Later, after becoming an example, I decided to pass out gospel tracts and invite people to church. I went to street corners, pool halls, and Burger King's and McDonald's to give out tracts. However, that was as far as it went. Praise God for gospel tracts, for surely many have been saved through them. However, a lot of people will not read a tract, or perhaps, can't read, therefore, we cannot stop with just giving out tracts. We must go farther still.

3. The cocoon stage - active witnessing

   At this point I began to give my testimony and witness to the sinner as I passed out tracts. I would tell of God's love for us and what Christ had done on the cross. I would explain how Christ changed my life. Very often I would see the conviction of the Holy Spirit come upon the person, but that was as far as I could go. I would walk away saying, "I hope you accept Christ as your Savior some day."

4. The butterfly stage - persuading

   This is getting the soul across the line for Christ. I am not referring to tricking him into a profession of faith or roping someone into church. I do not mean to confuse a soul into having an emotional experience. I am talking about letting the Holy Spirit work through our lives in the capacity of presenting the gospel of Christ and then persuading the person to step out by faith and receive Christ as Savior then and there.

2 Corinthians 5:11, *"Knowing, therefore, the terror of the Lord, we* ***PERSUADE*** *men."* Acts 18:4, *"And he* (Paul) *reasoned in the synagogue every Sabbath, and* ***PERSUADED*** *both Jews and Greeks."* Proverbs 11:30, *"The fruit of the righteous is a tree of life, and he who* ***WINS*** *souls is wise."* Luke 14:23, *"Then the master said to the servant, 'Go out into the highways and hedges, and* ***COMPEL*** *them to come in, that my house may be filled."*

Three Reasons Many Spiritual Christians Are Not Winning Souls

1. Spiritual Christians often are not going after lost souls.

Psalm 126:6, *"He who continually GOES FORTH weeping, bearing seed for sowing, shall doubtless come again with rejoicing, bringing his sheaves with him."* Mark 16:15, *"GO into all the world and preach the gospel to every creature."* Acts 20:20, *"And from HOUSE TO HOUSE..."* Matthew 4:19, *"Follow Me, and I will make you FISHERS OF MEN."*

Nowhere in the Bible does God tell the sinner to go to church. Instead, He tells the church to go to the sinner. Many spiritual Christians could be winning souls to Christ every week if they would heed the GO of soulwinning. It is a matter of discipline. The Apostle Paul confessed, *"I keep under my body that I might bring it into subjection"* (1 Corinthians 9:27). The devil will seek to hinder you by distractions, company, business and many other ways. He does not want you to engage in this all-important work. Therefore, you MUST resolve in your heart to give certain hours per week to the task of contacting the lost. You must go where they are. You must seek them. They will not come to us except on rare occasions.

You say, "But I do go out on visitation, yet I never seem to win anyone to Christ. What is wrong in my life?"

2. Going Christians often are not presenting Christ.

If we are going to get people saved, we must talk to them about Jesus and about being saved. We must give them the gospel of Christ. We must talk to them about being born-again, about accepting Jesus in their hearts.

In our visitation we often talk about the weather, current events, or even religion and the church. We must get down to business and pinpoint the matter of receiving Christ as Savior. The Gospel must be imparted to the sinner if the Holy Spirit is to perform His ministry of wooing him to Christ.

Romans 1:16, *"For I am not ashamed of the GOSPEL OF CHRIST, for it is the power of God to salvation for everyone who believes..."* 1 Corinthians 2:2 *"For I determined not to know anything among you except Jesus Christ and Him crucified."* Acts 8:35, *"Then Philip opened his mouth, and beginning at this Scripture, preached JESUS to him."* John 12:32, *"IF I AM LIFTED UP from the earth, will draw all peoples to Myself."*

Soulwinning is bringing the sinner and Christ together. We must talk about Jesus. Philip preached Jesus to the eunuch and got him saved. Paul was determined to stick to the subject of Jesus, and he won a multitude to Christ. If we start telling the story of Jesus' dying on the cross, the Holy Spirit will begin convicting and saving. So the next time you are out on visitation exalt the Lord Jesus Christ.

You say, "But I have been telling the sinner about Jesus, yet I am still not getting them saved. What is wrong?"

3. Witnessing Christians often are not inviting the person to make a decision

It is not enough to present Christ to the sinner. We must also give an invitation for him to receive Christ as his Savior then and there. We must persuade him to make a decision. We must lead him to take that step of faith and settle it now. We must help get the prospect across the line to Christ by encouraging him to release his faith. Salvation comes when a sinner, who realizes he is lost, exercises faith in Christ.

A lot of people stop short of winning souls because they don't now how to draw the net (give an invitation). I have left seeking souls who really wanted to be saved because I could not draw the net. They were convicted and ready, but I could not lead them to step out by faith and receive Christ there on the spot. When I learned to draw the net, it revolutionized my life and ministry. I began to win souls to Christ.

The following Scriptures indicate that there is more to soulwinning than just giving a straightlaced witness and "leaving it all in the Lord's hands."

2 Corinthians 5:11, *"Knowing, therefore, the terror of the Lord, we PERSUADE men..."* Acts 18:4, *"And he* (Paul) *reasoned in the synagogue every Sabbath, and PERSUADED both Jews and Greeks."* Acts 26:28, *"Then Agrippa said to Paul, 'You almost PERSUADE me to become a Christian.'"* Acts 18:13, *"They got an indictment against Paul saying, 'This fellow PERSUADES men to worship God contrary to the law.'"* Acts 19:26, *"Paul has PERSUADED and turned away many people, saying that they are not gods which are made with hands."* Luke 14:23, *"Then the master said to the servant, 'Go out into the highways and hedges, and compel them to come in, that my house may be filled.'"*

Start giving an invitation after you present the gospel of Christ. You will be surprised to find that some will accept Him there on the spot.

Man's Responsibility in Contrast to the Holy Spirit's Responsibility

1 Corinthians 3:9: *"For we are God's fellow workers."*

What a thought - that God would stoop low enough to use men in His work of reconciliation! Could not the Sovereign One have filled men with the Holy Spirit before birth, as with John the Baptist? Could He not with light smite Paul to the earth? God, who humbles Himself to behold the things done in Heaven, makes a believer into the meet vessel.

"Who humbles Himself to behold the things that are in the heavens and in the earth?" (Psalm 113:6). *"Therefore if anyone cleanses himself from the latter, he will be a vessel for honor, sanctified and useful for the Master, prepared for every good work"* (2 Timothy 2:21).

God uses men to farm His husbandry (1 Corinthians 3:9, *"For we are God's fellow workers; you are God's field, you are God's building"*) and to find new stones for His building, to enlist new soldiers, to find lost sheep, to pick His vineyard. He does the work they cannot do - giving rain on the farm, shaping the new stones, clothing the soldiers, calling the sheep, ripening the grapes. What a joy to roll the stone from the door before our Lord says, "Come forth!"

The Holy Spirit does not perform his work of convicting, wooing and performing the new birth until we do our part of giving out the gospel. We are co-laborers in the ministry of soulwinning. Confusion here concerning our separate responsibilities is to court disaster and fruitlessness. IN GOD'S ECONOMY OF REACHING SOULS FOR CHRIST, THERE ARE THREE INSTRUMENTS INVOLVED.

1. The instrument of the Gospel – (the seed)

    a. It is the message of Christ's death, burial, and resurrection.
    b. It is the truth of God's love in giving His Son to die for us.
    c. It is the light of redemption through His shed blood.
    d. It is the knowledge of His substitutionary death for us.

    1 Corinthians 15:1-4, *"Moreover, brethren, I declare to*

you the gospel which I preached to you, which also you received and in which you stand. For I delivered to you first of all that which I also received: that Christ died for our sins according to the Scriptures, and that He was buried, and that He rose again the third day according to the Scriptures." 1 Corinthians 4:15, *"I have begotten you through the gospel."* Romans 1:16, *"For I am not ashamed of the gospel of Christ, for it is the power of God to salvation for everyone who believes, for the Jew first and also for the Greek."*

2. The instrument of the Holy Spirit.

   a. He convicts the sinner, making real his lost condition.
   b. He draws the sinner to Christ.
   c. He seals Christ to their heart as Savior.
   d. He gives the new birth.

   John 16:8, *"HE WILL CONVICT the world of sin, and of righteousness, and of judgment."* John 3:5, *"Jesus answered, 'Most assuredly, I say to you, unless one is born of water and the Spirit, he cannot enter the kingdom of God.'"* John 12:32, *"And I, if I am lifted up from the earth, will draw all peoples to Myself."* 1 Corinthians 2:4, *"And my speech and my preaching were not with persuasive words of human wisdom, but in DEMONSTRATION OF THE SPIRIT..."* 1 Thessalonians 1:5, *"For our gospel did not come to you in word only, but also IN POWER, AND IN THE HOLY SPIRIT."*

3. The human instrument of the Believer (the carriers)

   a. We are the messengers of the Gospel.
   b. We are the vessels that God works through.
   c. We are ambassadors of Christ.

   1 Corinthians 3:9, *"For WE ARE GOD'S FELLOW WORKERS..."* Matthew 28:19, *"GO THEREFORE and*

make disciples of all the nations, baptizing them..." Luke 24:48, *"And YOU ARE WITNESSES of these things."* Romans 1:14-15, *"I am a debtor....so, as much as is in me, I am ready to PREACH THE GOSPEL to you who are in Rome also."* Acts 20:20, *"...From house to house (TESTI-FYING)."* Romans 10:14, *"How then shall they call on Him in whom they have not believed? And how shall they believe in Him of whom they have not heard? And how shall they hear without a PREACHER?"*

d. We are the instrument carrying the seed (gospel) and are referred to as preachers, witnesses, fishermen, ambassadors, messengers, soulwinners, and teachers. The Holy Spirit brings His work of convicting and drawing AFTER we have given the seed. If this were not the case, we could say the Holy Spirit is lagging when souls are being saved. But the truth is we must initiate the soulwinning effort by sowing or watering the seed. Then the Holy Spirit accompanies the seed, convicting the sinner and drawing him to Christ.

e. When souls are not being saved in our churches, it is not the Holy Spirit's fault, nor is it the gospel's fault, nor is it always the sinner's fault. Most of the time it is OUR fault for not carrying out our responsibility for sowing the seed.

Consider the Holy Spirit's Response to the Believers Meeting His Responsibility.

WHEN WE DO THIS	**THE HOLY SPIRIT DOES THIS**
We sow the seed	.He impregnates the heart
We water the seed	.He gives life to it
We fertilize the seed	.He causes it to grow
We dig around	.He prunes it
We weep	.He ripens it
We go	.He accompanies
We tell the story	.He brings conviction

We lift up Jesus	.He reveals Him to their heart
We declare the Good News	.He draws
We plead	.He woos
We pray	.He empowers
We draw the net or give an invitation	.He performs the spiritual birth

Mental Attitudes That Defeat Us in Soulwinning

> *"Casting down arguments and every high thing that exalts itself against the knowledge of God, bringing every thought into captivity to the obedience of Christ"* (2 Corinthians 10:5).

There are certain attitudes which must be acquired if we are to be successful in soulwinning. Our success depends upon our attitude. We need to think right before we can become consistent soulwinners.

These correct attitudes make the difference between being "duty driven" or "love impelled." A person's attitude determines his manner of thinking, feeling, and acting. Wrong attitudes will defeat and discourage you in the work of soulwinning.

1. The attitude of feeling incompetent

   "I can do all things through Christ who strengthens me" (Philippians 4:13). Many Christians take this pessimistic attitude of feeling inadequate because of a lack of education or talent or training. They feel unable to witness for Christ, not to mention giving an invitation to a sinner. Their pet phrases are, "I can't," "I don't know how," "I'm too ignorant," "I'm scared." Now it is true that we are incompetent in ourselves but remember that Jesus lives within us, and we can do all things through Christ who strengthens us. These attitudes are the voice of Satan to keep us from going out and bearing fruit for Christ.

2. The attitude of not feeling led to go

   And He said to them, 'Go into all the world and preach the gospel to every creature'" (Mark 16:*15). "Go therefore and make disciples of all the nations, baptizing them in the name of the Father and of the Son and of the Holy Spirit, teaching them to observe all things that I have commanded you; and lo, I am with you always, even to the end of the age. Amen"* (Matthew 28:19-20).

There are many who are sitting down waiting for God to give them some kind of feeling whereby they will know that He wants them to win souls. This nation is very foolish because God has already commanded us in His Word to go into all the world and preach the gospel to every creature. "Feeling" should not even enter the picture since His explicit command is "Go." Other areas of our life are not monopolized by "feeling led." We go to work whether we feel led or not. We brush our teeth whether we feel led or not. We pay our bills whether we feel led or not. Why should we relegate God's great command to win souls to our "feeling led"? It is ridiculous. It is warped thinking.

3. The attitude that soulwinning is a talent

"But you shall receive power when the Holy Spirit has come upon you; and you shall be witnesses to Me in Jerusalem, and in all Judea and Samaria, and to the end of the earth" (Acts 1:8).

"I'm not gifted with gab" is the cry from this group. Their attitude is that soulwinning is only for certain ones who have the talent or gift. "This is not my calling," they say. Soulwinning is not a talent! It is not a gift of gab! It is not a calling to certain ones! Soulwinning is the command of God to every believer.

4. The attitude that soulwinning is hard and gruesome

"For this is the love of God, that we keep His commandments. And His commandments are not burdensome" (1 John 5:3).

Soulwinning is only hard and gruesome when we make it that way. Dr. R. G. Lee said, "Look on soulwinning as a business, not an incidental matter; as work, not play; as time well spent, not wasted; as a privilege, not a boresome duty." A psychologist in California gave an arithmetic test to two classrooms of the same mentality and age level. To one class he said the test would be extremely hard, while to the other class he stated the test would be very easy. The class who approached the test with the attitude that it would be easy made far better grades than the class who approached it thinking it would be hard.

5. The attitude that it is no use trying to win them unless they are drawn

Some teach that God must initiate soulwinning with a personal invitation to the sinner, otherwise all our efforts are futile. They make much of the Scripture, *"No man can come to me, except the Father draw him,"* John 6:44. They fail to realize that God has already initiated a personal invitation to every sinner in giving His Son to die on the cross and extending a "whosoever will may come" to the entire human race.

The Holy Spirit does the drawing. We turn the switch on. The Holy Spirit will draw any man that we will give the gospel to. As we lift up Christ, He begins drawing him. The Holy Spirit accompanies the gospel. It is our privilege to turn on the drawing power by proclaiming the gospel. While we are waiting for the Holy Spirit to start drawing the sinner, He is at the same time waiting for us to give the sinner the gospel so that He can start drawing. His drawing follows our giving out the gospel.

6. The attitude that a sinner must have an emotional experience.

It is nice to see a person cry or shout when accepting Christ; however, crying and shouting are not the criteria of a genuine conversion. We do not want to become warped with Satan's lie that unless there is an obvious emotional experience the sinner was not saved. People are different in their personalities and emotions. Some are more expressive than others.

If a person believes from the heart in Jesus Christ and confesses Him to be his Lord, we have no right to doubt their salvation until they disprove it by their fruit. We are to preach Christ to them and extend an invitation to receive Him by faith, not by feeling. After this, it is entirely between the person and the Holy Spirit.

7. The attitude that you should only deal with prepared hearts

"Oh, I believe in soulwinning, but I don't think you should just go out and talk to anyone. I think you should let God direct you to prepared hearts that are convicted and ready." This attitude reflects inner selfishness. Who wouldn't like to deal only with those who are ready, ripe, and convicted? How nice that would be.

Did it ever occur to you why these "prepared hearts" became prepared? It was because someone was willing to go to them before they were prepared and give them the gospel. Someone was willing to break the fallow ground, sow the seed, take the cursing, endure the insults, and have a door slammed in his face before that heart was prepared in order that it might become prepared.

Fears That Stop Most Christians from Soulwinning

Of all the many fears and excuses that Christians use for not winning souls, these are what I believe to be the four big ones. In one sense, these four fears are legitimate fears. For this reason, we will give a possible solution to counteract them.

1. The fear of offending the sinner

This is the fear that if we approach a sinner in an attempt to win him we may "bungle the job" and offend him thus driving him further away. Many times Christians are honest in this fear because they lack knowledge or have personality problems.

How to Cope with Arousing Resentment in the Sinner.
The solution for this fear is to learn and practice the principles of making people like you. Here are ten ways that anybody can make people like them:

a. Become genuinely interested in the person, have feeling for him.
b. Be friendly. (Proverbs 18:24, *"A man who has friends must himself be friendly, but there is a friend who sticks closer than a brother."*)
c. Smile.
d. Be a good listener and let him talk freely at first.
e. Talk in terms of his interests (his job, family, home, hobbies. etc.).
f. Be complimentary. Show sincere appreciation. Brag on something.
g. Make him feel important and do it correctly.
h. Use his name often and pronounce it correctly.
i. Be understanding and try to see things from his point of view.
j. Don't rush him; lead gently.

2. The fear of making the spiritual approach

This is the fear of beginning the spiritual conversation. You can talk about things in general, but when it comes to making the transition, you freeze. You seem to be at a loss when it comes to bringing up the subject of salvation. You find yourself plagued with fear when attempting to ask them about their personal relationship with Christ. You have no difficulty talking about current events - but changing the conversation to the spiritual is frightening. Is this the case with you? One solution for this fear is to master some fixed approach questions.

How to Cope with Making the Spiritual Approach.
The solution for this fear is to have your approach questions mastered. Here are some good approach questions to lead into the spiritual conversation.

a. "If you were to die today, are you really sure that you would go to heaven?"
b. "Have you accepted the Lord Jesus Christ as your personal Savior?"

c. "Have you received Christ as your Savior and been baptized?

d. "If you were to die right now, are you one hundred percent sure that you would go to heaven?"

e. The gradual approach questions given by Gene Edwards.

f. The strategy of the gradual approach questions is to draw the prospect out by letting him talk as much as possible. Ask the question and be silent. When he finishes, go to the next question. Do not correct him or disagree with him at any time. Your aim is to listen to him during the first six questions and hope he will listen to you after the seventh.

1. "Do you ever give much thought to spiritual things?"
2. "What would you say is a person's greatest spiritual need?"
3. "Have you heard of the four spiritual laws?"
4. "Has there ever been a time in your life when you seriously considered your need of eternal life?"
5. "In your opinion, what would you say a person must do to inherit eternal life and go to heaven?"
6. "What I really had in mind was, 'How does one go about receiving the experience of salvation?'"
7. "Could we look at a few verses of Scripture and see just what God says about this matter?"

g. "My friend, can you tell me the way to heaven?"

h. "Do you have eternal life?"

i. "Have you ever noticed how up-to-date and even ahead-of-the-times the Bible is, though it was written long ago?"

j. "Do you know that if you are born once, you will die twice, whereas if you are born twice, you will die only once?" (John 3:3, *"Jesus answered and said to him, 'Most assuredly, I say to you, unless one is born again, he cannot see the kingdom of God.'"* Revelation 20:6,14, *"Blessed and holy is he who has part in the first resurrection. Over such the second death has no power, but they shall be priests of God and of Christ, and shall reign with Him a thousand years. Then Death and Hades were cast into the lake of fire. This is the second death.")*

k. "My friend, would you be kind enough to tell me what you think this verse means?"

NOTE: Following the approach question, you will want to get their permission to read from God's Word (Romans Road). This may be done by asking two additional questions, such as: (1) Would you like to be one hundred percent sure of going to heaven? and (2) If I could show you in the Bible how you can be one hundred percent sure, would you believe it?

3. The fear of not knowing how to present the Gospel.

At this point, the Christian is afraid he cannot show the prospect from the Bible how to be saved. Although he knows that the sinner must believe in Christ, he does not know how to lead him step by step into this relationship. He does not know where to begin in the Scriptures. He is not familiar with the things a sinner should know in order to he saved. The solution for counteracting this fear lies in mastering a presentation of the gospel.

How to Cope with Not Knowing How to Present Christ.
The solution for this fear is to decide what the soulwinner's message really is and then develop a plan of presenting it.

I fully realize that salvation is not a plan, but a Person. However, there must be a way of introducing this person. You might say, "Jim, I want you to meet my friend Jesus. Jesus, this is Jim," except for the fact that getting saved is more than just a casual acquaintance. It involves committing one's life and destiny into the hands of that person. It involves making a break with sin. It involves taking Christ as Lord as well as Savior and friend. It must be clearly understood that human merit has no part in it, that salvation is all of grace.

Not only must one know what the message for the sinner is, but one should also develop a simple presentation of it. We should know the proper Scriptures to use. You would not read just any passage in the Bible if you were endeavoring to show a person the truth on tithing, would you? No, you would turn to those certain Scriptures pertaining to tithing. Likewise, there are certain Scripture passages to use in pointing a sinner to accept Christ as his Savior. There is a simple presentation of the gospel called the "Roman Road" that many soulwinners use. It is called the Roman Road because you convey the four basic points of the soulwinning message from the book of Romans.

The Roman Road shows the person the fact that he is a sinner. (Romans 3:10-12, 23, *As it is written: "There is none righteous, no, not one; There is none who understands; there is none who seeks after God. They have all turned aside; they have together become unprofitable; there is none who does good, no, not one, for all have sinned and fall short of the glory of God, and God's judgment for sin.")* (Romans 6:23, "*For the wages of sin is death, but the gift of God is eternal life in Christ Jesus our Lord.")* Then it leads him to understand that Christ died for our sins (Romans 5:8, "*But God demonstrates His own love toward us, in that while we were still sinners, Christ died for us")* and that we can receive salvation by accepting Christ by faith. (Romans 10:9-10, 13, "*That if you confess with your mouth the Lord Jesus and believe in your heart that God has raised Him from the dead, you will be saved. For with the heart one believes unto righteousness, and with the mouth confession is made unto salvation. For whoever calls on the name of the Lord shall be saved.")* We will study this presentation in more detail later, but Romans is only one book in which we might lead a person through such a presentation of the Gospel.

Other books of the Bible to lead a soul to Christ:

	John Road	**Hebrews Road**	**Revelation Road**	**1 John Road**	**Isaiah Road**
Fact of Sinnership	3:18	10:26	21:8	1:8	53:6
Judgment for Sin	3:36	10:27-31	21:8	5:16	53:12
Christ Died for Our Sin	3:16	10:10-12	5:12	4:9	53:4-10
Accept Christ By Faith	1:12	11:1	3:20	4:15	55:6-7

4. The fear of not knowing how to draw the net or give an invitation

Here the Christian is afraid that, after presenting Christ to the sinner, he cannot lead him to make the decision of accepting Him NOW. It is the fear of asking the prospect to exercise his faith now and call upon the Lord. The tendency is to call the preacher for help or walk away saying, "I hope you will come to church Sunday and get it settled." The solution to this fear is to learn to give an invitation each time you present the gospel.

The Soulwinner's Message

The sinner must know certain things in order to be saved. Regardless of how sincere and fervent he may be, if he does not have the knowledge of certain facts about Christ and about himself, he cannot be saved. There are some things the sinner must realize. In the tenth chapter of Acts, there is an account of a very religious man by the name of Cornelius. He was very devout and deeply sincere but still lost. (Acts 11:14, *"Who will tell you words by which you and all your household will be saved.")* He was lost because he was without the knowledge of certain facts. He had to hear something. (Romans 10:17, *"So then faith comes by hearing, and hearing by the word of God.")*

1. The sinner must know that he is lost.

Romans 3:10, *"As it is written: 'There is none righteous, no, not one'"*; Romans 3:23, *"For all have sinned and fall short of the glory of God";* 1 John 1:8, *"If we say that we have no sin, we deceive ourselves, and the truth is not in us";* Isaiah 64:6, *"But we are all like an unclean thing, and all our righteousnesses are like filthy rags; we all fade as a leaf, and our iniquities, like the wind, have taken us away"*; Ecclesiastes 7:20, *"For there is not a just man on earth who does good and does not sin"*; Romans 5:12, *"Therefore, just as through one man sin entered the world, and death through sin, and thus death spread to all men, because all sinned."*

2. The sinner must know that he is under the wrath of God because of his sin, and that the price on sin is judgement and hell.

   Romans 6:23, "*For the wages of sin is death, but the gift of God is eternal life in Christ Jesus our Lord";* Revelation 20:14, "*Then Death and Hades were cast into the lake of fire. This is the second death";* John 3:36, "*He who believes in the Son has everlasting life; and he who does not believe the Son shall not see life, but the wrath of God abides on him";* Romans 1:18, "*For the wrath of God is revealed from heaven against all ungodliness and unrighteousness of men, who suppress the truth in unrighteousness";* Ezekiel 18:4, "*Behold, all souls are Mine; the soul of the father as well as the soul of the son is Mine; the soul who sins shall die.*"

3. The sinner must know that works cannot save him.

   Titus 3:5, *"Not by works of righteousness which we have done, but according to His mercy He saved us, through the washing of regeneration and renewing of the Holy Spirit*"; Romans 3:20, "*Therefore by the deeds of the law no flesh will be justified in His sight, for by the law is the knowledge of sin*"; Ephesians 2:8, "*For by grace you have been saved through faith, and that not of yourselves; it is the gift of God.*" Romans 11:6, "*And if by grace, then it is no longer of works; otherwise grace is no longer grace. But if it is of works, it is no longer grace; otherwise work is no longer work*"; Galatians 2:16, "*Knowing that a man is not justified by the works of the law but by faith in Jesus Christ, even we have believed in Christ Jesus, that we might be justified by faith in Christ and not by the works of the law; for by the works of the law no flesh shall be justified";* Romans 6:23, "*For the wages of sin is death, but the gift of God is eternal life in Christ Jesus our Lord";* 1 John 5:11, "*And this is the testimony: that God has given us eternal life, and this life is in His Son.*"

4. The sinner must know that only Jesus Christ can save him.

   John 14:6, "*Jesus said to him, 'I am the way, the truth, and the life. No one comes to the Father except through Me'"*; 1 Timothy 2:5, "*For there is one God and one Mediator between God and men, the Man Christ Jesus"*; Acts 4:12, "*Nor is there salvation in any other, for there is no other name under heaven given among men by which we must be saved"*; Hebrews 7:25, "*Therefore He is also able to save to the uttermost those who come to God through Him, since He always lives to make intercession for them"*; Hebrews 10:10, "*By that will we have been sanctified through the offering of the body of Jesus Christ once for all"*; Hebrews 10:19, "*Therefore, brethren, having boldness to enter the Holiest by the blood of Jesus"*; 1 John 1:7, "*The blood of Jesus Christ His Son cleanses us from all sin"*; John 10:9, "*I am the door. If anyone enters by Me, he will be saved, and will go in and out and find pasture"*; John 12:46, "*I have come as a light into the world, that whoever believes in Me should not abide in darkness*"; John 8:24, "*Therefore I said to you that you will die in your sins; for if you do not believe that I am He, you will die in your sins"*; John 6:51, "*I am the living bread which came down from heaven. If anyone eats of this bread, he will live forever; and the bread that I shall give is My flesh, which I shall give for the life of the world.*"

5. The sinner must know that he is saved by grace through faith.

Acts 16:31, "*So they said, 'Believe on the Lord Jesus Christ, and you will be saved, you and your household.'"*; John 3:16, "*For God so loved the world that He gave His only begotten Son, that whoever believes in Him should not perish but have everlasting life"*; John 3:18, "*He who believes in Him is not condemned; but he who does not believe is condemned already, because he has not believed in the name of the only begotten Son of God*"; John 3:36, "*He who believes in the Son has everlasting life; and he who does not believe the Son shall not see life, but the wrath of God abides on him*"; Galatians 3:26, "*For you are all sons of God through faith in Christ Jesus*"; John 1:12, "*But as many as received Him, to them He gave the right to become children of God, to those who believe in His name*"; Romans 10:9, "*That if you confess with your mouth the Lord Jesus and believe in your heart that God has raised Him from the dead, you will be saved";* Romans 3:28, *"Therefore we conclude that a man is justified by faith apart from the deeds of the law."*

The Warm-Up Conversation

The soulwinner must know how to win the prospect's confidence in order to get his permission to let you take him through the Roman Road. We must win a hearing if we are going to win the sinner to Christ. We must win his favor so that he will listen to what we have to say. This is to be done through our "warm-up" conversation.

Craig W. Massey, in his book *How To Do Effective Visitation,* says conversation is an art to be studied and practiced until it becomes an effective instrument in your life. It may be thought of as a bridge, for it links your mind with the minds of others. This bridge is built of words. The better you learn to use words, the stronger the bridge and the greater your influence for Christ.

As you seek to win people to Christ, you will meet with negative attitudes such as indifference, prejudice, ignorance, unbelief, antagonism, embarrassment, and argumentation. Your first task is to "disarm" the prospect and make him feel comfortable in your presence so that when Christ is introduced, his mind will be receptive.

1. Try to know a little bit about many subjects.

   The more words you know and the more knowledge you have increases your ability to think. Alert, clear, quick thinking becomes an important factor in conversation. A successful insurance salesman does not hurry off to make the contact without thinking of his approach. If the prospect were in the steel business, this salesman would go to the library and refresh his mind in the particular field of his potential customer. If the prospect were a lawyer, the salesman would follow the same procedure. He makes it his business to find common ground for the opening conversation. He takes time and thought, but the quantity of his sales proves it worthwhile. Can Christians afford to do less than a salesman does when their motives are so much higher?

2. Show a genuine interest and concern.

   Talk in terms of his interests. Ask him about his job, his family, his hometown, and his hobbies. Try to make him feel important and be sincere in it. As you talk, use his name often and be sure that you pronounce it correctly. Smile and show friendliness. Be complimentary and show appreciation. Find something to brag on in the house. You have not come to talk about yourself and tell him your likes and dislikes. He does not care how great you think you are. Talk about him. Listen to him. Laugh at his jokes. Let everything revolve around him at first and around Christ at the last.

3. Ask open-ended questions.

   This type of question forces people to talk and to reveal themselves. Open-ended questions begin with words such as WHERE, WHO, HOW, WHAT, WHEN, WHY, and WHICH. The open question produces an answer that generally supplies a springboard for another question. It also makes it easier for the timid Christian to do less talking.

4. Avoid dead-end questions.

   The dead-end questions begin with words such as ARE, IS, WILL, DO, HAS, CAN, and SHALL. Saying "yes" or "no" can answer this type of question simply. It leads to a dead-end in conversation. It tends to cross-examine the prospect. Notice too that the burden of the conversation falls completely on the soulwinner. It is a poor type of question to draw out the prospect during the warm-up conversation.

   To illustrate, suppose you are talking to a young man who has just graduated from high school. A closed question would be asked and answered like this: "Do you expect to go on to college?" The answer, "No." End of conversation.

Now, here is an open question: "What are your plans now that you are out of high school?" "Well, I expect to get a job for the summer. Next fall I plan to join the Air Force and get my college training there." This offers several springboards for more questions, while the closed question makes it more difficult to go on in conversation.

5. Be a good listener.

  a. When the prospect is speaking, look directly at him so he knows he has your attention.
  b. Use audible responses such as: "Um-hmm," "I see,'" "Yes," "Is that so?" "That's interesting!"
  c. Use also silent responses such as an expression on your face of question, shock, or interest. Also, a slight nod of the head.
  d. Beware of interrupting the prospect.
  e. Beware of reflecting boredom, even though he may he uninteresting.
  f. Never give the impression that you can't wait until he is finished so you may have an opportunity to talk.

If you can become a good listener you can become a soulwinner. A good listener will win the sinner's confidence, and he will feel that he has found a true friend who really cares. This is groundwork for soulwinning.

The Roman Road

The Roman Road is a simple presentation of the gospel from the book of Romans. It shows the sinner four important things that will help him to come to a saving knowledge of Christ.

1. Show him that he is a sinner.

   Romans 3:10-12, 23, "*As it is written: There is none righteous, no, not one; There is none who understands; there is none who seeks after God. They have all turned aside; they have together become unprofitable; there is none who does good, no, not one for all have sinned and fall short of the glory of God.*"

   It is very important that he acknowledge his lost condition. Ask him if he realizes that he is a lost sinner. Trust God to convict him of this fact.

2. Show him the punishment for sin.

   Romans 6:23, "*For the wages of sin is death...*" Revelation 20:14-15, "*Then Death and Hades were cast into the lake of fire. This is the second death. And anyone not found written in the Book of Life was cast into the lake of fire.*" Revelation 21:8, "*But the cowardly, unbelieving, abominable, murderers, sexually immoral, sorcerers, idolaters, and all liars shall have their part in the lake which burns with fire and brimstone, which is the second death.*"

   Point out to the prospect that the terrible consequence of being a sinner is death. We go outside of the book of Romans to show him that this death is hell or the lake of fire. He should be aware of this future punishment.

3. Show him that Jesus paid the penalty for his sin.

   Romans 5:8, "*But God demonstrates His own love toward us, in that while we were still sinners, Christ died for us.*" John 3:16, "*For God so loved the world that He gave His only begotten Son, that whoever believes in Him should not perish but have everlasting life.*"

   Explain the substitutionary death of Christ. Lift up Jesus on the cross. Tell of God's great love for sinners in giving His only begotten Son to die for them. Emphasize the finished work of Christ on Calvary.

4. Show him that he must receive Christ by faith.

Romans 10:9-10, "*That if you confess with your mouth the Lord Jesus and believe in your heart that God has raised Him from the dead, you will be saved. For with the heart one believes unto righteousness, and with the mouth confession is made unto salvation.*" Romans 10:13, "*For whoever calls on the name of the Lord shall be saved.*"

Point out that since Christ has died for his sin, all he must do is open his heart and receive Him as Savior and Lord. Make clear that even though Jesus has already died for his sins, he must still appropriate this forgiveness by a single act of faith.

Drawing the Net

After presenting the gospel to the sinner, we give him an invitation to trust Jesus. In some cases, the sinner will not be ready to take Christ on the first witness, but since we cannot know what is going on inside his heart, we should endeavor to draw the net and see if he is ready.

This term, "Drawing the Net," is derived from the old fishermen who meant "landing the fish." Too often we witness and never get the prospect across the line to salvation. We do not land the fish. We may wrestle with him, argue with him, yank on him and even reprimand him only to walk away and say, "I hope you get saved some day."

I am convinced that many souls could be landed for Jesus if the worker would only draw the net. In my early attempts at soulwinning, I let many slip through because I did not know how to draw the net. I would give the gospel and invite them to church but that was as far as it went. The turning point in my soulwinning came when I realized that the sinner must take Christ by FAITH, and that I could help encourage him to exercise his faith in the Lord Jesus. Faith is the arm that connects us to Christ, but there must be a time when faith reaches out. There must be a releasing of faith. Passive, intellectual head-faith must become an active, heart-faith in order for salvation to come to that life. Mere belief must be acted upon.

After presenting Christ to the sinner as the way of forgiveness for his sins by simple faith, we must help him to trigger that faith into action. We must help him to appropriate what Christ has already purchased for him on the cross.

How can we help the sinner to exercise faith in Christ? How do we get him across the line to Jesus? How do we get him to decide now? The answer is an "Invitation Appeal" designed to show what God has promised to do and then lead him gently to step out on these promises and judge God faithful and honest to fulfill them. Faith is taking someone at his promise. Faith is acting on someone's word.

The "Invitation Appeal" has three peaks to which the prospect is brought to the place of releasing his faith in Jesus. We lay the foundation with promises of what God will do and then encourage him to step out on God's Word, receiving Christ as his Savior.

The sinner must move from intellectual and emotional faith into volitional faith. Intellectually, he believes Christ can save him because He died on the cross; emotionally, he wants Christ to save him because he is a lost sinner heading to hell. This is not enough! His will must be involved; there must be a definite choice. The sinner who knows he is lost and heading to Hell must now step out and believe volitionally on Christ, thus bringing regeneration. We can encourage this by drawing the net.

Memorizing the following "Invitation Appeal" will give the soulwinner confidence and wisdom to draw the net. In order to simplify the learning of this appeal, we have broken it down into fifteen points. Determine to master the entire talk. Please note in quotation, under each point, an actual demonstration of drawing the net on a prospect.

1. Recap the Roman Road.

As you begin the invitation summarize briefly the Roman Road

Map to salvation.

EXAMPLE: "Now, John, I have shown you in the Bible where God says we are all sinners. I know I am a sinner. John do you know that you are a sinner? (Yes.) We have also seen in the Bible that because we are sinners we are lost and heading to Hell. You understand that, don't you? (Yes.) John, we have also seen in the Scripture that Jesus Christ died on the cross for our sins so that we would not have to go to Hell. You believe that, don't you? (Yes, I do.) We read in the Bible that if a person believes in his heart and confesses with his mouth Jesus to be his Lord, that he will be saved. John, you believe that, don't you? (Yes.)"

2. Start talking slower and softer.

From this point on it is important that we slow down, lower our voice, and become very earnest. We want to cultivate an atmosphere of sacredness in order that the Holy Spirit may bring a holy hush into the room. All joking and frivolity is laid aside. It is as if we were earnestly contending with a man who is about to jump off a ten-story building. It is as if we were in the operating room and the surgeon is about to begin. It is serious business.

3. Read the net Scriptures (1 John 5:11-12 and Revelation 3:20).

We point out in 1 John 5:11-12 that eternal life is wrapped up in the person of Jesus Christ. ("*And this is the testimony: that God has given us eternal life, and this life is in His Son. He who has the Son has life; he who does not have the Son of God does not have life.)* Then we explain Revelation 3:20: that if he will open his heart, Jesus will come in and make His abode within his heart thus imparting eternal life. ("*Behold, I stand at the door and knock. If anyone hears My voice and opens the door, I will come in to him and dine with him, and he with Me.*")

EXAMPLE: "John, I want to turn to 1 John 5:11-12 and show you a very precious promise. *'And this is the record that God hath GIVEN...'* John, notice that word '*given.*' It is an important word because it reveals to us that salvation is a gift. We cannot earn it, buy it, or work for it, can we? God has given to us eternal life. That means it will last for how long, John? (Forever.) That's right, if it is eternal life then it will last forever and forever. And John, this is what we all want... *'eternal life'* to live forever in Heaven with our Lord Jesus Christ, isn't it? (Yes.) John, notice in verse eleven, he tells us where this eternal life is to be found. *'and this life is in his Son.'* John, this life is in his what? (His Son.) That's right, 'His Son.' And what is the Son's name? (Jesus.) That is right, 'Jesus.' Now in verse twelve we read, *'He that hath the Son hath life and he that hath not the Son of God hath not life.'* John, wouldn't you agree that this verse is teaching that eternal life is all wrapped up in the person of Jesus Christ, God's Son? If we have Jesus in our heart, we have life; but if we don't have Jesus, then we don't have anything. You see, going to heaven involves a relationship with Jesus. Isn't that right? (Yes.)

"Now read verse thirteen with me, John, *'These things have I written unto you that believe on the name of the Son of God; that ye may KNOW that ye have eternal life...'* He did not say that we would 'hope so, guess so, think so or maybe so,' but that we may **KNOW** that we have eternal life. Verses eleven and twelve were written so that we can know and be one hundred percent sure that we have eternal life. Isn't that wonderful? (Yes.) Now, John, I know that I have eternal life, because I have the Son, Jesus Christ, in my heart. You can also know you have eternal life by letting the Son come into your heart."

4. Lay a foundation for faith by pointing out the two distinct responsibilities in the net verse.

If the sinner is going to exercise faith he must have something for faith to rest on. Faith is not an intangible that leaps out into the dark. Rather, faith has a solid foundation, namely the Word of God. "*So then faith comes by hearing, and hearing by the word of God,*" (Romans 10:17). Since faith is taking someone at his word, we want to point out that God has made a definite promise to save, but that it is a conditional promise. This means His saving us is dependent upon our fulfilling our responsibility of exercising faith in Christ.

EXAMPLE: "John, I want you to notice that Christ has given us a great promise in Revelation 3:20, "*Behold, I stand at the door and knock. If anyone hears My voice and opens the door, I will come in to him and dine with him, and he with Me.*" Jesus says if we will do something, He will do something. We have a part, and He has a part. Can you show me in this verse what your part is, John? (Open the door.) That's right, now what is Jesus' part? (To come in.) That's right. If we open the door of our heart, Jesus will come in and save us. We cannot do His part, nor will He do our part.

5. Get him to vouch for the honesty of God.

We continue to lay the foundation for faith to be released by building the sinner's confidence in God's Word. By showing him from the Bible what God has already done (in giving His Son to die) and what He will do if a sinner will trust Him, we bring the prospect to vouch for the fact of God's willingness to save him. We give him personal assurance that God will back up His promise and keep His Word. We get the sinner to acknowledge this in the following manner.

EXAMPLE: "John, Jesus promises here that if you will open the door of your heart, He will come in and save you. Do you believe the Bible is true? (Yes.) Do you think Christ would lie to us? (No.) In other words, you believe the Lord is honest and will do what he has promised? (Yes.) John, when Jesus invited 'any man,' who does that mean? (Anybody.) Then it also includes you and me, doesn't it? (Yes.) If he promises to save anyone who opens the door of his heart for Him, we could guarantee it to be a fact, since He is God and cannot lie. John, suppose you were to open the door of your heart and invite Jesus in, what do you think He would do, according to this verse? (Come in.) That's right. If we do our part, He will certainly do His part."

6. Ask him if he would like for Jesus to come into his heart.

EXAMPLE: "John, would you like for the Lord Jesus to come into your heart today and forgive all your sins, making you his very own? (Yes.)"

7. Ask him to let you pray.

EXAMPLE: "John, would you be willing for us to bow our heads and let me offer a prayer on your behalf, that God will help you to open your heart to Christ? (Yes.)"

8. Ask him to put his finger on Revelation 3:20 before you pray.

EXAMPLE: "John, before we pray (lay your Bible on his lap or in front of him) would you place your finger on verse twenty where He says that if we open the door, He will come in. By doing this you are saying to God, 'I believe you are honest and will keep your word and I am claiming this promise for my life today.' And now with our heads bowed and our eyes closed, I am going to pray. While I pray, if you want to, you can open your heart for Jesus. If you don't want to, you don't have to. This is strictly up to you."

9. Pray a simple prayer for his salvation.

EXAMPLE: "Dear heavenly Father, thank you for this opportunity of talking with John today about becoming a Christian. Father, here is a man that Jesus died for. We know you love him and want to make him your child. Now Lord, I pray that You will help John to realize that he is a lost sinner on the road to hell, and that only Jesus can save him. Dear Lord, help John to open his heart and receive Christ as his Savior'... (Pause.)

10. Stop in the middle of your prayer and ask him to pray.

NOTICE: This is the first peak in the net appeal where the sinner is brought to the point of releasing his faith. It is hoped that as he prays he will exercise faith in Christ. It is faith that saves — not just a prayer. Realizing it is possible for him to say a prayer and not really trigger his faith in Christ, there are yet two other peaks in the appeal where he may release his faith in Jesus.

EXAMPLE: "Now, John, before I finish my prayer, would you be willing to invite Jesus into your heart today? The verse you have your finger on promises that if you will open the door He will come in. In your own words, would you ask the Lord to come into your heart? Go ahead, right now."

11. When he finishes his prayer, ask him to clinch his decision for Christ by taking your hand.

NOTICE: This is the second peak in the invitation appeal where the sinner is brought to the place of releasing his faith in Christ. If he did not believe during the prayer, it is possible that when he reaches out to grasp your hand, he will release his faith. This simple gesture has been the means of many to trigger their faith. However, it is still possible that he may grasp your hand and not really believe from the heart. Therefore, we have one other peak where the prospect may be brought to the place of appropriating the salvation obtained at Calvary.

EXAMPLE: "John, while our heads are bowed and our eyes are closed and just before I finish my prayer, if you really meant the prayer that you just prayed and the best you know how you are opening the door of your heart for Jesus... would you signify it by taking my hand?"

12. Finish your prayer by thanking God for his decision.

EXAMPLE: "And now, dear heavenly Father, I want to thank you for John's accepting Christ as his personal Savior. I pray, dear Lord, that You will help him to know in his heart that he is saved and may he be a hundred percent Christian the rest of his life. In Jesus' name, Amen."

13. After finishing your prayer, lead him to assurance from the Word.

This is the third time the sinner is brought to the place of exercising faith in Christ. If, perhaps, he failed to "believe" when he prayed and even when he took your hand, it is possible he will release his faith at this time. It is not wise to get up from the prayer meeting and say, "Now, John, you are a Christian." We do not want to put words in his mouth and give him a false assurance. It has been my experience many times, that while leading the person into assurance through the Word, he actually exercised the initial faith unto salvation.

EXAMPLE: "John, according to this verse (pointing to Revelation 3:20, "*Behold, I stand at the door and knock. If anyone hears My voice and opens the door, I will come in to him and dine with him, and he with Me")* where would you go if you were to die right now? (To heaven.) Why would you go to heaven? (Because Jesus came into my heart.) Well, John, how do you know that He came into your heart? (Because He said so right here.) In other words, you are taking Christ at His promise today? You believe then that since you have opened your heart for Jesus, you are convinced that He has kept His promise and has come into your heart and saved you? (Yes.) All right, John, tell me, who saved you? (Jesus did.) What did He save you from? (Sin and Hell.) That is right. And John, since Jesus has come into your heart today, what has He given you? (Eternal life.) That's right—eternal life. If it is eternal, how long will you have it? (Forever.)

"John, suppose that someone tomorrow would ask you, 'John, are you a Christian?' What would you say? (Yes.) Suppose they ask you when you became a Christian. What would you say? (Yesterday.) In other words you believe that right here today is the time that you have gotten it settled for men and eternity? (Yes.) You believe that today has been your day of salvation? (Yes.) John, this is what I would do if I were you. I would take my Bible and write in the front cover today's date. Put down, 'November 1, 2,___ at 4:00 p.m. in my living room.' I would also write Revelation 3:20, the promise that you claimed today. And, John, jot another verse down there: Hebrews 13:5 where Jesus says that He will never forsake nor leave us. If He came into your heart today, and He has promised never to leave you, then He is yours forever. If you are tempted to doubt your salvation later, you can come back to your Bible and open it to these two verses and stand on His precious promises."

14. Offer to pick him up for Sunday School this Sunday.

    EXAMPLE: "John, how about letting me come by Sunday morning and pick you up for Sunday School? Will that be all right? I would like for you and the wife to plan to come and have dinner with us after the service. How about that? Okay?"

15. Sit with him in the church service.

    This is very beneficial in that during the invitation, if necessary, you can speak a word to him without causing a scene and embarrassing him.

    EXAMPLE: "John, would you like for me to go down front with you as you make your public stand for Christ? I will be very happy to go along with you. Okay?"

How to Get the Convert to Make a Public Profession in Church

The fact is that a new convert is a babe in Christ and needs to be taught what he is to do for Jesus. We expect a brand new Christian to know all the rules and responsibilities of Christianity, although we didn't when we were first saved. They must have the milk of the word and be helped along.

Here are the steps in leading the new convert to make his public stand for Christ. These steps are to be taken immediately after winning him to Christ and leading him to assurance.

1. Ask him what Jesus has done for him.

   EXAMPLE: "John, has Jesus done something for you today? (Yes.) What is that, John? (He came into my heart.) Well, that is certainly a wonderful thing to know that Jesus Christ has come into your heart and saved you from sin and hell. Think about it. You will not have to go to hell. Your name has been written in the Lamb's Book of Life, John. Doesn't this make you love and appreciate Jesus very much? (Yes.)"

2. Tell him he can do something for Jesus.

   EXAMPLE: "John, there is something that you can do for Jesus now that will please Him very much. Jesus has done something wonderful for you today in forgiving you of your sins and coming into your heart. In return there is something you can do for Him as an expression of your love and appreciation. John, would you like to do something for Jesus that would mean a whole lot to Him? (Yes.)"

3. Tell him the first thing Jesus wants us to do after we have been saved is to tell people publicly.

   EXAMPLE: "John, the first thing that Jesus wants us to do after we have been saved is to make a public stand for Him. You see, Jesus says in Matthew 10:32, "*Therefore whoever confesses Me before men, him I will also confess before My Father who is in heaven*." Jesus doesn't want us to be ashamed of Him. John, you are not ashamed of the Lord Jesus Christ, are you? (No.)"

   "Would you be willing to make a public declaration of your faith in Christ? (Yes.) Well, John, let me tell you how you can do this. There are several ways it might be done. You might put a speaker on your car and drive around the neighborhood telling your decision for Jesus; or you might get on the radio and tell people that you have accepted Christ. But, the way most people make a public stand for Christ is at church on Sunday morning.

   "You see, John, during the invitation after the Sermon has been preached, you can walk down the aisle and take the preacher by the hand. Tell him that you have trusted Jesus, and you want it made public before the whole church. He will have you sit down at the front, and later he will tell the congregation about your choice for Christ. John, although you will not be making a speech, it will be a public stand for Christ. You will simply be coming forward and letting the preacher tell the people that you have trusted Jesus as your personal Savior and that you are happy about it."

4. Get a definite commitment to do it the coming Sunday.

EXAMPLE: "John, do you have to work this Sunday? (No.) So as far as you know you could come to church this Sunday? Right? (Yes.) All right, John, providing that there is no sickness or death in the family between now and this Sunday, would you be willing to come and make your stand for Christ? You will not be doing this for me, but for Jesus. He has done something wonderful for you and this is an opportunity to do something that will please Him. How about it, John? Will you do it for Christ this Sunday? (Yes.)"

5. Seal the commitment with prayer.

EXAMPLE: "John, let's bow our heads for a word of prayer, asking God to bless this commitment that you have just made. 'Dear heavenly Father, we thank you for saving John today. We rejoice that he has received Christ as his personal Savior. Father, we thank You also that John has decided to come forward this Sunday and make his public stand for You in the midst of the brethren. We pray there will be no sickness or accidents to keep him away Sunday. In Jesus' name, Amen.'

"John, I will be looking for you this Sunday. God will bless you for taking your stand for Christ."

NOTICE: In some cases, you may want to have the convert pray and promise the Lord that he will come and make his public stand for Christ. C.W. Fisk does this quite often.

EXAMPLE: "John, while our heads are bowed and our eyes are closed, before I finish my prayer, would you tell Jesus that you will be there Sunday and walk the aisle to let the pastor tell the people that you have been saved? (If he hesitates, encourage him to make a verbal promise to God like this:) 'Dear Lord, I will be in Your house this Sunday and walk the aisle to make my stand for Jesus.'"

How to Direct the Convert to Follow Christ in Baptism

1. If he comes forward in the service and you are baptizing at that service, here is what you say to him:

   EXAMPLE: "John, you have accepted Christ as your Lord and Savior and that means He is to be your boss and captain. It means that we seek to follow Him and do as He wishes for our life. Is that right? (Yes.) The first thing our Lord asks of us is that we follow Him in baptism. Baptism pictures our being buried and resurrected with Christ to walk in a new life. It is also an open confession of our faith in Him. John, we are going to be baptizing in a few minutes. We furnish the robes, towels and everything you need. "John, God commands us to 'repent and be baptized' in Acts 2:38. (*"Then Peter said to them, 'Repent, and let every one of you be baptized in the name of Jesus Christ for the remission of sins; and you shall receive the gift of the Holy Spirit.'"*) You have repented, now are you ready to be baptized? Are you ready for Christ to start being Lord of your life? Our Captain has given the marching orders, namely to be baptized. I've said yes to Him, how about you? (Yes.) Fine. Come with me and I will show you to the dressing room."

2. How to get a commitment in the home to follow Christ in baptism.

   In churches where they do not baptize every Sunday or keep the baptistry filled, it sometimes becomes necessary to get the convert committed to take this step in the home. In this case, we endeavor to get him to understand the meaning of baptism and give his consent to follow Christ in baptism at the next service. This will give you time to fill the baptistry.

   EXAMPLE: "John, you have accepted Christ as your Savior and that is a wonderful thing. There is something else that you will certainly want to do. It will mean a lot to your spiritual growth and be pleasing to Christ. John, I am referring to baptism. You see, baptism is a beautiful symbol picturing our union with Christ and sharing in His death, burial, and resurrection. It pictures our identification with Him. As you go down in the water it is saying, 'I have been buried with Christ, all my sins have been washed away by His blood.' And as you come up out of the water it is saying, 'Now I have a new life, a resurrected life, to live for Jesus.'

"More than that, John, baptism is like putting on a uniform. For instance, when a man joins the army, they give him a uniform. Everyone who sees him in that uniform knows he belongs to Uncle Sam. Now what about a fellow who refuses to wear the uniform? That uniform is an identification badge. John, when we go down in the baptismal water, it is putting on the uniform of Christ. (Galatians 3:27, "*For as many of you as were baptized into Christ have put on Christ.*") It is letting people know that we are on the Lord's side and we belong to Him. It actually becomes a public testimony.

"John, we are going to be baptizing this Sunday so that new Christians can follow our Lord's command. He is our Captain and His marching orders are, 'repent and be baptized.' Are you going to let Jesus start being Lord of your life this week? (Yes.) Fine. Then you will plan to come Sunday and be baptized. Right? (Yes.)"

The Six Objectives in a Soulwinning Visit

Suppose we are going to a home in an attempt to win a man to Christ. First, we must realize that we do not always win the person on the first visit. Therefore, we have several objectives in view as we make this all-important "first visit." There is groundwork to be accomplished, which may bring about his salvation at a later visit. Memorize these six objectives and keep them in mind as you go into the house.

1. Endeavor to make the prospect to like you and be your friend.

   It is so important that he likes you. We must sell ourselves first if we are going to sell Christ. We must win the confidence of the sinner. If he resents you, it is very likely that you will not be able to minister Christ to him.

2. Discern his true spiritual condition.

   We want to know just where he really stands in relation to God.

Is this man a born-again believer, or is he just a religious-but-lost church member? Maybe he is a discouraged believer who needs encouragement or a hardened backslider who needs jolting.

Your giving special attention to his answers to your questions will help you discern his true condition. Often his expressions and reactions to your questions will be revealing. One big question that will usually let you know where a person really stands is "What are you counting on to get you to heaven?" If the answer is anything other than Christ and His substitutionary work on the cross, this person probably needs to be saved.

Depend upon the Holy Spirit to open your understanding and give you discernment to know his condition. If, in your own mind, you are not sure he is saved, set out to deal with him as if he were lost.

3. Expose him to the Gospel.

In order for the Holy Spirit to produce conviction and draw the sinner to Christ, we must do our part in presenting the message of the gospel to him. The Holy Spirit works with and accompanies the Gospel of Christ. Our part is to give the gospel out. The Holy Spirit's part is to take the gospel and drive it into the heart, convicting and wooing the sinner to Jesus.

In the event you are not able to open your Bible and read the gospel message, you could possibly quote the Scripture or tell the gospel in your own words. If the person absolutely does not want to hear it, you might ask for permission to have prayer before leaving and in your prayer relate the gospel. You can thank God for giving His Son to die on the cross for our sins. But whatever you do, expose him to the gospel so the Holy Spirit can begin His work of convicting.

4. Get him to decide for Christ NOW!

After you have presented the Gospel of Christ, it is always wise to give an invitation for him to accept Christ there on the spot. You cannot always tell by a person's outward appearance if he will do it. The sinner may seem outwardly disinterested, yet within may be hungry for the Lord. I have made it a practice to always try and draw the net before leaving the man. "Jim, wouldn't you like to go ahead and settle it today by asking Christ to come into your heart and be your Savior?" If be says no, there is no harm done so long as I do not continue to press him. After all, he may say yes.

One day I visited with a deputy sheriff and during the whole conversation he appeared unconcerned and bored. Since I had listened for twenty minutes as he told of his son's baseball achievements, now he would listen to me. I had earned a hearing. When I finished presenting the Roman Road plan of the Gospel, my human impulse was to cut it off and make my graceful exit. I really did not expect this man to respond to the invitation appeal. But out of habit, I asked this big man if he would like to kneel with me right there in his living room and receive Christ as his Savior. He replied, "Yes, I would. I have needed to do this for a long time." He accepted Christ as his Savior, and we rejoiced together for another twenty minutes!

5. Get him to attend church next Sunday.

After you have finished your conversation, as you are preparing to leave his home, invite him to church Sunday. Do not let it be a vague invitation such as, "Jim, we would like to have you and your family visit with us at church sometime." Be definite and specific by saying, "Jim, how about you and the family coming this Sunday and visiting with us in our church service? Would you let me come by and pick you up? We are going to have a good service Sunday and I surely would like for you to be there." Aim to get him in your next church service. Get a commitment from him.

6. Leave the door open for future ministry.

Just because he did not accept Christ do not lose your cool and insult him. Remember it may take several visits to bring this person to Christ. Perhaps you have sowed the seed today and someone else will come along and reap the harvest. R. A. Torrey said anyone who expects to win a soul to Christ every fifteen minutes had better go into some other business. If you become upset because the sinner would not accept Christ and start scaring him with threats of "sinning away his day of grace" or "this is your last chance," you could possibly do great damage. You may be closing the door for others to deal with him. After you have done your part in the visit, be sure to leave a good taste in his mouth for another visit. Be careful that you do not stay too long, as this may close the door for another visit.

Proverbs 25:17, ***Seldom set foot in your neighbor's house, lest he become weary of you and hate you.***

Don'ts in Soulwinning

1. Don't argue. You never get anywhere arguing. You will put a barrier between the sinner and yourself. Either agree with him and go on or ask him if you can "set that question or issue on the shelf" and come back to it later.

2. Don't talk over his head. Don't use big theological words that he does not understand.

3. Don't talk down to the sinner. That is, don't act self-righteous and Pharisaical. (That you are better than he is.)

4. Don't chase rabbits. Don't get sidetracked on opinions, doctrines, sins, etc. Stay with the Gospel.

5. Don't put him on the defense. Do not criticize or condemn his religion or opinion, or you will put a barrier between the two of you.

6. Don't talk too fast. Don't be like a nervous, overanxious salesman.

7. Don't start frying the fish before he is landed. That is, don't try to get him baptized and in the church before he is saved.

8. Don't be rude to the sinner. Don't talk to the sinner in his home like the preacher would preach from the pulpit.

9. Don't rush him. If he gets this feeling, he will balk.

10. Don't embarrass him or you will certainly make him resent you, thus forfeiting your opportunity to win him.

11. Don't salve his conscience by implying that he is a good fellow. He must be made to realize that he is a lost sinner.

12. Don't lean or lay on the sinner. Avoid intimate contact. One sinner said, "The first half-hour I was concerned about my heavy load of sin, but the last half-hour I was more concerned about that heavy Christian laying on me."

13. Don't pray long prayers with the sinner. I heard about one soulwinner who prayed on and on, and when he got through, he found that the sinner had slipped out and had stolen the soulwinner's hat and coat.

14. Don't be guilty of having bad breath or body odor.

15. Don't preach denomination. The issue is Christ. If you have truly made a friend, the convert will usually do what you want him to after you win him to Christ.

16. Don't let him do the preaching. Once you start the Roman Road, stay in the driver's seat.

17. Don't take his excuses seriously. Don't call him a liar, but let his excuses go in one ear and out the other.

18. Don't be harsh like an attorney on cross-examination. Show tenderness and love for the sinner.

19. Don't let the "Silent Partner" interrupt the presentation. Decide which one will do the soulwinning and the other sit back and pray.

20. Don't try to get the sinner to have an experience just like yours. Give him the gospel and get him to seek Jesus, not an experience.

21. Don't allow your thoughts to dwell upon the honor of being used. Keep self out of the way and remember you are simply an instrument.

22. Don't push the sinner beyond his measure. Your part may be to sow seed or to water. The increase may come later.

23. Don't scold the sinner for not "seeing" all at once.

24. Don't be dogmatic over doubtful things. (Controversial issues.)

25. Don't try to get the sinner to give up certain specific sins. Show him he is a lost sinner and needs to repent and turn to Christ.

26. Don't raise unnecessary objections such as: "You must go down the aisle," or "Are you willing to quit your smoking?" or "Are you willing to give up your mother at home?" However, if any of these things are already an issue with him, then point out that he must be willing to settle it in God's favor in the long run.

27. Don't talk about home and mother too much. Don't push the point of his being saved in order to please his mother or to be a better husband. Work rather from the truth that he is lost and dishonoring God in his sin.

28. Don't look upon any as hard cases.

29. Don't tell them to think about it for a while. Always ask them if they would like to receive Christ now. Attempt to draw the net.

30. Don't be a spiritual psycho (religious nut). Don't be yelling, jerking, and shouting while visiting with the prospect. You will scare him away from Christ. He will think he must act like that if he becomes a Christian and will run from it. Exhibit a sane, sensible, pleasing disposition that will cause him to want what you have.

31. Don't wear out your welcome. If you notice he is restless and keeps looking at his watch, make your graceful exit. In doing this you will leave the door open for another visit.

32. Don't operate on last week's experience. Get with God in prayer and receive fresh life each day.

Spiritual Preparation for Soulwinning

1. Be sure you have a changed life.
2 Corinthians 5:17,"*Therefore, if anyone is in Christ, he is a new creation; old things have passed away; behold, all things have become new.*"

If a person is to be successful in soulwinning, he must know Christ. A life that has been changed by the power of God can win souls. Many who vainly tried to win souls later found that they themselves were lost. A personal, experimental knowledge of Jesus as your own Savior is a must.

2. Make sure you have confessed your sins and are walking with God.

2 Timothy 2:21, *"Therefore if anyone cleanses himself from the latter, he will be a vessel for honor, sanctified and useful for the Master, prepared for every good work."*

If we are to have God's maximum blessing upon our soulwinning effort, we need to be clean outwardly and inwardly. All the secret sins, especially the thought life, should be brought under subjection to the Lord Jesus. The "little foxes spoil the vine." Sin in your life will deteriorate your soulwinning zeal in time.

3. Be surrendered to the Lord.

Romans 12:1, *"I beseech you therefore, brethren, by the mercies of God, that you present your bodies a living sacrifice, holy, acceptable to God, which is your reasonable service."*

It is one thing to be clean; it is another thing to be surrendered to the Lord. The Apostle Paul said, *"For me to live is Christ"* (Philippians 1:21). Being submissive to the call and will of God is vital in the matter of soulwinning. The young lad brought his five loaves and two fishes to Jesus. Have you brought your all to Christ?

4. Have a burden for the lost.

Romans 9:2, *"...that I have great sorrow and continual grief in my heart. For I could wish that I myself were accursed from Christ for my brethren, my countrymen according to the flesh."*

It certainly helps to have a burden for lost souls. Paul had a heavy heart over his generation. However, you should not wait until your heart is broken before starting out in soulwinning. God will bless the gospel regardless of our unconcern. We are to go primarily because it is our responsibility to go. As we go, God will burden us for souls of others.

5. Develop genuine love and compassion for sinners.

Matthew 9:36, *"But when He saw the multitudes, He was moved with compassion for them."*

We are not talking about enthusiasm or human love patched up. We are talking about genuine love flowing from within because of the Christ-nature. Men will not put you off if they really believe you love them. However, they will never believe that you love them unless you really do. It is strange how love attracts. If we are filled with God's love, the result will be an untiring effort in soulwinning. How do we get love? The fruit of the Spirit is love; therefore, we need to be filled with the Spirit.

6. Be convinced of the urgency of your task.

1 Corinthians 9:22, *"To the weak I became as weak, that I might win the weak. I have become all things to all men, that I might by all means save some."*

Billy Sunday was asked the secret of his success in reaching so many souls for Christ. It is said that he walked over to the window and looked out at the masses of people on the streets and said, "They are going to Hell! They are going to Hell! They are going to Hell! They are going to Hell!" And then he said, 'If there is a secret to my winning so many souls, it is because I really believe that men without Christ are going to Hell." My friend, when this truth really lays hold of your heart, it will stir you to rescue the perishing.

7. Be patient and perseverant in presenting the Gospel.

1 Corinthians 2:2, *"For I determined not to know anything among you except Jesus Christ and Him crucified."*

The Apostle Paul said, "but one thing I do" (Philippians 3:13). He was determined to be a soulwinner. His mind was made up about the matter. R. A. Torrey said, "Anyone who wishes to win souls at the rate of one every fifteen minutes had better go into some other business." Soulwinners need patience. Sometimes it takes weeks or months or even years of sowing and watering and fertilizing before we see that soul accept Christ as Savior. A group of soulwinners set out to win a selected hundred lost prospects. They kept records of every visit made. When all of the hundred had been reached for Christ and all of the visits had been totaled up and averaged out, surprisingly each prospect had been visited an average of thirteen times.

8. Know the Scriptures you will present.

Psalm 119:130, *"The entrance of Your words gives light; it gives understanding to the simple."*

It is very important to know the Scriptures whereby you can direct a person in how to be saved. Without the Word, they cannot be saved. In Romans 10:17 we are told, *"Faith cometh by hearing, and hearing by the Word of God."* We are told in Luke 8:11 that, *"The seed is the Word of God."* It is important that we know the right Scriptures to use at the right time.

9. Pray, pray, pray, pray, and pray.

Jeremiah 33:3, *"Call to Me, and I will answer you, and show you great and mighty things, which you do not know."*

God is a prayer-answering God. When we pray over souls, we will see things happen. God bids us to call unto Him and He will do great things. (Note: Refer to the section in the book on "How to Pray for the Lost."

10. Rely on the power of the Holy Spirit in all that you say and do.

Acts 1:8, *"But you shall receive power when the Holy Spirit has come upon you; and you shall be witnesses to Me..."*

How much more effective is the Christian who takes time to wait upon God for the anointing of the Holy Ghost. *"Not by might nor by power, but by My Spirit," says the LORD* (Zechariah 4:6). Ask God to fill you with the Holy Spirit and believe that He will do it. Claim the Spirit's fullness.

Personality Preparation for Soulwinning

In trying to reach people for Christ we want to display a pleasant personality. A grouchy disposition can close the door to winning them.

1. Be friendly and polite.

   Demonstrate what you want to give them. Friendliness will prevent the drudgery in visiting. A friendly attitude will warm a cold heart. We are told in Proverbs 18:24, "*A man who has friends must himself be friendly.*"

2. Smile.

   A smile will open a closed door. A smile will demand attention and respect from strangers. A smile breaks down defenses and opens the door to their hearts. You can smile if you want to. It will help.

3. Be brisk, not brusque.

   By brisk, we mean to be stimulating and enthusiastic. No one appreciates a deadpan visiting him nor a "fishtail" handshake. Perk up and come alive.

4. Treat him as you would want to be treated.

   It is important that we are courteous and kind in our dealings with the unsaved. We should watch our manners. Be gentle and considerate.

5. Use tact and discretion.

   Tact is the wisdom or skill of saying or doing the right thing at the right time. It has been defined as spiritual intelligence. If you want to gather honey, don't kick over the beehive. Pray for tact. The opposite of tact is crudeness, which is defined as lacking grace or not being refined.

6. Be bold and courageous, not fearful and timid.

   In Joshua 1:7, we are told, *"Only be strong and very courageous."* The Apostle Paul reminds us in Romans 8:31, "*If God is for us, who can be against us?*" *"The fear of man brings a snare"* (Proverbs 29:25).

7. Be sympathetic to the other person's situation.

   This word ***sympathetic*** means "fellow feeling" or "showing interest." It is more felt than heard. It is weeping with the sad and rejoicing with the glad. It is entering into the feeling of others. This does not mean to sit for hours listening to someone's life history. However, if there is a problem he wishes to share, we do well to listen and help. In so doing, we win their confidence and win them to Christ.

How to Pray for the Lost

We can win anyone for whom God gives us a burden. If God burdens our heart for a soul, it is evident that He intends to save that soul. It is also evident that He desires to work through us as the human vessel since He gave us the burden. Many times the soul is actually won in prayer. It is one thing to pray; it is another thing to "pray right." Here are seven pointers for praying for the lost to be saved.

1. Pray believing.

   Mark 11:24, *"Therefore I say to you, whatever things you ask when you pray, believe that you receive them, and you will have them."*

   Prayer is the key, but faith unlocks the door. We must pray believing that God is working in the sinner's heart and preparing him for our visit.

2. Pray realizing that God is able to do anything.

   Mark 10:27, *"But Jesus looked at them and said, 'With men it is impossible, but not with God; for with God all things are possible.'"* Recognize God in the picture, for nothing is too hard for God. In our praying, most of us never get beyond human limitations and boundaries. We whittle God down to our own size and power. We are like the woman who said, "It's no use for you to talk to my husband. He won't listen to me."

3. Pray asking the Lord to glorify Himself by saving the person.

   John 14:13, *"And whatever you ask in My name, that I will do, that the Father may be glorified in the Son."*

   We should not pray for a soul to be saved that he or she might be a better husband or wife. This is selfish praying. We should pray for souls to be saved so that they will no longer dishonor God in their sins. Our great concern should be that they will stop trampling over the precious blood of Christ and stop spurning God's love. This should be the real motive in soulwinning rather than to put another "notch" on our belt or add a few more figures to our report.

4. Pray that the sinner's eyes, ears, and heart would be opened.

Matthew 13:13,15, *"Therefore I speak to them in parables, because seeing they do not see, and hearing they do not hear, nor do they understand. For the hearts of this people have grown dull. Their ears are hard of hearing, and their eyes they have closed."* Every sinner needs the Holy Spirit to reveal his sinful condition. Then Christ will be revealed to the heart. We should pray that the Holy Spirit would "quicken" their conscience, plow up their heart, and ring conviction in their soul. We should pray that God would give them "hearing ears" and "believing hearts." Pray that God shall open their understanding

5. Pray claiming redemption for that soul which the blood of Christ has purchased.

2 Timothy 2:26, *"And that they may come to their senses and escape the snare of the devil, having been taken captive by him to do his will."*

In one sense, every soul is God's purchased possession, though still held by Satan through unbelief. We must through prayer claim and take for God that which is rightfully His. This is praying on the ground of redemption.

6. Pray claiming the tearing down of Satan's strongholds.

2 Corinthians 10:4, *"For the weapons of our warfare are not carnal but mighty in God for pulling down strongholds."*

The devil has built up lies, false doctrine, stumbling blocks, and many other strongholds in the minds of the unsaved to keep them from receiving Christ. He has them blinded lest the light of the glorious gospel should shine unto them. We must through prayer rebuke the devil and claim the tearing down of his lies and warped ideas that are keeping the sinner from trusting Christ as Savior.

We must exercise our authority in Christ.

7. Pray with perseverance.

Luke 18:7, "Shall God not avenge His own elect who cry out day and night to Him, though He bears long with them?"

Perseverance is "not giving up." We persevere not to persuade God, but we persevere because of the enemy. In persistent intercession, we are pushing back the forces of evil. We are getting the Devil off of God's territory. Daniel prayed for three weeks before he received his answer from God, though the Scripture says that God answered his prayer on the first day. Daniel spent three weeks wrestling with the forces of evil and hanging onto God in order that he might receive his "package."

Three Suggestions for Winning Relatives and Close Friends

Usually it is more difficult to win relatives and close friends because they know us for what we used to be. It is hard for them to believe that we have suddenly changed and become new creatures. Therefore, it is very important to go the second mile in reaching them. The fact is that you have a better chance of reaching them than a stranger does. However, you must first prove to them that Christ is real in your own life. When they are convinced that you are really honest and sincere in your profession, you can easily win them. Here are three big pointers in reaching relatives and close friends:

1. Be the best example of a Christian you can in front of them.

You must demonstrate what you profess. There must be no profane language, no arguing, no wrangling, no gossiping, and no shouting at others in their presence. What you DO speaks so loudly they cannot hear what you say.

You must prove yourself before them with a consistent life. Jesus told the Gadarene demoniac, "Go home and show thy friends what great things the Lord hath done for thee." We, too, must "show" our friends and relatives that God has really done something in our lives.

2. Be a servant to them.

Perform continuous acts of service for them. Serve them. Do little things that are not expected of you. The convincing proof of your change is your willingness to go out of your way to serve them. Oh, we are willing to do nice things for outsiders, like the preacher, but when it comes to our own immediate family, how we gripe and pull back. But this is the very thing that will convince them that you have something they need. This kind of generosity will shock them.

Jump in and do your part of household chores voluntarily instead of being pushed. Offer to help with their part. Go out of your way to be considerate. Actually search for something nice to do for them. Be willing to sacrifice your time and money doing little niceties for them. While doing it, you convince and prove to them without a shadow of a doubt that something has happened in your life.

This is really what our Lord commanded, "In love serve one another." We are denying ourselves and becoming servants as Jesus said we should. Let them have the best chair, the biggest piece of pie, and the first choice of chicken. Offer them the first drink of water on that hot day. "In love preferring one another," you will win a hearing with them and thereby be able to lead them to Christ.

3. Don't put them down or condemn them.

Do not nag them, or they will dread being around you. Do not judge or criticize them, or you will build a barrier between the two of you. Do not cast remarks like, "You are not living right, you know." "You shouldn't be smoking and drinking and dancing, etc." "You know you should be going to church." "Why don't you stop living the way you are and straighten up?"

This kind of thing not only irritates them with you, but also builds resentment against the church. It gives them the impression you are acting "holier than thou." They feel that you think you are better than they are and are setting yourself up on a pedestal. You may not mean to display this attitude. However, if they take it this way, it will still drive them away from you. You will forfeit your opportunity to win them.

It is important to exercise patience with relatives and close friends. It may take several months to let them see the change that Jesus Christ has made in your life. They want to know if it will last. Show them it will. So love them, and in your loving them, serve them. In your serving them, throw in some components. You will be laying the foundation to win them to Christ.

After you have convinced them that you are real and they are willing to listen to you, sit down with them and go through the Roman Road presentation of the Gospel. Deal with them the same as you would any other sinner. The problem is to gain a hearing from them. The three suggestions given in this lesson are simply means of getting to them. There is still the task of leading them to Christ and drawing the net.

Three Suggestions for Winning Co-workers

Winning people you work with on the job is somewhat more difficult than winning strangers. It takes more than just preaching to them because you can undo all your preaching in five minutes by improper action on the job. It is not like going out on visitation and witnessing to a man and then leaving him. You are with him all day long every day of the week. He has time to observe you and see if you are living what you preach. Here are three suggestions for reaching those on the job:

1. Let them see the joy of the Lord.

   Walk in victory. Keep your cup running over. Let them see that you have victory in all areas of your life and work. Do not magnify your problems before them at work. The Apostle Paul demonstrated his victory and faith before the two hundred and seventy-six passengers on board the ship in the midst of the storm (Acts 27). He exhorted them to be of good cheer and they were all of good cheer. He proved to them that his God was real and that he had a personal relationship with Him.

   Be careful how you suffer setbacks. They are watching to see if your religion will hold up in the testing time. If you are telling them how big your God is one minute, and the next minute you are down in the dumps, crying and discouraged, you are not going to make a big impression on them.

Ephesians 5:18-20, "*And do not be drunk with wine, in which is dissipation; but be filled with the Spirit, speaking to one another in psalms and hymns and spiritual songs, singing and making melody in your heart to the Lord, giving thanks always for all things to God the Father in the name of our Lord Jesus Christ.*"

2. Carry your load at work because you do your work as unto the Lord.

Be diligent and conscientious over your responsibilities at work. Be honest and of strong character. Give a full day's work. We are told in Romans 12:11, "*Not lagging in diligence, fervent in spirit, serving the Lord.*" A lazy Christian on the job is a reproach to Christ. He will hurt the testimony of the church. He becomes a stumbling block. All the witnessing you have done will go out the window when they see you shirk your responsibility and thereby overburden the other fellow. Your testimony is certainly ruined with him. He will size you up as being dishonest, lazy, and unwilling to do your part of the work. You will not win him to Christ.

Respect your boss and those in authority. This is taught in the Bible. Ephesians 6:5, "*Bondservants, be obedient to those who are your masters according to the flesh, with fear and trembling, in sincerity of heart, as to Christ; not with eyeservice, as men-pleasers, but as bondservants of Christ, doing the will of God from the heart.*" The Apostle Paul is saying that we should be eager to give our employer our very best. Serve them as you would Christ. He is exhorting employees to work hard even when the boss is not looking. Work hard with gladness all the time, as though you are working for Christ. If a Christian undermines his employer and joins in with the others in criticizing him, he hurts himself in their eyes. Remember you are supposed to be different. They are watching.

3. Be an example of humility.

If there is anything that will make the fellows on the job despise you, it is a self-righteous, Pharisaical, "holier than thou" attitude. It is good to take regular inventory of yourself concerning this ugly attitude. Stand guard against it. It will build a wall between you and the fellows and close the door of opportunity. This disastrous spirit will not only cause you to forfeit your chance to win them, but will also put a bad taste in their mouth toward Christianity as a whole.

The opposite of self-righteousness is humility. Be humble. Humility is the awareness that you are absolutely nothing within yourself. It is realizing that you have become somebody in Christ and that the only good thing in you now is Jesus. Humility is an awareness that were it not for the grace of God I would be in his condition on the road to Hell. Humility says, "I am no better than you are. My heart is wicked and deceitful the same as yours. The only difference is I have received Christ as my Savior and Jesus makes the difference."

Four Suggestions for Winning Those of Another Religious Faith

There will be times that you will be confronted with winning someone of a different faith from your own. It is easier for me to win an unsaved Baptist to Christ than an unsaved Catholic, because we are already wearing the same religious tag. We have something in common. The Catholic would probably think I am trying to make a Baptist of him and therefore would not be as willing to listen. Four suggestions to help win them are as follows:

1. Begin by focussing on your common ground.

   Be very nice and friendly. Be sure to observe all the "Don'ts" in soulwinning. Be extremely careful not to criticize their religious faith even though they may not be active in it. Don't put them on the defense. Get them going with you, agreeing with you.

2. Keep the conversation focussed on Christ, not denomination or religion.

   The truth of the matter is that we are not trying to make a Baptist of anyone, but to make a Christian. We may say something like this, "John, I want you to know I am not here to make a Baptist of you. Just being a Baptist will not take anyone to heaven. As a matter of fact, many Baptists are lost and on the road to hell themselves because they have never really taken Jesus Christ as their personal Savior. You see, it isn't the church name or tag we wear that makes us right with God. It is what we do with the Lord Jesus Christ."

3. Ask a clarifying transition question.

EXAMPLE: "John, let me ask you a question that I ask all the Baptists. If you were to die today, are you one hundred percent sure of going to heaven?" If he says yes, then put the big question to him that follows:

4. "John, for just a few minutes, would you be willing to forget your religion, and I will forget mine as we look into the Bible and see what God says about going to Heaven?"

If he gives consent, take him through the Roman Road as you would anyone else. If he accepts Christ as his Savior, follow through with the public profession talk. (See previous section on public profession.) Try to get him to come to your church Sunday to make his public stand for Christ.

EXAMPLE: "John, since I have had the joy of being with you today and helped you to find Christ, I would love to see you make your public profession of Christ. Would you be willing to visit my church this Sunday and walk the aisle for Jesus. I will go down with you and we will tell my preacher together that you have been saved. You will not be joining the church unless you want to."

Five Ways to Encourage Yourself to Continue Soulwinning

1. Set aside one day a week to devote to sharing the Gospel.

This does not mean that you cannot witness for Christ the rest of the week; it simply means that one day a week is completely devoted to the ministry of soulwinning. If you cannot take an entire day, give the afternoon or the entire evening. Let nothing interfere with this time of soulwinning. If company comes in, make them go along with you or tell them you will be back later and to make themselves at home.

Here is the advantage of this. All week long you can be putting aside prospects to visit. Jot them down on a card and keep it with you all week. By Friday, you will have plenty of people lined up to visit. During the week you can be praying for these prospects and building momentum to win them.

2. Have a soulwinning partner.

   You are nailing yourself down by taking on a steady partner. Have it understood that the two of you will visit on this certain day of each week. If you are tempted to skip visitation, the fact of his depending on you to go with him will produce an added effort on your part. At the same time, you will be training your partner to become a soulwinner also.

3. Set a goal to share the Gospel with three people each week and win one to Christ.

   You may want to increase this later, but to start out, don't overstep yourself. This could cause you to lose heart. The joy of winning souls each week will become an addiction and keep you going back. If you fail to win one for the week, do not become discouraged but seek to win two the next week. Remember that God wants to save them more than we want them saved.

4. Write these four facts in the back of your Bible and read them constantly.

   a. Christ Commanded Me to Go and Blesses Me When I Go. Matthew 28:19, *"Go ye therefore, and teach all nations, baptizing them in the name of the Father, and of the Son and of the Holy Ghost."*

   b. The Spirit Empowers Me to Tell as I Go. Acts 1:8, *"But ye shall receive power, after that the Holy Ghost is come upon you: and ye shall be witnesses unto me."*

   c. The Spirit Will Convict the Sinner. John 16:8, *"And when He is come. He will convict the world of sin and of righteousness and or judgment."*

   d. Some Soul Is at Stake and I Can Be the Instrument Used to Change the Course of His Destiny. James 5:20, "L*et him know that he who turns a sinner from the error of his way will save a soul from death and cover a multitude of sins.*

How to Get into the House

We are often faced with the problem of getting into the house. It is important that we get in, for we are not likely to win them to Christ talking through the screen door. Determine to master the following pointers on getting into the house and what to do when you get in.

1. Approach the house quietly.

   Do not be noisy, thus giving them full warning of your coming. You do not want them to get braced and have time to make up excuses.

2. Observe the yard for clues about the people.

   If there are toys, you know there are children. If there is a boat, maybe there is a fisherman. Certain tools reveal certain hobbies and often tell us what type of work they do. All of these make conversation, and many times will help to get us in the house.

3. Knock loudly and boldly.

   A Bible salesman taught me years ago that if you knock loudly you are more apt to get invited in. He said a loud and long knock gives a psychological reaction that there is somebody important out there. Whereas, a soft knock tends to give the impression that there is a timid, scared, and unimportant person out there.

4. Smile.

   A warm, friendly smile has gotten soulwinners in the house when nothing else would. Do not underestimate the power of a smile.

5. Introduce yourself and explain your visit.

   EXAMPLE: "Good evening, we are from the Southcrest Baptist Church. Is this where Mr. and Mrs. Bill Smith live?" You notice this question brings forth a yes answer and this is what we want because if they give a yes answer to our next question we are in the house. As you give your introduction, shift your weight backward and do not lean toward the door. Speak naturally, clearly and with a pleasant voice tone.

"My name is Buddy Murphrey, and this is Bob Smith. We are out doing some visiting for our church and if you have a few minutes we would like to come in and visit with you. Would that be all right?"

6. Get into the house if possible; however, don't force your way in.

After you introduce yourself, take a step toward the door and raise your hand as if to touch the door. They will likely invite you to come in.

What to Do When You Walk into the House

1. Be friendly and introduce yourself to everyone in the room.

You will become the host for the first few minutes. Be radiant and glow. Be gentle and gracious. Be polite and well-mannered.

2. Subtly direct the seating arrangement.

If two of you are visiting together, the one who plans to do the talking should sit by the prospect. This usually means heading for the couch, thus leaving the silent partner to sit in the chair

3. Do not be distracted over an upset house.

If she says, "My house is a mess; I am so embarrassed," do not reply, "Oh, it's not so bad, you ought to see mine." Instead, change the subject immediately by saying "My! That's a beautiful picture on the wall," or (pointing to one of the children) "Is this the boss of the house?"

4. Find something in the house to compliment.

As you walk in, scan the house immediately to determine the most appropriate thing to brag on. Be sincere in giving your compliment for flattery is easily detected and will offend. A sincere compliment on a picture, a piece of furniture, the carpet, or a child will open the way for a warm general conversation. It will set them at ease and cause them to feel good toward you.

5. Remove distractions, especially the television.

You are in the house about to sit down and you notice the television is blaring. Now what are you going to do? It is obvious you will not do very much witnessing until it is either turned off or at least turned down. The following methods have been used successfully by many soulwinners to get the television turned off.

a. Apologize for interrupting.

"Oh, are we interrupting your favorite television program? If so we could come back another time?" The chances are that it is not their favorite program, and they will automatically turn the set off or down. This approach is to be used almost immediately upon entering the house.

b. Whisper.

Talk so softly that he can't hear you. The prospect, realizing he cannot hear you, will become aware that the television is blaring and reach over to turn it down.

c. Take charge.

Stand up between the prospect and the television. Get his attention and let the silent partner ease over and turn it down. This could be done by getting up to look at something in the room (a picture, a piece of furniture, or a child) and then, before sitting down, stand directly between the prospect and the television set. While you have his attention, the silent partner does his job.

d. Ask directly.

Ask the man, "Do you mind if we turn the television down for a few minutes?" If he refuses to grant the request, you may take it that he does not intend to listen to you tonight. I suggest you make your graceful exit and try to find a more interested prospect.

6. Carry on a general conversation for five or ten minutes.

This is very important because it is here that we warm them up for a hearing to take them through the Roman Road presentation of the gospel. If you fail in the warm-up conversation, you may be denied the opportunity to even read the Scripture. (Use your warm-up conversation covered previously in this chapter.)

7. Don't talk about the church or membership until leaving.

   You mentioned you were from the church at the beginning and that is enough until you start out the door. We are primarily interested in getting them to Jesus. The average person already thinks that joining the church is synonymous with being saved, and we certainly don't want to instill this error any deeper.

8. Make your transition from the casual to the spiritual.

   Don't let your general conversation ramble on and on. After you have talked in general awhile, begin your spiritual approach. Do not let the warm-up conversation exceed 20 minutes. If you have difficulty making the transition, study carefully the questions on "How to Cope with Making the Spiritual Approach" earlier in this chapter.

When Not to Go into the House

In making a visit with the purpose of winning a soul to Christ, it is important to get into the house if possible. However, there are times when it is best not to go in.

The soulwinner should size up the situation quickly, and then make his decision whether to go in or come back at another time. Here are four situations when it might be best to offer to come back later:

1. When the family is seated at the dinner table.

   EXAMPLE: "I see you folks are having your evening meal and I will not disturb you. Let me come back at another time." They will appreciate you for it. The chances are you will be better received when you return.

2. When they have company.

   It is very difficult to win a person to Christ in the presence of other people. There is a real danger of embarrassing the prospect.

EXAMPLE: "I see you have company tonight, so I will not disturb you. Let me come back another time. Okay?"

3. When only the wife or lady is home.

This takes for granted that the visitor is a man who comes upon a situation where only the wife is at home. Unless the soulwinner has a partner, it is wise not to go in.

4. When the couple or family is leaving.

If they are about to leave for a previous engagement, offer to come back another time. If the prospect plainly states he has a commitment elsewhere and you force your visit on him, he is sure not to appreciate it.

There are times when the Holy Spirit may overrule any of these "Don'ts" and you may go right in and win the soul to Christ. If the prospect really seems interested and wants you to come in, go in and win them to Jesus.

The Duties of the Silent Partner

The silent partner is the other person visiting with the soulwinner. What does he do while the soulwinner is at work?

1. He participates in the general, warm-up conversation.

The silent partner may chime in now and then during the preliminary conversation but is not to take the lead. He stays in the background as much as possible.

2. He helps to get the soulwinner and prospect seated together.

Upon entering the house he quickly scans the room to spot the seating arrangement. If there is a couch and a single chair, he goes for the chair. He is concerned that the soulwinner and prospect get seated together at first in order to prevent unnecessary shuffling later.

3. He is silent when the soulwinner begins the spiritual conversation.

He does not butt in. He does not take the lead from the soulwinner. He keeps quiet. He is to remain silent until the soulwinner gives him the signal to take over. Sometimes two soulwinners may alternate, but only as one gives the other permission to do so. It is very improper and impolite to interrupt the soulwinner.

4. He will take care of children if necessary.

   If the baby needs attention the silent partner jumps to the occasion. He may hold the baby, feed the baby, change the diaper, entertain, turn the beans off, answer the door, etc., and anything else that needs attention so the soulwinner can continue leading the prospect to Christ.

5. He may ask for a cup of coffee or glass of water at the appropriate time.

   Suppose the soul winner is trying to win the husband, and the wife keeps butting in. You notice things aren't going so well so you endeavor to get her out of the room. You ask for a glass of water and try your hand at witnessing to her in the kitchen. At least you will detain her a bit.

6. He prays silently and looks interested.

   He does not make a scene. He does nothing to attract the prospects attention. He prays silently and appears to enjoy what the soulwinner is saying.

7. Witnessing to someone else.

   He can find a second person in the house to win or alternate with the soulwinner on the next visit. He can take a new Christian with him.

How to Win Souls in the Church Invitation

One of the best places to win souls is at church during the invitation.

1. Who should go?
   a. Only those who are living the life.

b. Only those who are burdened for the soul.
c. Only those who witness outside the church too.
d. Only men deal with men and women deal with women.

2. When to go?
   a. When heads are bowed.
   b. When you feel that someone is under conviction.
   c. When the person can be easily reached without making a scene.
   d. When you are sure the Holy Spirit has given you the green light.

3. How to go?
   a. Go quietly.
   b. Try to come from behind.
   c. You may put your hand on his shoulder, but don't lunge on him.

4. What to say?
   a. Introduce yourself, if you have not met the person already.
   b. Be gentle, polite, and courteous.
   c. Say something like this, "John, would you like to receive Christ as your Savior today? I would be happy to go forward with you and we could tell the pastor. Okay?"

5. Don'ts.
   a. Don't nag him about coming forward.
   b. Don't give the impression that coming forward is being saved.
   c. Don't make a scene. Avoid embarrassing him.
   d. Don't go to small children. Let God move on them. They are more tender than adults and will respond when the Spirit begins dealing with them.

How to Win Souls at the Altar

1. Be ready.
   a. Be prayed up.
   b. Be seated near the front on the end of a pew.
   c. Be watching the pastor and come quickly when signaled.

2. Introduce yourself to the seeker.
   a. Smile and shake hands.
   b. Say, "John, I'm glad you have come."
   c. Take him to the designated place where you deal with the lost.

3. Give the soulwinner's message briefly (by asking the following questions):
   a. "Do you realize that you are a sinner?"
   b. "Do you understand that if you were to die in your sins, you would be lost forever?"
   c. "Do you realize that Christ paid the price for your sins on Calvary?"
   d. "Do you believe that if you would receive Christ into your heart today he would come in and cleanse you from your sin?" Open your Bible and read Revelation 3:20, "*Behold, I stand at the door and knock. If anyone hears My voice and opens the door, I will come in to him and dine with him, and he with Me*" and point out the two distinct parts. Explain that Christ will do His part of "coming into his heart" if he will do his part and "open the door."
   e. "Let's bow our heads and ask the Lord Jesus to come into your heart."
   f. "Would you be willing to ask God to be merciful to you, a sinner, and ask Jesus to come into your heart?"
   g. "John, if you are accepting the Lord Jesus Christ as your personal Savior right now, would you signify it by taking my hand?"
   h. "Now, John, let me offer a prayer of thanksgiving."
   i. "According to God's promise (Revelation 3:20), John, where would you go now if you were to die?"
   j. "Who saved you?" "What did He save you from?"

4. Direct him to take a seat on the front pew.
   a. Pull out the decision card.

Explain baptism and get a commitment from him to be baptized.
Take him to the baptismal dressing room.

CONCLUSION

A NEW ADVENTURE

The most exciting venture in life begins when a person comes to Jesus Christ in faith and is born again. Nothing compares to the awesome privilege of being a member of the holy family of God. Getting to know the awesome God of the universe and discovering the privileges, gifts and responsibilities of a Christian is a never ending source of joy and wonder. Being able to share your faith in a way that causes others to come to salvation in Christ is the most indescribable thrill you could imagine. Our God is magnificent, His Word is exhaustless and our life in Him is fabulous.

In the words of Steven Curtis Chapman's most popular song of the decade, *"Saddle up your horses, we've got a trail to blaze. To the wide blue yonder of God's amazing grace. We're following our leader into the glorious unknown. This is life like no other – this is the great adventure."* The hymn writer expressed it this way, *"Every day with Jesus is sweeter than the day before. Every day with Jesus I love Him more and more. Jesus saves and keeps me and He's the One I'm living for. Every day with Jesus is sweeter than the day before."*

My prayer for you is that this book will create a thirst for an awesome God who wants to do awesome works through you.

"Jesus is ..... What?"

"AWESOME!"

NOTES

NOTES

NOTES

NOTES

NOTES

NOTES

NOTES

NOTES

NOTES

NOTES

NOTES

NOTES

NOTES

NOTES

NOTES

NOTES

NOTES

NOTES

NOTES